Essentials *of* Human Rights

The daring publisher, Universal Law Publishing Company, among the foremost in the law publishing field and progressive in venturing to bring out rare legal literature of avant garde *character has rightly enriched the* corpus juris *of India*

Justice V R Krishna Iyer
Random Reflections, page 14

Essentials *of* Human Rights

Raj Kumar Gupta
Advocate, Supreme Court of India

Universal
Law Publishing Co. Pvt. Ltd.
NEW DELHI - INDIA

2013 Edition

ISBN: 978-93-5035-346-2

Published by

Universal
Law Publishing Co. Pvt. Ltd.
NEW DELHI - INDIA

A-58, G.T. Karnal Road Industrial Area,
(Near Azadpur Metro Station), Delhi-110033
Tel. : 011-47082254, 27458529, 27215334 Fax : 011-27458529
e-mail: unilaw@vsnl.com

- Showroom : C-27, Connaught Place, New Delhi-110001
  e-mail: sales@unilawbooks.com
- Editorial : edit@unilawbooks.com
- Website : **www.unilawbooks.com**

Join us on Facebook
www.facebook.com/unilawbooks

Recommended citation: Raj Kumar Gupta, *Essentials of Human Rights* (New Delhi: Universal Law Publishing Co. Pvt. Ltd., 2013).

Computer Typeset at Aesthetic and *Printed* at Mudrak, Delhi.

Dedicated to my respected father
Late Shri Mahabir Prasad Agrahari Ji
and respected mother
Late Smt. Reshma Devi Ji

Altamas Kabir
Judge
Supreme Court of India

17, Safdarjung Road
New Delhi-110011
Ph.: 23017059
23015962

FOREWORD

Mr. Raj Kumar Gupta, the author of this book, *"Essentials of Human Rights"*, is an Advocate practising in the Supreme Court of India. In this book, he has dealt with a subject which throughout history has been the subject of great concern and importance in the march of civilization. Human rights are of different hues. Some are basic in nature, while others are capable of being regulated. When a human being is born, he or she has the right to breathe fresh unpolluted air, to drink pure and uncontaminated water, to be provided with shelter, clothing, food and nutrition and health care, as at birth and even for quite some time thereafter, a human baby is not in a position to fend for itself, as are progeny of the animal kingdom. Other rights are fundamental in nature and are essential for the development of the human personality, but are capable of being regulated and even suppressed, depending on the established Government.

In this book, the author has referred to and dealt with the different facets of human rights that could and should be made available to all human beings, with particular reference to India. He has dealt with the historical development of the concept of human rights and their violation throughout history. Shri Gupta has referred to the *Magna Carta* promulgated by King John of England on 15-6-1215. Though essentially, the Charter dealt with the protection of privileges of the English aristocracy, it is one of the first documents which recognized certain rights of the English nobility over their estates.

Shri Gupta has also dealt with human rights and their impact on women and children, religious harmony, education, preventive detention, physically disabled people and even people who are infected with the HIV Syndrome. That apart, in Chapter 4 of the book, Shri Gupta has dealt with human rights and the rule of law and has very appositely referred to the rule of law being the foundation of the Indian legal system. I would go a step further to add that the rule of law is, in fact, the foundation of our democratic process which exists in India today. In his discourse, Shri Gupta has referred to the various conventions which had impacted world society at large. While referring to the French Declaration of Rights and the American Bill of Rights, Shri Gupta has also referred to the various Conventions and Declarations of the United Nations, such as the Universal Declaration of Human Rights, 1948, the International Covenant on Civil and Political Rights, 1966, the International Covenant on Economic, Social and Cultural Rights, 1966, the International Convention on the Elimination of All forms of Racial Discrimination, 1966, the American Convention on Human Rights, 1969, the African Charter on Human Rights and People's Rights, 1981, as also the Convention for the Elimination of All Kinds of Discrimination against Women, commonly known as CEDAW. In addition to the international conventions, Shri

Gupta has also dealt with the various human rights enactments within the country, such as, the Protection of Human Rights Act, 1993, enactments related to marriage, dowry prohibition, adoption and maintenance, pre-natal diagnosis relating to sex selection, and the general laws, such as, the Indian Penal Code, and, lastly, the Constitution of India, the fountain-head of all laws within the country.

The book contains reference to the basic laws relating to human rights and their violation, within its covers. It will be useful to all people, who are in any way involved in human rights activities, in understanding the concept of human rights and the solutions available where they are violated, the role of the National Human Rights Commission, as also the judiciary, in the protection of human rights. Having gone through the contents of the book, I can say that it deserves a place on the shelves of all law libraries and I can also recommend the same not only to those who are involved in human rights activities, but also to those who want to have a basic understanding of the concept of human rights in a condensed form in one composite volume.

Altamas Kabir

PREFACE

I gratefully acknowledge the help and assistance rendered by my wife Smt. Saroj Gupta, my both sons Abhishek and Abhinav, my learned Junior Shri Biswajit Kumar Shahi, Shri Mukesh Kumar Singh and Shri Anand Kumar Singh Advocates and Shri Pawan Kumar, my Stenographer.

I am deeply grateful to Mr. Altamas Kabir, Judge of Supreme Court of India for sparing his valuable time to write foreword of this book.

My sincere thanks go to the Authors namely Shri Palok Basu, Former Justice of Allahabad High Court, Mr. Khwaja A. Muntaqim, Mr. V.N. Shukla, the Editor of Times of India and the authors of the Books wherefrom relevant extracts quoted in this book and thanks are also to the publishers of those Books.

My thanks are due to Universal Law Publishing Co. Pvt. Ltd., the publisher of the book, without whose support it would not have been possible for me to take up this venture.

It is just possible that some mistakes remain for which I remind the respected readers "to err is human, to forgive divine."

I do hope that this Book will be of some use and interest to its readers.

Raj Kumar Gupta
NOIDA

August, 2013

CONTENTS

Foreword		vii
Preface		ix
Table of Cases		xiii
Chapter 1	Human Rights and its Historical Background	1
Chapter 2	Human Rights and the Children	4
Chapter 3	Human Rights and the Women	8
Chapter 4	Human Rights and the Rule of Law	15
Chapter 5	Human Rights and Religious Harmony	19
Chapter 6	Human Rights and Law Enforcing Officials	24
Chapter 7	Compensation for Violation of Human Rights	28
Chapter 8	Horizon of Human Rights	31
Chapter 9	Corporate Governance and Human Rights	34
Chapter 10	Human Rights and Education to Children	40
Chapter 11	Human Rights and Custodial Crimes	47
Chapter 12	Human Rights and the Detainee	62
Chapter 13	Public Interest Litigation as Aid to the Protection of Human Rights	70
Chapter 14	Social Justice and Human Rights under the Indian Constitution	74
Chapter 15	Human Rights of Physically Disabled and AIDS/HIV-affected Persons	77
Chapter 16	Human Rights and the Fundamental Rights of Indian Constitution	82
Chapter 17	Human Rights and Directive Principles of State Policy of Indian Constitution	96
Chapter 18	Role of National Human Rights Commission in Protection of Human Rights in India	102
Chapter 19	Role of Judiciary in Protection of Human Rights	107
Appendix 1.—	The Magna Carta (The Great Charter)	116
Appendix 2.—	The Declaration of Independence, 1776 (4-7-1776)	123
Appendix 3.—	The Bill of Rights of Constitution of the United States of America	126
Appendix 4.—	The French Declaration of the Rights of Man and Citizen	133
Appendix 5.—	Universal Declaration of Human Rights, 1948	135
Appendix 6.—	International Covenant on Civil and Political Rights, 1966	139
Appendix 7.—	International Covenant on Economic, Social and Cultural Rights, 1966	153
Appendix 8.—	English Bill of Rights, 1689	161
Bibliography		166
Subject Index		167

TABLE OF CASES

A

A.K. Gopalan *v.* State of Madras, AIR 1950 SC 27: 1950 SCR 88 58, 87, 112

A.P. Christian Medical Educational Society *v.* Government of Andhra Pradesh, (1986) 2 SCR 749 93

Ahmedabad St. Xavier's College Society *v.* State of Gujarat, (1974) 1 SCC 717 94

Air India, Statutory Corporation *v.* United Labour Union, (1997) 9 SCC 377 96

Aruna Roy *v.* Union of India, (2002) 7 SCC 368 40

B

Babu Lal *v.* State of Maharashtra, AIR 1961 SC 884 86

Bachan Singh *v.* State of Punjab, (1982) 3 SCC 24 15, 109

Bandhua Mukti Morcha *v.* Union of India, AIR 1997 SC 2218: (1997) 10 SCC 549 42, 90

Bhim Singh MLA *v.* State of Jammu and Kashmir, (1985) 4 SCC 677 25, 53, 114

Bodhisatwa Gautam *v.* Subhra Chakraborty, (1996) 1 SCC 49 72

C

C.E.S.C. Ltd. *v.* S.C. Bose, 1991 Supp (2) SCR 267 75

Chaitanya Singh *v.* M.D.S. University, AIR 1998 Raj 129 28

Chakradhar Paswan *v.* State of Bihar, (1988) 2 SCC 214 84

Chameli Singh *v.* State of Uttar Pradesh, (1996) 2 SCC 549 75, 108

Charan Lal Sahu *v.* Union of India, (1990) 1 SCC 613 33

Citizens for Democracy through its President *v.* State of Assam, (1995) 3 SCC 743 25

Consumer Education and Research Centre *v.* Union of India, (1995) 3 SCC 42 74, 108

D

D.K. Basu *v.* State of West Bengal, (1997) 1 SCC 416 29, 52, 55, 57, 59, 62, 112, 113

E

Emperor *v.* Bisheswer Prasad Sinha, AIR 1933 All 678 (FB) 111

G

Grih Kalyan Kendra Workers' Union *v.* Union of India, (1991) 1 SCC 619 97

H

Hooney *v.* Kolohan, (1935) 294 US 103 111

Hussainara *v.* Home Secretary, State of Bihar, (1980) 1 SCC 98 98

I

Indra Sawhney *v.* Union of India, 1992 Supp (3) SCC 217 84

J

J.P. Unnikrishnan *v.* State of Andhra Pradesh, AIR 1993 SC 2178 43

Javed Abidi *v.* Union of India, AIR 1999 SC 512 80

Joginder Kumar *v.* State of Uttar Pradesh, AIR 1994 SC 1349: (1994) 4 SCC 260 49, 51, 54

K

Kartar Singh *v.* State of Punjab, (1994) 3 SCC 569 58
Keshvananda Bharati *v.* State of Kerala, (1973) 4 SCC 225 21
Kharak Singh *v.* State of Madhya Pradesh, (1964) 1 SCR 352 86
Kishore *v.* State of Himachal Pradesh, (1991) 1 SCC 286 98

M

M.C. Mehta *v.* State of Tamil Nadu, (1996) 6 SCC 756 90, 97
Mahant Ram Kishan Dass *v.* State of Punjab, AIR 1981 SC 1576 92
Maharishi Awadesh *v.* Union of India, 1994 Supp (1) SCC 713 14, 99
Makhan Singh Tarsikka *v.* State of Punjab, AIR 1952 SC 27 58
Maneka Gandhi *v.* Union of India, (1978) 1 SCC 248 33
Mohan *v.* Union of India, 1992 Supp (1) SCC 594 101
Mohd. Ahmed Khan *v.* Shah Bano Begum, (1985) 2 SCC 556 99
Mohd. Yunus Khan *v.* State of Uttar Pradesh, (2010) 10 SCC 539 15, 63
Mumbai Kamgar Sabha *v.* Abdul Bhai Faizullabhai, (1976) 3 SCC 832 101

N

Nandini Satpathy *v.* P.L. Dani, (1978) 2 SCC 424 51
National Federation of Blind *v.* Union Public Service Commission, AIR 1993 SC 1916 80
National Human Rights Commission *v.* State of Gujarat, AIR 2009 (Supp) SC 318 33

P

Paschim Bangal Khet Mazdoor Samity *v.* State of West Bengal, AIR 1996 SC 2426 72
PGI Chandigarh *v.* Faculty Association, (1998) 4 SCC 1 84
Prem Shankar Shukla *v.* Delhi Administration, AIR 1980 SC 1535 53, 115

R

R.S. Sodhi *v.* State of Uttar Pradesh, 1994 (Supp) 1 SCC 142 53
Ramchandra Tandai *v.* State of Orissa, AIR 1994 Ori 228 80
Randhir Singh *v.* Union of India, (1982) 1 SCC 618 96
Rati Lal Panachand Gandhi *v.* State of Bombay, 1954 SCR 1055 92
Reynold Rajamani *v.* Union of India, AIR 1982 SC 1261 14
Romesh Thappar *v.* State of Madras, AIR 1950 SC 124: 1950 SCR 594 76, 108, 110
Rudal Sah *v.* State of Bihar, (1983) 4 SCC 141 53
Rural Litigation and Entitlement Kendra *v.* State of Uttar Pradesh, AIR 1987 SC 359 101

S

S.G. Jaisinghani *v.* Union of India, AIR 1967 SC 1427: (1967) 2 SCR 703 15, 108
SAHELI, a Women's Resources Centre *v.* Commissioner of Police Delhi, (1990) 1 SCC 422 28, 53
Samir *v.* State of West Bengal, AIR 1975 SC 1165 89
Sanjeev Coke *v.* Bharat Coaking Coal, AIR 1983 SC 239 97
Satish *v.* State of Uttar Pradesh, 1992 Supp (2) SCC 94 100
Selvi *v.* State of Karnataka, (2010) 7 SCC 263 30
Sham Khan *v.* State of Maharashtra, 1992 Supp (2) SCC 521 59

Sheela Barse *v.* Secretary, Children's Aid Society, (1987) 3 SCC 50	33
Srinivasa *v.* State of Karnataka, (1987) 2 SCC 692	97
Stainislaus *v.* State of Madhya Pradesh, (1977) 1 SCC 677	91
State of Haryana *v.* Jagdish, (2010) 4 SCC 216	48
State of Madhya Pradesh *v.* Thakur Bharat Singh, AIR 1967 SC 1170	86
State of Rajasthan *v.* Sukhpal, (1983) 1 SCC 393	58
State of Rajasthan *v.* Vidyawati, AIR 1962 SC 933	29, 115
State of Tamil Nadu *v.* K. Shyam Sunder, (2011) 8 SCC 737	44
State of Tamil Nadu *v.* L. Abu Kavur Bai, AIR 1984 SC 326	97
Sunil Batra *v.* Delhi Administration, (1980) 2 SCR 557	62
T	
Trilokinath *v.* State of Jammu and Kashmir, AIR 1967 SC 1283	84
U	
Union Carbide Corporation *v.* Union of India, (1989) 1 SCR 730	89, 107
Urquhart *v.* Brown, (1906) 205 US 179: 51 Law Edn. 760	111
V	
Vishaka *v.* State of Rajasthan, (1997) 6 SCC 241	9

CHAPTER 1

HUMAN RIGHTS AND ITS HISTORICAL BACKGROUND

According to great author D.D. Basu, "Human Rights are those minimal rights which every individual must have against the State or other public authority by virtue of his being a member of the human family irrespective of any other consideration".

The natural rights relating to dignity, life, liberty and equality of individuals guaranteed by the Constitution, the International Covenants and enforceable by courts, are ordinarily known as Human Rights. Human beings are an integral part of the society. In India, even in the ancient period, the principles of Fundamental Human Rights were followed and it was known as *"Vasudhaiva Kutumbakam"* (entire world is a family).

According to Mr. Justice S.H. Kapadia, Chief Justice of India, "Human Rights are needed not just for life but for life with dignity. They shape political society. Human Rights Jurisprudence is a mechanism to attain human dignity. Human rights are based on the philosophy of value. They are not absolute. They are not unchanging. The basic feature of Human Rights is universality."

Justice Ashok Bhan, Supreme Court of India rightly summarized "Human Rights" as under:

> "In animal world there are two basic rights – right of self-preservation and right to procreate. In the said world the might is right. Human beings by evolutionary process started living in socially and politically organised society where strong and weak could live in peace and harmony. In an organised civil society the right to live with dignity is the basic human right. Human Rights have been defined under section 2(1)(d) of the Protection of Human Rights Act, 1993 to mean rights relating to life, liberty, equality and dignity of the individual guaranteed by the Constitution or embodied in the international covenants and enforceable in a Court of Law. Human Rights are not absolute. They change with the changing times according to the need of an individual *viz-a-viz* societal rights. In an organised society right to life, liberty, equality and dignity would be the basic Human Rights and their applicability is universal in nature".

Human Rights have been defined under section 2(1)(d) of the Protection of Human Rights Act, 1993 as under:—

> "Human Rights mean the rights relating to life, liberty, equality and dignity of the individual guaranteed by the Constitution or embodied in the International Covenants and enforceable by Courts in India."

In this regard, the views of Mr. Justice A.K. Sikri, Acting Chief Justice, Delhi High Court about human rights, published in "Human Rights" Year Book, 2007 is very relevant, which is reproduced as under:- "The most important lesson which was learnt as a result of Second World War was the realization by the Governments of various countries about the human dignity which needed to be cherished and protected. It is for this reason that in the U.N. Charter, 1945, adopted immediately after the Second World War, dignity of the individuals was mentioned as of core value. The almost contemporaneous Universal Declaration of Human Rights (1948) echoed same sentiments. After emphasis on human dignity in the U.N. Charter, Universal Declaration of Human Rights, and several International Conventions as well as in the Constitution of India, in the last 50-60 years the concept of Human Rights has acquired new and dynamic meaning, comprehending in its sweep various facets. The underlined message in the aforesaid documents is the acknowledgement that human rights are individual and have a definite linkage of human development, both sharing common vision and with a common purpose. Respect for Human Rights is the root for human development and realization of full potential of each individual, which in turn leads to the augmentation of human resources with progress of the nation. Empowerment of the people through human development is the aim of human rights.

Our constitutional governance, as envisaged, respects basic Human Rights and promotes human development in all situations wherein the dignity and the worth of an individual lies at the core of a democratic value. The members of our Constituent Assembly were great visionaries. They were fully convinced that respect for Human Right is not merely in theory but in practice from the standpoint of good governance was the only lasting solution that would guarantee peace and tranquillity in independent India. Granville Austin while analysing the functioning of Indian Constitution in first 50 years has described three distinguished strands of Indian Constitution; (i) protecting national unity and integrity; (ii) establishing the institution and spirit of democracy; and (iii) fostering social reforms. The strands are mutually dependent, and inextricably intertwined in what he elegantly describes as "a seamless web".

In the Constitution of India, "Human Rights" have not been defined. However, in Part-III of the Constitution of India, Fundamental Rights are set out in Articles 14-32, which include equality before the law, prohibition of discrimination on the grounds of religion, caste, place of birth, sex, in the matter of public employment, freedom of speech and expression, to practice any profession, to carry out any occupation, trade and business, to form association or union, right to life, right to freedom of religion. It is pertinent to mention here that International Covenant on Civil and Political rights, economic, social and cultural rights, international treaties and other declarations and importantly Universal Declaration of Human Rights adopted by the United Nations General Assembly on 10-12-1948 have largely expanded the arena of Human Rights and these are based on Universality of human rights. It is also to be noted that most of fundamental rights as mentioned in Constitution of India are similar to human rights as described in Universal Declaration of Human Rights.

Mr. P.P. Rao, Senior Advocate, Supreme Court of India has expressed his views on the development of "Human Rights" in the Book "Human Rights in the Changing World" as under:—

"From a panoramic view of the development of Human Rights, it is clear that the scope of Human Rights stands vastly expanded, they extend not just to the basic civil and political rights but also to a wider range of new rights which include not only socio-economic rights (such as the right to health, the right to education, the right to work and employment and the right to rest and leisure) but also the right to secure the requisite conditions necessary for the enjoyment of all the declared rights by the members of the human family".

"Creating a world free from colonial domination, free from wars and nuclear weapons, free from terrorism and communal clashes, free from environmental pollution and ecological imbalances, free from poverty and illiteracy, free from famine and epidemics and in short, free from fear and want is a difficult task. The pre-requisites for the enjoyment of human rights can be secured only by promotion of universal respect for Human Rights, organised public opinion and sustained work by States and citizens alike".

In 1993, at Vienna the World Conference on Human Rights had approved the principles as described in Universal Declaration of Human Rights adopted by the United Nations General Assembly on 10-12-1948, which provides that all human rights are universal, indivisible, inter-dependent and inter-related.

Every human being has right since his birth to have clean water, unpolluted air, to enjoy liberty, freedom of speech and expression etc., whether he is born in any developed country, developing country or under-developed country.

The United Nations Organisation is an international body for the promotion and protection of Human Rights. It monitors their enforcement through several agencies/organisations and creates global human rights standard. It has always tried for international brotherhood and peaceful co-existence and a single world family. It is very sad to say that inspite of honest desire of United Nations and its different agencies, Human Rights are violated day and night and innocent and helpless human beings suffer by the cruel violators of Human Rights and United Nations Organisation is helplessly seeing the blatant violations of human rights.

At the time of King Conrad II, the struggle for human rights started when a Charter determining the rights of the Parliament in 1037 AD was issued. Other important documents were Draft of Rights 1689, English Bill of Rights 1689, American Declaration of Independence 1776, the Bill of Rights of Constitution of the United States of America, French Declaration of the Rights of the Man and of the Citizen, 1789, Universal Declaration of Human Rights, 1948, International Covenant on Civil and Political Rights, 1966, International Covenant on Economic, Social and Cultural Rights, 1966. (Kindly *see* Appendix).

In the history of Human Rights, *Magna Carta* enjoys very important status. Henry I, Stephen and Henry II could not keep their promise to accept this charter continued to promise. On 15-6-1215, King John of England granted *Magna Carta* to the English Baron that their privileges will not be encroached. This Charter was also issued in the years 1216, 1217 and 1325, after being modified.

CHAPTER 2

HUMAN RIGHTS AND THE CHILDREN

In 1924, Geneva declaration was promulgated for education and protection of the children. In the same year League of Nations endorsed codification in one text the fundamental condition to which children had right. In 1948, it was revised. On 20-11-1959 General Assembly of United Nations adopted ten- point declaration on the rights of children. Universal Declaration of Human Rights adopted in 1948 is of great importance to consider the situation of the children and probably it proceeded on the basis that children rights are an integral part of Human Rights. Article 25(1) of the said declaration provides that everyone has the right to a standard of living adequate for the health and well being of himself and his family, including food, clothing, housing and medical care and necessary social services, and the right to security in the event of employment, sickness, disability, widowhood, old age or other lack of livelihood in circumstances beyond his control. Article 25(2) provides that motherhood and childhood are entitled to special care and assistance. All children, whether born in or out of wedlock, shall enjoy the same social protection. This article gives emphasis to prove special care and assistance to motherhood and childhood. Article 26(1) of the said declaration says that everyone has right to education. Education shall be free, at least in the elementary and fundamental stages. Elementary education shall be compulsory. Technical and professional education shall be made generally available and higher education shall be equally accessible to all on the basis of merit.

In 1979, on the eve of International Year of the Children, Poland started its proposal for a convention on the Rights of Children. In the year 1979 itself the working group set up by U.N Commission on Human Rights examined several aspects and interacted with non-governmental organisations and several other organisations who were serious about the problems of rights of children. Thereafter the United Nations conventions on the Rights of the Children were held in 1989, which duly recognised the necessity to have job, understanding and happiness. Article 1 says that every human being under 18 years of age is a child. Article 2 says the children with protection against discrimination. Article 3 provides the supremacy of children interest in all cases.

On 29-30 September, 1990 at United Nations Organisation, New York Headquarter, the world summit for children was held to find solutions regarding increasing problems of children.

In India, there is not a single town where children are not engaged/employed at tea stalls, Dhabas, servants at home, servant at stationery shops or even pulling rickshaw, although Article 24 of the Indian Constitution says that no child below the age of 14 years shall be employed to work in any factory or mine or engaged in hazardous employment. Similarly Article 39 of the Indian Constitution contemplates that State shall in particular direct its policy towards securing the health and strength of workers, men and women, and at the tender age children are not abused and that citizens are not forced by economic necessities to enter avocations unsuited to their age or their strength. Lot of seminars, symposiums, lectures are organised at Five Star Hotels/air-conditioned halls to find out the ways to stop child abuse. Long resolutions are passed but never implemented or even if implemented to a minor extent. Similarly the cases of child abuse are increasing day-by-day without any check. Children are victims of sexual exploitation, drug abuse and child labour. Involvement of children in such nefarious activities deprives them of their innocence.

Mr. Justice A.K. Sikri, Acting Chief Justice, Delhi High Court while discussing the social malaise of child trafficking aptly pointed out that Children are the most vulnerable human asset of any nation. Therefore, their nurture and solicitude becomes the responsibility of the State, nay it is the responsibility of the entire society. Today's children constitute tomorrow's future and to ensure a brighter future of our children, we have to ensure that they are properly educated and not exploited. For this reason, they are entitled to special care and assistance, more so, because of their physical and mental immaturity. However, at the same time, children are most vulnerable members of any society. Because of this vulnerability, many children are exploited in various forms. In this article, the author wants to focus on the menace of child trafficking. The problem is more complicated in developing countries like ours, where child trafficking exists in relationship with illiteracy and poverty.

Trafficking in women and children is the gravest form of abuse and exploitation of human beings. Thousands of Indians are trafficked everyday to some destination or the other and are forced to lead lives of slavery. They are forced to survive in brothels, factories, guesthouses, dance bars, farms and even in the homes of well-off Indians, with no control over their bodies and lives. The Indian Constitution specifically bans the trafficking of persons. Article 23, in the Fundamental Rights, Part III of the Constitution, prohibits "traffic in human beings and other similar forms of forced labour", as published in Human Rights Year Book, 2011.

Mrs. Minna Kabir, a renowned voluntary worker for Child Rights, who has been working for the upliftment and betterment of the poor and unprivileged children, in her thought provoking article "the Rhetoric and the Reality of the Children's Rights' published in Human Rights Year Book, 2011 has rightly mentioned as below: "In order to make "India fit for children" all members of society have to ensure that we will put children first, care for every child, and leave no child behind. On this day of celebration of Human Rights Day let us make a pledge to fight this war for justice for all our children. Let us all give them back their rights and not think of it as charity to them. We owe it to them, as we feel we owe it to our own children, the promise of a bright future and the chance to stand on their own feet with pride and dignity. Let us try to make it possible, one child at a time if necessary, for no child to have to go to sleep with an empty stomach, or without a shelter over his or her head. Let us make the rhetoric of child rights into a reality for every child."

The serious problems of child labour—exploitation, lack of food, education, health services, shelter, and under nourishment are the problems calling the attention of the worlds' leaders. A poet has rightly said: "*Jis Desh ka Bachpan Bhukha Hai, Us Desh Ki Jawani Kya Hogi*" (If childhood of a country is hungry, then, what will be its adulthood.)

It is a not a secret fact that every year mostly in under-developed and developing countries, Lakhs of children are facing death due to disease, shortage of medicine, malnutrition, lack of drinking water and sanitation. China has largest child population and the second position comes to India.

In India the Supreme Court has taken great lead over resolving the complex and serious problems of bonded labour, child labour, child adoption and contract labour etc. Emphasizing the role of holy Constitution of India and part played by the Indian Judiciary, eminent senior lawyer of Supreme Court of India Mr. Keshav Dayal has truly pointed out in his remarkable article "Children Human Rights, Constitutional Provisions and International Documents" published in Human Rights Year Book, 2011 that "childhood is an age of innocence, vulnerability and an age which is best suited for moulding an individual's personality. This is right time for adequate socialization to integrate the children with the ways of the world. A child needs love, care and protection. The children are the most vulnerable group in India and are in urgent need of social care. Due to poverty and over-dependence, children can be ill-treated, exploited and even forced into undesirable acts."

The Constitution of India has also taken care of the children and there are various principles enshrined in the Constitution which deal with the rights of the children. The Constitutional concept of children in India is the realization of a healthy childhood with a pace for all round growth and development, and protection from exploitation and abuse by child labour forced on them due to economic necessity.

Children are engaged in manufacturing of carpets at Bhadohi, U.P., Muzzafarpur, Bihar and Kashmir. They are to work continuously for 12 hours, if not more. Children are also engaged in match and crackers industry in Shivkasi, Tamil Nadu, gem polishing industries in Rajasthan, manufacturing of bidis in whole India.

Due to more children in the family and also due to poverty, the parents/ guardians of children do not send them to school but they send them to above mentioned industries or other working place to earn. The soft period of life (childhood) is spent at working place by male child and girl child also.

There is no dispute that the Central Government, State Governments and several non-governmental organisations are doing well to solve the child labour problem, but more strong and bold actions are needed from Central Government to protect the god-gifted childhood and inflict harder punishment to those who are responsible for employment of children either directly or indirectly.

In India, Right of Children to Free and Compulsory Education (RTE) Act, 2009 came in force on 1-4-2010. It gives every child right to a quality elementary education. All children aged 6-14 years shall have the right to free and compulsory elementary education at a neighbourhood school. The Government will provide schooling free of cost until a child's elementary education is completed. No school fee or cost of uniforms, textbooks, mid-day-meals and transportation need be borne by the child or parents to obtain elementary education.

There are regular and repeated cases of sexual exploitation of girl child. Therefore, educated persons, self-employed people, Government employees, professionals should give at least one hour per week to teach the children regarding their health and hygiene and basic ideas of reading.

Certain laws namely Child Labour (Prohibition and Regulation) Act, 1986 and others are enacted to regulate the child labour problems. This 1986 Act has taken care of the problems of children, which includes child health, hours of works and rest, conditions of employment etc. Section 7 of the said Act provides that no child shall be permitted or required to work between 7 p.m. and 8 a.m. and no child shall be required or permitted to work overtime. Section 8 says that every child employed in an establishment shall be allowed in each week, a holiday of one whole day. Section 14 of the said Act imposes penalty upon violators of the beneficial provisions mentioned in the said Act.

Plantation Labour Act, 1951 was enacted to protect the interest of plantation labourers particularly women and children. Section 25 of the said Act contemplates that except with the permission of the State Government. No women or child worker shall be employed in any plantation otherwise than between the hours of 6 a.m. to 7 p.m. provided that nothing in this section shall be deemed to apply to midwives and nurses employed as such in any plantation.

Section 21 of the Motor Transport Workers Act, 1961 provides that no child shall be required or allowed to work in any capacity in any motor transport undertaking.

The Children (Pledging of Labour) Act, 1933 was enacted to protect the interest of child. In this Act child means a person who is under the age of 15 years. Section 4 of the said Act says that whoever being the parent or the guardian of a child makes an agreement to pledge the labour of that child, shall be punished with fine which may extend to fifty rupees. Sections 5 and 6 also impose penalty regarding pledging the labour of a child.

In 1948, the Factories Act was enacted. Section 67 of the said Act provides that no child who has not completed his 14th year shall be required or allowed to work in any factory. Section 71 of the said Act also provides that no female child shall be required or allowed to work in any factory except between 8 a.m. and 7 p.m.

Kerala has lowest child labour population. It has highest child literacy percentage in India. In Bihar, Orissa, Chhattisgarh, Rajasthan, child labour is a well-organised phenomenon. It is the need of the hour that more emphasis should be given on education and health of the children.

When I think over to give free education to child and to restrict child labour, a question comes to my mind as to whether the problems of child labour has any connection with increasing population. It is a fact that the increasing population is also one additional factor of child labour problem. Children constitute the most important segment of society, the main enemy of the children are poverty, hunger, disease and illiteracy. The rights of the children are a priority for adult responsibility. Children are like buds of flowers. They should be properly nursed and taken care of, so that the buds become complete flowers.

CHAPTER 3

HUMAN RIGHTS AND THE WOMEN

According to Indian tradition and culture, women are treated as Goddess. There is a saying in Sanskrit language that where women are treated with honour, there God lives. It is well said that all the rights of women are Human Rights. The Universal Declaration of Human Rights proclaims the equality of the sexes. The Fourth World Conference on women held in Beijing in 1995, was an important step forward in terms of Human Rights for women. The declaration adopted there turned the focus on this gender. But, in practice, even now women rights are not being implemented in the manner they ought to have been implemented.

Promoting women rights calls for special attention. It has been an important area of focus for the whole world and the international organisations. Now there is global recognition to the rights of women, which are considered as an integral and an inalienable part of Universal Human Rights. This principle was approved earlier at the World Conference on Human Rights in Vienna in 1993. But it is sad to note that still, women are subjected to sexual offences like rape, sexual slavery, forced prostitution, forced pregnancy and subject to gender bias in almost every walk of life. Women are half of the total population of the world but they are deprived of their legitimate claims.

Keeping in view the spirit of the Universal Declaration of Human Rights that affirms the principle of the inadmissibility of discrimination and proclaims that all human beings are born free and equal in dignity and rights and that everyone is entitled to all the rights and freedoms set forth therein, without distinction of any kind, including distinction based on sex. Convention on the Elimination of all Forms of Discrimination against Women was adopted by the General Assembly on 18.12.1979, but it came into force on September 3, 1981. Under this Convention, the State parties are required to eliminate discrimination against women in all its forms and manifestations. The State parties are also required to embody the principle of the equality of men and women in their Constitutions and other laws so that the women may enjoy the same political, social, economic and cultural rights which the men enjoy. In this Convention, obligations have also been imposed to eliminate discrimination against women in marriage and family life. Even earlier, the UN General Assembly had adopted "Convention on the Political Rights of Women" on 20th December, 1952. The convention provided that women shall be entitled to vote in all elections on equal terms with men without any discrimination and they shall be eligible for election to all publicly elected bodies, established by national law, on equal terms with men, without any discrimination and they shall also hold public office and shall discharge their legal functions and duties freely.

In this context reference of Article 14 of the Constitution of India is very relevant, which says as under:—

> "The State shall not deny to any person equality before the law or the equal protection of the laws within the territory of India".

This Constitutional provision is based on Irish and American Constitutions. Article 14 aforesaid provides equality before the law and equal protection of law for women and men. The Indian Parliament has passed several laws beneficial to the women, such as Special Marriage Act, 1954 under which marriage is solemnized between a Hindu and a Muslim, Christian or Parsi and the said marriage is treated as valid marriage. The Hindu Marriage Act, 1955 under which a marriage can be solemnized between Hindus only. The Hindu Succession Act, 1956 under which the rights of the succession among the Hindu female and male both are determined. The Hindu Minority and Guardianship Act, 1956 under which custody of a minor child of a Hindu is dealt with. The Hindu Adoption and Maintenance Act, 1956, under which the maintenance matters are regulated. The Suppression of Immoral Traffic in Women and Girls Act, 1956 is applicable to all the Indians irrespective of their castes or religions. The Dowry Prohibition Act, 1961 is a penal law applicable to all the Indians for taking and giving dowry at the time of marriage of women. The Medical Termination of Pregnancy Act, 1971 under which abortion is prohibited. The Equal Remuneration Act, 1976 is a beneficial legislation to the working class regarding the protection of remunerations for their survival in organised or non-organised sectors. The Child Marriage Restraint Act, 1929 under which marriage of minors is prohibited unless the boy and girl attain 21 years and 18 years respectively. Maternity Benefit Act, 1961 for pregnant women is another example.

Supreme Court of India has delivered a landmark judgment in the case of *Vishaka* v. *State of Rajasthan*, (1997) 6 SCC 241. In this case, a writ petition under Article 32 of the Constitution of India was filed before the Supreme Court of India for the enforcement of the fundamental rights of working women guaranteed under Articles 14, 19 and 21 of the Constitution of India. In the said Writ Petition the issue of prevention of sexual harassment of working women at their place of work was also raised. After hearing learned Solicitor-General for Government of India and other learned Counsels, the Hon'ble Supreme Court for effective enforcement of the basic Human Right of gender equality and against sexual harassment and abuse at the place of work issued Guidelines until a legislation is enacted for this purpose. The said Guidelines were issued under the power exercised under Article 32 of the Constitution of India and it was treated as the law of the land under Article 141 of the Constitution of India. The guidelines and norms prescribed herein are as under:—

> "Having regard to the definition of 'Human Rights' in section 2(1)(d) of the Protection of Human Rights Act, 1993, taking note of the fact that the present civil and penal laws in India do not adequately provide for specific protection of women from sexual harassment in work places and that enactment of such legislation will take considerable time, it is necessary and expedient for employers in work places as well as other responsible persons or institutions to observe certain guidelines to ensure the prevention of sexual harassment of women".

1. Duty of the employer or other responsible persons in work places and other institutions:

It shall be the duty of the employer or other responsible persons in work places or other institutions to prevent or deter the commission of acts of sexual harassment and to provide the procedures for the resolution, settlement or prosecution of acts of sexual harassment by taking all steps required.

2. Definition:

For the purpose, sexual harassment includes such unwelcome sexually determined behaviour (whether directly or by implication) as:

(a) physical contact and advances;

(b) a demand or request for sexual favours;

(c) sexually coloured remarks;

(d) showing pornography;

(e) any other unwelcome physical, verbal or non-verbal conduct of sexual nature.

Where any of these acts is committed in circumstances whereunder the victim of such conduct has a reasonable apprehension that in relation to the victim's employment or work whether she is drawing salary, or honorarium or voluntary, whether in government, public or private enterprise such conduct can be humiliating and may constitute a health and safety problem. It is discriminatory for instance when the woman has reasonable grounds to believe that her objection would disadvantage her in connection with her employment or work including recruiting or promotion or when it creates a hostile work environment. Adverse consequences might be visited if the victim does not consent to the conduct in question or raises any objection thereto.

3. Preventive steps:

All employers or persons in-charge of workplace whether in the public or private sector should take appropriate steps to prevent sexual harassment. Without prejudice to the generality of this obligation they should take the following steps:

(a) Express prohibition of sexual harassment as defined above at the work place should be notified, published and circulated in appropriate ways.

(b) The rules/regulations of government and public sector bodies relating to conduct and discipline should include rules/regulations prohibiting sexual harassment and provide for appropriate penalties in such rules against the offender.

(c) As regards private employers steps should be taken to include the aforesaid prohibitions in the standing orders under the Industrial Employment (Standing Orders) Act, 1946.

(d) Appropriate work conditions should be provided in respect of work, leisure, health and hygiene to further ensure that there is no hostile environment towards women at workplaces and no woman employee should have reasonable grounds to believe that she is disadvantaged in connection with her employment.

4. Criminal proceedings

Where such conduct amounts to a specific offence under the Indian Penal Code or under any other law, the employer shall initiate appropriate action in accordance with law by making a complaint with the appropriate authority.

In particular, it should ensure that victims, or witnesses are not victimized or discriminated against while dealing with complaints of sexual harassment. The victims of sexual harassment should have the option to seek transfer of the perpetrator or their own transfer.

5. Disciplinary action

Where such conduct amounts to misconduct in employment as defined by the relevant service rules, appropriate disciplinary action should be initiated by the employer in accordance with those rules.

6. Complaint mechanism

Whether or not such conduct constitutes an offence under law or a breach of the service rules, an appropriate complaint mechanism should be created in the employer's organisation for redress of the complaint made by the victim. Such complaint mechanism should ensure time-bound treatment of complaints.

7. Complaints committee

The complaint mechanism, referred to in (6) above, should be adequate to provide, where necessary, a Complaints Committee, a special counsellor or other support service, including the maintenance of confidentiality.

The Complaints Committee should be headed by a woman and not less than half of its members should be women. Further, to prevent the possibility of any undue pressure or influence from senior levels, such Complaints Committee should involve a third party, either NGO or other body who is familiar with the issue of sexual harassment.

The Complaints Committee must make an annual report to the Government Department concerned of the complaints and action taken by them.

The employers and person in-charge will also report on the compliance with the aforesaid guidelines including on the reports of the Complaints Committee to the Government Department.

8. Workers' initiative

Employees should be allowed to raise issues of sexual harassment at workers' meeting and in other appropriate forum and it should be affirmatively discussed in employer-employee meetings.

9. Awareness

Awareness of the rights of female employees in this regard should be created in particular by prominently notifying the guidelines (and appropriate legislation when enacted on the subject) in a suitable manner.

10. Third party harassment

Where sexual harassment occurs as a result of an act or omission by any third party or outsider, the employer and person in-charge will take all steps necessary and reasonable to assist the affected person in terms of support and preventive action.

11. **The Central/State Governments are requested to consider adopting suitable measures including legislation to ensure that the guidelines laid down by this order are also observed by the employers in private sector.**

12. **These guidelines will not prejudice any rights available under the Protection of Human Rights Act, 1993.**

These directions would be binding and enforceable in law until suitable legislation is enacted to occupy the field.

It is true that women have always been an object of gross and severe violence in the hands of men. The biological weakness of a woman makes her an easy prey particularly to physical domination. She is often a victim of physical violence not only outside her home but also in her home. The constant neglect of the female children, which apart from having adverse affect on their health also creates mental conditions for them in which they cannot resist any physical violence or several forms of injustices. They continue to be the weaker and the suppressed of the human species. What is, therefore, fundamentally necessary is to see that in matters of health and education they are treated at par with male children.

Women are victims of exploitation by the male members in the whole world. Women are tortured and exploited in the name of religion and social sanctions etc.

Universal Declaration of Human Rights declares that all human beings are born free and equal in dignity and rights. Everyone is entitled to all the rights and freedoms set forth therein, without distinction of any kind based on sex. United Nations General Assembly had adopted "Convention on the Political Rights of Women" on 20-12-1952. Again on 18-12-1979 Convention on the Elimination of all Forms of Discrimination against Women was adopted by the General Assembly but it came into force on 3-9-1981. Under this Convention, the State Parties are required to eliminate discrimination against women in all its forms. In this Convention, obligations have also been imposed to eliminate discrimination against women in marriage and family life.

Article 51A of the Constitution provides that the State shall endeavour to foster respect for international law. But till today the benefit of Article 51A has not been achieved fully.

In the year 1990, the National Commission for Women Act was enacted to constitute a National Commission for Women. Section 10 of the said Act provides as below:

(1) The Commission shall perform all or any of the following functions, namely:

   (a) investigate and examine all matters relating to the safeguards provided for women under the Constitution and other laws;

   (b) present to the Central Government, annually and at such other times as the commission may deem fit , reports upon the working of those safeguards;

   (c) make in such reports recommendations for the effective implementation of those safeguards for improving the conditions of women by the Union or any State;

   (d) review from time-to-time, the existing provisions of the Constitution and other laws affecting women and recommend amendments thereto so as to suggest remedial legislative measures to meet any lacunae, inadequacies or shortcomings in such legislations;

(e) take up the cases of violation of the provisions of the Constitution and of other laws relating to women with the appropriate authorities;

(f) look into complaints and take *suo moto* notices of matters relating to—

(i) deprivation of women's rights;

(ii) non-implementation of laws enacted to provide protection to women and also to achieve the objective of equality and development;

(iii) non-compliance of policy decisions, guidelines or instructions aimed at mitigating hardships and ensuring welfare and providing relief to women;

and take up the issues arising out of such matters with appropriate authorities.

(g) call for special studies or investigations into specific problems or situations arising out of discrimination and atrocities against women and identify the constraints so as to recommend strategies for their removal;

(h) undertake promotional and educational research so as to suggest ways to ensuring due representation of women in all spheres and identify factors responsible for impeding their advancement, such as, lack of access to housing and basic services, inadequate support services and technologies for reducing drudgery and occupational health hazards and for increasing their productivity;

(i) participate and advise on the planning process of socio-economic development of women;

(j) evaluate the progress of the development of women under the Union and any State;

(k) inspect or cause to be inspected a jail, remand home, women's institution or other place of custody where women are kept as prisoners or otherwise, and take up with the concerned authorities for remedial action, if found necessary;

(l) fund litigation involving issues affecting a large body of women;

(m) make periodical reports to the Government on any matter pertaining to women and in particular various difficulties under which women toil;

(n) any other matter which may be referred to it by the Central Government.

(2) The Central Government shall cause all the reports referred to in clause (b) of sub-section (1) to be laid before each House of Parliament along with a memorandum explaining the action taken or proposed to be taken on the recommendations relating to the Union and the reasons for the non-acceptance, if any, of any of such recommendations.

(3) Where any such report or any part thereof relate to any matter with which any State Government is concerned, the Commission shall

forward a copy of such report or part to such State Government who shall cause it to be laid before the Legislature of the State along with a memorandum explaining the action taken or proposed to be taken on the recommendations relating to the State and the reasons for the non-acceptance, if any, of any of such recommendations.

(4) The Commission shall, while investigating any matter referred to in clause (a) or sub-clause (f) of sub-section (1), have all the powers of a civil Court trying a suit and, in particular, in respect of the following matters, namely:—

(a) summoning and enforcing the attendance of any person from any part of India and examining him on oath;

(b) requiring the discovery and production of any document;

(c) receiving evidence on affidavits;

(d) requisitioning any public record or copy thereof from any Court or office;

(e) issuing commissions of the examination of witnesses and documents; and

(f) any other matter which may be prescribed.

It is good to say that since its Constitution, the Commission is actively involved in taking up issues relating to welfare and protection of the basic Human Rights of women in India. It has proposed several amendments in the law of Dowry Prohibition, Guardianship, Bigamy of Marriage, Hindu Marriage Act and Child Marriage Restraint Act etc.

There is need for introduction of Uniform Civil Code in India. Article 44 of the Constitution of India provides that "The State shall endeavour to secure for the citizens a Uniform Civil Code throughout the territory of India. The said Article 44 is part of Directive Principles of State Policy. Inspite of passing 58 years, the citizens of the country are not able to get Uniform Civil Code. Hindus, Muslims, Parsis, Christians are all having their own personal laws. Supreme Court of India in the case of *Maharishi Awadesh* v. *Union of India* reported in 1994 Supp (1) SCC 713 rejected a petition whereby Government of India was sought to be directed to introduce a Common Civil Code. It was held that it was a matter for the Legislature and the court cannot legislate the matters. Further in the case of *Reynold Rajamani* v. *Union of India,* reported in AIR 1982 SC 1261 the Supreme Court of India while interpreting section 10 of the Indian Divorce Act, 1869, which is applicable to the Christians, where question was raised to remove the discrimination between women and men, it was specifically held that a legislative provision enumerates the grounds of divorce, those grounds limit the Court's jurisdiction. They cannot legislate to add or delete the grounds of divorce.

With a view to provide protection to women against certain crimes, some new legal provisions *viz.,* sections 304B, 366A, 366B, 376A, 376B, 376C, 376D in the Indian Penal Code, likewise section 8A has been introduced in the Dowry Prohibition Act, 1961, section 66 has been introduced in the Factories Act, 1948.

CHAPTER 4

HUMAN RIGHTS AND THE RULE OF LAW

Great Jurist A.V. Dicey has said that British Constitution, though unwritten, is founded on rule of law and contains three conceptions, that is the law is supreme and there is no scope for arbitrariness, nobody is above law and that general rules of Constitutional Law are the result of ordinary law. Rule of law is a concept which is dear to all men of law, who cherish freedom. It is the concept which man has evolved to eschew the rule of arbitrariness in official and public conduct. It is to ensure the rule of reason. Golden principles of rule of law controls/checks the Government and other its organs from acting arbitrarily and against the due procedure of law. Arbitrary action of such authorities can be challenged before Court of law on the ground of violation of principle of rule of law. The rule of law forms part of the basic structure of the Constitution of India.

Dr. B.S. Chauhan, Judge Supreme Court of India in his Judgment in the case of *Mohd. Yunus Khan* v. *State of Uttar Pradesh,* (2010) 10 SCC 539 has held as follows:

> "Arbitrariness is an anathema to the principles of reasonableness and fairness enshrined in our constitutional provisions. The rule of law prohibits the exercise of power in an arbitrary manner and/or in a manner that travels beyond the boundaries of reasonableness. Thus, a statutory authority is not permitted to act whimsically/arbitrarily. Its actions should be guided by the principles of reasonableness and fairness. The authority cannot be permitted to abuse the law or to use it unfairly."

Supreme Court of India in a landmark decision in the case of *S.G. Jaisinghani* v. *Union of India,* (1967) 2 SCR 703 has specifically observed that in a system governed by rule of law, discretion when conferred upon executive authorities, must be confined within clearly defined limits. The rule of law from this point of view means that decisions should be made by the application of known principles and rules, in general, such decisions should be predictable and citizen should know where he is. If a decision is taken without any principle or without any rule it is unpredictable and such a decision is the antithesis of a decision taken in accordance with the rule of law.

Similarly Supreme Court in *Bachan Singh* v. *State of Punjab,* (1982) 3 SCC 24 has held that the rule of law has really three basic and fundamental assumptions, *one* is that law making must be essentially in the hands of a democratically elected Legislature, *Second* is that even in the hands of democratically elected Legislature, there should not be un-fettered legislative power and *thirdly* there must be an independent judiciary to protect the citizens against excesses of Executive and Legislative power.

The origin of concept of Rule of Law is from France. Rule of Law means for every action of the Government; there should be a valid reason and legal support. Article 14 of the Constitution of the India provides that every citizen is equal before the law and entitled equal protection of laws. Therefore, no person is small or tall in the eye of law and every person is equal and is entitled of equal treatment by the hands of law.

General Assembly of the United Nations, meeting in Paris proclaimed the Universal Declaration of Human Rights and urged that it be adopted, "as a common standard of achievement for all peoples and all nations".

Former President of India Shri R. Vankataraman while delivering inaugural address in the Seminar on Human Rights Day celebrations organised by International Law Association, Regional Branch, India at New Delhi stated that Universal Declaration of Human Rights is a document of unprecedented historical importance. It sets forth the fundamental liberties and rights common to all people on earth. It is the fountain- head for new rules of international law. It heralded the beginning of a new legal order and codifies, in a single instrument, those fundamental principles which the modern world believes to be at the very core of human existence. These principles constitute a categorical imperative for our present and future and are part of what has aptly been called "the Common Law of Mankind."

The Charter of the United Nations accepted certain basic Human Rights and reaffirmed faith in fundamental Human Rights, the dignity and worth of human persons, in the equal rights of men and women and of nations, large and small, and to establish conditions under which justice and respect for the obligations arising from treaties and other sources of international law can be maintained and to promote social progress and better standard of the life in freedom.

Article 1 of Universal Declaration of Human Rights reiterates that all men are born free and equal in dignity and rights. Article 2 pleads for equality, which similar to Article 15(1) of the Constitution of India relating to non-discrimination on the ground of religion, race, sex etc., and Article 3 ensures everyone's right to life, liberty and security. It is similar to the provisions of Article 21 of the Constitution of India. Article 4 is against slavery or servitude. Article 7 of the Declaration provides that all are equal before the law and are entitled without any discrimination to equal protection of law. It is similar to Article 14 of the Constitution of India which is based on principle of equality before the law. Article 8 of the Declaration speaks that everyone has the right to an effective remedy by the competent National Tribunals for act violating the fundamental rights granted to him by the Constitution or by law. It is similar to Article 32 of the Constitution of India, the right to judicial remedy against violation of Fundamental Rights. Article 9 of the said declaration specifically says that no one shall be subjected to arbitrary arrest, detention or exile. Article 11(1) of the said declaration provides that everyone charged with a penal offence has the right to be presumed innocent until proved guilty according to law and Article 11(2) provides that no one shall be held guilty of any offence on account of any act or omission which did not constitute a penal offence, nor any heavier penalty shall be imposed than the one which was applicable at the time of commission of the offence. The provisions of Article 11 of the Declaration are similar to Articles 20-22 of the Constitution of India relating to life and liberty. Declaration 19 says that everyone has the right to freedom of opinion and expression and is similar to Article 19(1)(a) of the Constitution of India relating to freedom of speech and expression.

It is very clear to say that the State can protect civil, social, cultural, economic and political rights of individuals and their dignity which are commonly known as fundamental Human Rights as mentioned above and are part of Universal Declaration of Human Rights. Rule of law and Human Rights are closely linked. Even preamble of said declaration declares right to rebellion against tyranny or oppression and need the protection of Rule of Law. Long time ago Father of the Nation, Mahatma Gandhi said: "I learnt from my illiterate but wise mother that all rights to be deserved and preserved come from duty well done. Thus, the very right to live accrues to us only when we do the duty of the citizenship of the world. From this fundamental statement perhaps it is easy enough to define the duties of man and woman and correlate every right to some corresponding duty to be first performed."

Principle of rule of law applies to every Government and its agencies/organs in every legal or judicial system. By maintaining rule of law, a State can protect the basic Human Rights of its citizens and can make life of human beings much better, can provide happiness and smile on the faces of poor children and helpless aged people. If the principle of rule of law is disregarded by the States, it will automatically hurt the basic Human Rights of the citizens.

Former Chief Justice of India Mr. Sabyasachi Mukherji while delivering speech on Human Rights' Day Celebrations at New Delhi said that, "Long time ago, Plato proclaimed: "I proclaim that might is right, justice is the interest of the stronger." Human nature has since changed, in natural state perhaps, a man will and perhaps should take whatever he can. But with civilisation we should change. But still we have apartheid in practice. Apartheid is denial of Human Rights. Slavery has a long history and abolition of slavery is not possible by proclamations. Indeed, the abolition of slavery has gone on for a long time. Rome abolished slavery. America abolished it and Russia did it but only the words were abolished not the thing. Harijans in India are still prosecuted. The social discrimination against Harijans is decried in its name. Not perhaps much has been done about the cry of poverty stricken people who are unable to get food, education and medical aid for their children. Refusal of immigration is an offence against Human Rights.

Justice Claire L Heureux Dube, Canada Supreme Court has said that "Human Rights are yardsticks against which all people must measure their conduct and that of their Governments and public officials and against which the global community as a whole must measure its progress."

In its report in 1961, the Law Commission of India has admitted the importance of rule of law as under:

> "The rule of law and Judicial review acquire greater significance in a welfare State. The maintenance of law and order and the prevention from external aggressions are but a part of the functions of such a State. It has a variety of other functions, which bring it into constant touch with the life of the citizens. The greater, therefore, is the need for ceaseless enforcement of the rule of law, so that the Executive may not, in a belief, in its monopoly of wisdom and its zeal for administrative efficiency, overstep the bounds of its power and spread

its tentacles into the domains where the citizens should be free to enjoy the liberty guaranteed to him by the Constitution."

Rule of law is the foundation of Indian legal system. According to the principle of separation of powers, all the three organs namely Legislature, Executive and Judiciary are expected to perform their duties and functions in their territory. They should not encroach upon the area of other organs. There should be cohesive arrangement between all the three organs and they should act within parameters of Constitution and they are expected to respect each other. The Legislature should not make law which discriminate people on the ground of religion, caste, race or sex. Legislature is expected to legislate to recognize the Fundamental Human Rights as described in Universal Declaration of Human Rights, 1948 and International Covenant on Civil and Political Rights, 1966, International Covenant on Economic, Social and Cultural Rights, 1966, International Convention on the elimination of all Forms of Racial Discrimination, 1966, American Convention on Human Rights, 1969, African Charter on Human Rights and People's Rights, 1981. Legislature should make law for the welfare of its citizens protecting their fundamental rights.

Executive includes Ministers of the Central Government as well as State Governments in India and also the bureaucracy and all Governmental/Semi-Governmental Officers and Staffs. They are the enforcing authorities of the law made by Parliament or the Assemblies of the State. They implement the law in reality. The benefits of the beneficial law are reached at the doors of citizens by the Executive Authorities and they are direct link between Government and the public.

Judiciary plays a very important role in dispensing justice to the needy people, who come to Court being harassed by Executive and other Governmental organs. Judiciary also interpret the law of the Parliament and the Assembly and ordinances issued by President of India or any Governor of the State. Independence of Judiciary must be absolute and there should not be any kind of interference in its functioning by Executive. In India, even today Judiciary is not given financial autonomy. For their budget, Judiciary has to seek sanction of the Executive Authorities. According to me, this is not good for independence of Indian Judiciary. There should be complete financial Autonomy so that there should not be any slightest control over the Judiciary by the Executive. Justice delivery system should be more simple and easy, less expensive and less time consuming.

CHAPTER 5

HUMAN RIGHTS AND RELIGIOUS HARMONY

Communalism is the basic feature of fundamentalism and it is a part of religious fanaticism. The Preamble of the Constitution of India provides liberty of thought, expression, belief, faith and worship and therefore, religious harmony is the basic feature of the Indian Constitution.

The word fundamentalism is explained in the *Oxford Reference Dictionary* that strict maintenance of traditional orthodox religious beliefs, a religious movement which developed among various Protestant bodies in the USA after the first world war, based on strict adherence to certain tenets (*e.g.*, the literal inerrancy of Scripture) held to be fundamental to the Christian faith. The *Encyclopaedia of Social Sciences* elaborates the origins of fundamentalism as follows:

Fundamentalism is the name of the aggressive conservation movement in the Protestant Churches of the United States which flourish during the decade after the world war.

In India, religious fundamentalism gains adherence only in the measure that reason retreats in politics, muscle power and money suffocates democracy. Ideological pluralism and ideological is sought to be snuffed out by fundamentalism expressed in religious terms, whether in the name of Hinduism or Islam or Christianity. It is a fact that any rigid dogma can degenerate into a fundamentalist mind set crushing liberty and democracy and fundamentalism can equally express itself in racist terms. The apartheid system in South Africa, Hitler's Nazism and Stalinist persecution are the examples of fundamentalism.

Whenever human beings in larger or smaller aggregates in any society perceive that their physical spiritual well being and their future cannot be achieved through reason in politics, thus became assailed by a sense of fear and uncertainty, they would tend to fall back upon fundamentalism as the only emotionally stabilising factor. It is directly relatable to massive frustration of hopes and aspirations of the peoples concerned for both bread and liberty.

Justice D.P. Madon of Supreme Court in his article "Anatomy of Communal Riots: Genesis, causes and Solutions" has said that Communalism is a way of thinking—the result of the perversions of religion and the distortions of history; and as people think, so do their children grow up to think. When this way of thinking gets translated into action, we have communal riots. As said before, no religion has continued or exists as its founder preached. Leaving aside other religions, Muslim fundamentalism is a common bye-word and is said to be a common phenomenon. If one wants to think of an intolerant religion, Islam is the first which comes to mind. Yet Prophet Mohammed never preached intolerance nor does the *Quran* proclaim it. Sura 2 verse 257 says, "There should be no compulsion in religion." Verse 286 of the Sura says, "We make no distinction between any of His Messengers". Sura 6 verse 109 states, "Revile not those unto whom they pray beside *Allah* lest they, out of spite, revile *Allah* in their ignorance".

Mr. R. Venkataraman, former President of India in his inaugural address of Human Rights day celebrations on 10.12.1988 at New Delhi had said: "The Universal Declaration was followed by the enunciation of the two legally binding instruments. The Covenant on Civil and Political Rights and the Covenant on Economic, Social and Cultural Rights. The standards set forth in these instruments were further amplified and expanded upon in treaties such as those on the Elimination of Racial Discrimination, on the suppression of Apartheid and on the Elimination of Discrimination against Women. The last decade has seen a fresh milestone being crossed every few years. The Convention against Torture has been followed by the Declaration on the Right to Development and we are now on the threshold of a Convention on the Rights of Migrant Workers and on the Rights of the Child. It has been pointed out not without justification that the proliferation of these legal codes and treaties has been somewhat more rapid than the actual implementation of existing instruments. I believe, however, that such codification is a reflection of the process of the progressive unfolding of a relatively new set of principles encompassing existing political realities and fresh ideas of our times."

The concept of Human Rights defines the limits of State action to protect an individual's freedoms. In the sphere of civil and political rights and the freedom of the individual, the concept claims a fundamental validity, even though it defines a State's responsibility in the area of Human Rights a trifle negatively. In this regard, the mention of Article 2 of the Universal Declaration of Human Rights, 1948 is most relevant. Article 2 aforesaid says that everyone is entitled to all the rights and freedoms set forth in this declaration, without distinction of any kind, such as race, colour, sex, language, religion, political or other opinion, national or social origin, property, birth or other status.

Further in the Charter of the United Nations, the nations of the world had determined to reaffirm faith in fundamental Human Rights, in the dignity and worth of the human person and to practise tolerance and live together in peace with one another as good neighbours.

It is seen that for the last 20-25 years or more religious fundamentalism had risen to great extent. Religious fanatics are killing innocent people in the name of religion in Iraq, Indonesia, in India, Kashmir and Punjab, which are clear infringement of basic Human Rights and religious harmony. There are repeated instances of conversion from one religion to another religion by allurement or by coercion or pressure. Such activities of forcible conversion of religion has been prohibited by India by legislation. Although, Article 18 in Universal Declaration of Human Rights, 1948 provides that everyone has the right to freedom of thought, conscience and religion; this right includes freedom to change his religion or belief, and freedom, either alone or in community with others and in public or private to manifest his religion or belief in teaching, practice, worship and observance.

The Preamble of the Indian Constitution solemnly resolved that India to be a Socialist, Secular, Democratic, Republic and to secure to all its citizens' liberty of thought, expression, belief, faith and worship. This is the basic structure of the

Indian Constitution as held by the Constitution Bench of the Supreme Court in the case of *Keshvananda Bharati* v. *State of Kerala*, (1973) 4 SCC 225. We all know, India is a country of several languages and different religions. It is a holy example of unity in diversity. Hindus make prayers in the East direction, Muslim makes prayer in the West direction but all live in India in peaceful and congenial atmosphere and they follow religious tolerance. This is the beauty of Indian culture and society.

Mr. P.N. Haksar in his article, "Fundamentalism and Secularism" has stated that "one can perhaps, formulate a generalization about cases generating fundamentalism expressed in religious terms. Whenever human beings in larger or smaller aggregates in any society perceive that their physical and spiritual well being and their future cannot be achieved through reason in politics, and thus become assailed by a sense of fear and uncertainty, they would tend to fall back upon fundamentalism as the only emotionally stabilizing factor. In so far as there is a growing potentiality of the rise of fundamentalism in countries where people profess Islam, it is directly relatable to massive frustration of hopes and aspiration of the peoples concerned for both bread and liberty. Historically speaking, these frustrations are the direct result of policies pursued by the West, including the United States, in the entire arena which embraces Pakistan, Iran, Turkey and the entire Arab World. Naturally, these frustrations might also grip those areas of the former Soviet Union in which people have Islamic faith."

Mr. P.N. Haksar in his above mentioned article further wrote that; "It is important to remember that the process of secularisation was powerfully helped by the elaboration of natural laws instead of laws derived from sanctity of religion. When, in the midst of this process, there emerged the modern nation State, the question arose, and certainly arises in our country with a particular sense of legitimacy, about the nature and character of our State. Is State an instrument for enforcing divine laws? Alternatively, is State an instrument for the enlargement and protection of the totality of national interest transcending religious or denominational divisions? It is from these considerations that there arose the need for the State confining itself to the affairs of this world, and thus being secular rather than being an instrument of any particular faith or dogma".

Professor Rasheeduzzafar, Vice-Chancellor, Hamdard University, New Delhi in his article "Role of the Education in Communal Harmony" has mentioned that in view of this global experience, it is significant that a strong defence of the concept of modern Indian nationalism, based on secularism, unity in diversity, and communal harmony, as against religious nationalism, is primarily in the interest of national unity and integrity and is a matter of great significance for the long-term survival and emergence of a united and strong India. The question is: how can education help in developing communal harmony and a united and strong India?

The aim of education is not merely to inculcate selective skills but to develop the complete man. Education should help our students to think clearly and be responsible citizens of India. The Spanish philosopher Ortega Y. Gasset was dead right when he said in his essay on The Mission of the University, "When you have been a member of a University in a true sense for any length of time, you will be thenceforward and for ever a different person."

It is in this broader context of educational objectives that we should seriously review as to where we have gone wrong in formulating and implementing our national education policy that it has failed to fulfil the goal and aspirations of communal harmony, so vital for the unity and strength of India.

Since education is essentially a community affair, stemming from the roots of society, striving to solve its problems, and to achieve its objectives and aspirations, it has a definite role to play in bringing about communal harmony and national integration in the country. Leaders in all walks of life, and a significant sector of the community, pass through the primary, middle and secondary schools, intermediate Colleges and Universities, and in this process are exposed to the impact of education. Education, however, can play an effective role in establishing communal harmony only when specific measures are taken which reduce and counter the divisive tendencies and create a degree of common cultural heritage from which members of every community may derive inspiration.

Ignorance about other religions is the main cause of religious fundamentalism. In India, Hindus, Muslims, Christians, Parsis, Sikhs, Buddhists and followers of other religions live together. But followers of every religion think that their religion is best and other is not to that mark. Although in the every religion supreme authority is God and a man should not hate other. Every religion teaches the principle of religious tolerance and brotherhood. But communal elements tried to create atmosphere of hatred and ill feeling among the people of different religions. Such activities are not good for the unity and stability of the country. Government should come forward with a proper scheme to provide education to all people that principles of all the religions is good for human beings so no one should hate other religion rather other religion should also be respected and honoured. Sometimes religion is misused by political leaders, to get their vote bank under their control. Now a days, it becomes true that educated/intellectual persons in India have no control over the common people and they have separated themselves from the common people and common people is under the control of persons who have petty interest in politics or earning their name or fame either by hook or crook.

Preamble of the Constitution and Articles 15-17 and 25-30 of the Indian Constitution provides that India is a secular country and all the religion should be honoured and respected. There is freedom of religions, belief and worship. Moreover, Article 51A of the Constitution of India contemplates that it shall be the duty of every citizen of India to abide by the Constitution and respect its ideals and institutions, the National Flag and National Anthem, to promote harmony and the spirit of common brotherhood amongst all the people of India transcending religious, linguistic and regional or sectional diversities, to renounce practices derogatory to the dignity of women, etc.

Further, religious feelings and sentiments of any citizen are not hurt and religious harmony is maintained/protected, several provisions in the Indian Penal Code, namely, sections 153A, 153B, 295, 295A, 296, 297 and 298 are incorporated. These are penal in nature and violators of those provisions if convicted will receive sentence of imprisonment and fine or both.

India is a country of more than one hundred crores people having several religions and many languages and the philosophy of *Sarv Dharam Sam Bhav* (treat all religions equally) is applicable. Lord Rama, Lord Buddha, Lord Mahavira, Guru Nanak were born in India and they preached for brotherhood, peace, amity and to honour the religion of each other. In *Ramayana*, it is specifically written that, "*Parhit Saris Dharam Nahi Bhai, Par Pida Sam Nahi Adhimai*" (There is no religion which does not help other and it is sin to cause pain to other). Communal harmony/religious harmony can only be obtained through co-operation of people of all the religions and for that it is to be tried from school level and every children should know about the other religion and the ideals of secularism be put in their mind from very initial stage. Ancient India propounded the philosophy of *Vasudhaiva Kutumbakam* (entire world is a family). Moreover there should be total ban on use of religion in politics. There must be inter-action between different religious heads to solve the problems which is likely to be aggravated. To maintain the religious harmony is very essential for unity of India.

CHAPTER 6

HUMAN RIGHTS AND LAW ENFORCING OFFICIALS

The term "law Enforcement Officials", as defined in International Code of Conduct for Law Enforcement Officials, includes all officers of the law, whether appointed or elected, who exercise police powers, especially the powers of arrest or detention. In case police powers are exercised by military authorities or by State security forces the term shall be regarded as including officers of such services. Law enforcing officials while discharging their duties are required to act according to national and international codes of conduct as also the municipal law and the rules made thereunder in the country where they have been entrusted with the job of law enforcement.

Power brings some sort of ego or arrogance or a feeling of superiority and strength in a person vested with such powers. Hence, it is essential that efforts must be to find some safety valves by which the ravages of power could be curtailed so that it could be anchored to certain ideals, which would make its use gainful and constructive. For thousands of years, the prophets, philosophers, thinkers and researchers have discovered inherent destructive propensities of power but it is common knowledge that the custodians of law whose duty is to protect and not to indulge in gross Human Rights violations become deprecators of civil liberties and flout the laws by resorting to committing acts of lawlessness.

International Code of Conduct for Law Enforcement Officials adopted by the United Nations *vide* Resolution No. 34/169 contains the following provisions:

Article 1. Law enforcement officials shall at all times fulfil the duty imposed upon them by law, by serving the community and by protecting all persons against illegal acts, consistent with the high degree of responsibility required by their profession.

Article 2. In the performance of their duty, law enforcement officials shall respect and protect human dignity and maintain and uphold the Human Rights of all persons.

Article 3. Law enforcement officials may use force only when strictly necessary and to the extent required for the performance of their duty.

Article 4. Matters of a confidential nature in the possession of law enforcement officials shall be kept confidential, unless the performance of duty or the needs of justice strictly require otherwise.

Article 5. No law enforcement official may inflict, instigate or tolerate any act of torture or other cruel, inhuman or degrading treatment or punishment, nor may any law, state of war or a threat of war, a threat to national security, international political instability or any other public emergency as a justification of torture or other cruel, inhuman or degrading treatment or punishment.

Article 6. Law enforcement officials shall ensure the full protection of the health of persons in their custody and, in particular, shall take immediate action to secure medical attention whenever required.

Article 7. Law enforcement officials shall respect the law and the present Code. They shall also rigorously oppose and combat all such acts.

Article 8. Law enforcement officials shall respect the law and the present Code. They shall also, to the best of their capability, prevent and rigorously oppose any violations of them.

Law enforcement officials who have reason to believe that a violation of the present Code has occurred or is about to occur shall report the matter to their superior authorities and, where necessary, to other appropriate authorities or organs vested with reviewing or remedial power.

As regards Indian Police, they have got their own code of conduct, the police rules and various legislations, such as, Indian Penal Code, Code of Criminal Procedure, Indian Evidence Act etc. and they are also expected to discharge their duties with utmost devotion within the permissible parameters. Like any other public servant, the police officials also indulge in the violation of laws and codes and the Supreme Court as also various High Courts have dealt with cases involving high handedness of the police. Various authorities on the subject as also relevant provisions of Code of Criminal Procedure, Indian Evidence Act have been quoted in the chapter entitled "Human Rights and Custodial Crimes'. However to make the things more crystal clear, some of the authorities concerning police atrocities are being quoted.

In the case of *Bhim Singh* v. *State of Jammu and Kashmir,* (1985) 4 SCC 677, the Supreme Court had expressed the following view:

> "We do not wish to use stronger words to condemn the authoritarian acts of the police. If the personal liberty of a Member of the Legislative Assembly is to be played with in this fashion, one can only wonder what may happen to lesser mortals. Police Officers who are the custodians of law and order should have the greatest respect for the personal liberty of citizens and should not flout the laws by stooping to such bizarre acts of lawlessness. Custodians of law and order should not become deprecators of civil liberties. Their duty is to protect and not to abduct."

Regarding inhumanity, unreasonableness and arbitrariness handcuffing and tying with ropes of the under trial prisoners, the Supreme Court in many cases held that it is violation of Human Rights guaranteed under international law and Constitution of India. In the case of *Citizens for Democracy through its President* v. *State of Assam,* (1995) 3 SCC 743, Supreme Court ruled as under:—

> "This Court has, clearly and firmly, laid down that the police and the jail authorities are under a public duty to prevent the escape of prisoners and provide them with safe custody but at the same time the rights of the prisoners guaranteed to them under Articles 14, 19 and 21 of the Constitution of India cannot be infracted. The authorities are justified in taking suitable measures, legally permissible to safeguard the custody of the prisoners but the use of fetters purely at the whims or subjective discretion of the authorities is not

permissible. This Court in *Batra's* case and *Shukla's* case elaborately dealt with the extreme situation when the police and jail authorities can resort to handcuffing of the prisoners inside and outside the jail. It is a pity that the authorities have miserably failed to follow the law laid down by this Court in the matter of handcuffing of prisoners. The directions given by this Court are not being followed and being treated as pious declaration. We take judicial notice of the fact that the police and the jail authorities are even now using handcuffs and other fetters indiscriminately and without any justification. It has, therefore, become necessary to give binding directions and enforce the same meticulously. The seven detenus who were lodged inside the ward of a hospital were likely to escape from custody. The antecedents of the detenus are not known. There is nothing on the record to show that they are prone to violence, general averments that they are accused of terrorist and disruptive activities, murder, extortion, hoarding and smuggling of arms and ammunition are not sufficient to place them under fetters and rope while lodged in a closed ward of the hospital as patients. Security guards were posted outside the ward. It is not disputed that while in jail the detenus were not handcuffed. They cannot be in a worse condition while in hospital under treatment as patients. In any case to safeguard any attempt to escape, extra-armed guards can be deployed around the ward of the hospital where the detenus are lodged. The handcuffing and in addition tying with ropes of the patient-prisoners who are lodged in the hospital is, the least we can say, inhuman and in utter violation of the Human Rights guaranteed to an individual under the International Law and the law of the land. Handcuffs or other fetters shall not be forced on a prisoner—convicted or under trial- while lodged in a jail anywhere in the country or while transporting or in transit from one jail to another or from jail to Court and back. The police and the jail authorities, on their own, shall have no authority to direct the handcuffing of any inmate of a jail in the country or during transport from one jail to another or from jail to Court and back."

Where the police or the jail authorities have well-grounded basis for drawing a strong inference that a particular prisoner is likely to jump jail or break out of the custody then the said prisoner be produced before the Magistrate concerned and a prayer for permission to handcuff the prisoner be made before the said Magistrate. Save in rare cases of concrete proof regarding proneness of the prisoner to violence, his tendency to escape, he being so dangerous/desperate and finding no other practical way of forbidding escape is available, the Magistrate may grant permission to handcuff the prisoner.

In all the cases where a person arrested by police, is produced before the Magistrate and remand—judicial—or non-judicial—is given by the Magistrate the person concerned shall not be handcuffed unless special orders in that respect are obtained from the Magistrate at the time of the grant of the remand.

When the police arrests a person in execution of a warrant of arrest obtained from a Magistrate, the person so arrested shall not be handcuffed unless the police has also obtained orders from the Magistrate for the handcuffing of the person to be so arrested.

The police officials, in discharging their duties have to comply with all the directions of the Court and provisions of the laws applicable to them and the persons with which they are dealing in matters of arrest, search of arrested persons, their examination, their detention, production before the Magistrate, cognizance of offences, attendance and examination of witnesses, confession etc.

The police code of conduct prescribed by the Government, also expects Policemen to be faithful to the Indian Constitution, discharge their duties with utmost devotion and sincerity without fear or favour or vindictiveness, to enforce the law, keep the welfare of the people always in mind and not to transgress the limits of the powers vested in them.

CHAPTER 7

COMPENSATION FOR VIOLATION OF HUMAN RIGHTS

According to Article 300 of the Constitution of India, Government is liable for its tortuous acts. Provisions of Article 300 aforesaid are set out as below:

> "300. *Suits and proceedings.*—(1) The Government of India may sue or be sued by the name of the Union of India and the Government of a State may sue or be sued by the name of the State and may, subject to any provisions which may be made by Act of Parliament or of the Legislature of such State enacted by virtue of powers conferred by this Constitution, sue or be sued in relation to their respective affairs in the like cases as the Dominion of India and the corresponding Provinces or the corresponding Indian States might have sued or been sued if this Constitution had not been enacted.
>
> (2) If at the commencement of this Constitution—
>
> (a) any legal proceedings are pending to which the Dominion of India is a party, the Union of India shall be deemed to be substituted for the Dominion in those proceedings; and
>
> (b) any legal proceedings are pending to which a Province or an Indian State is a party, the corresponding State shall be deemed to be substituted for the Province or the Indian State in those proceedings."

Supreme Court of India in the case of *SAHELI, a Women's Resources Centre* v. *Commissioner of Police Delhi,* (1990) 1 SCC 422 has categorically held that a suit lies against the Government for wrongs done by public servants in the course of business, such as death or injury caused to a person by Police Authorities.

But Rajasthan High Court in the case of *Chaitanya Singh* v. *M.D.S. University,* AIR 1998 Raj 129 has held that the compensation in proceedings for enforcement of fundamental rights cannot be claimed directly under Article 226 of the Constitution of India where alternative remedy of filing suit is available.

The doctrine of sovereign immunity of the State from its liability for torts committed by its servants has its roots in the feudal period of English history when England was ruled by absolute monarchs. The King was the dispenser of justice. All Courts of law were his Courts and as such the King could not be sued in his own Courts and because the King was the fountainhead of justice, he could not do any wrong. Immunity of the State for its sovereign acts is claimed on the basis of the old English maxim that the King can do no wrong.

But due to enacting of Crown Proceedings Act, 1947, the law relating to immunity in England has been changed. The doctrine of sovereign immunity and good faith clause used to ignore acts of malfeasance and misfeasance on the part of public authorities. These acts resulted in depriving the fundamental rights especially life and liberty.

Sections 201 to 229 of the Indian Penal Code provides offences against the public servant. It is well-settled that the State is not above the law. Any State or its servants cannot play with the life and liberty of a citizen and the property. State is a juristic person. There is no doubt that the State has extraordinary powers but it has statutory duties also. Maintenance of law and order, administration of justice and reduction of crimes are primary functions of the State. Violation of basic Human Rights and fundamental rights by the State authorities are wrong in public law and the State is legally bound to pay the compensation to the victims.

In *State of Rajasthan* v. *Vidyawati*, AIR 1962 SC 933, the Supreme Court rejected the maxim "the king can do no wrong" observing that there is no corresponding provision in the Indian law and further ruled that the doctrine of Sovereign immunity, in the absence of any express legislation to the contrary, does not apply.

So far as fundamental rights and Human Rights are concerned, the law has marched ahead like a Pegasus, but the Government attitude continues to be conservative and it tries to defend its action or the tortuous action of its officers by raising the plea of immunity for sovereign acts or acts of the State. The ever increasing abuses of power by the public authorities and arbitrary interference with life and liberty of the citizen came to be recognised by the Court and held such infringements to be wrong in public law and State was held liable to compensate the victims.

The rule requires that the wrongs should not remain un-redressed. All the individuals or persons committing wrongs should be liable to an action for damages for breach of civil law or for criminal punishment. Compensation means anything given to make things equivalent, a thing given or to make amends for loss, recognize, remuneration or pay. The expression compensation is not ordinarily used as an equivalent to damage although compensation may often have to be measured by the same rule as damages in an action for a breach. Compensation is a return for a loss or damages sustained. Justice requires that it should be equal in value, although not alike in kind. The object of providing compensation is to place the claimant as far as possible in the same position financially as he was before the accident. In the case of death, basis of compensation is loss of monetary benefits to the dependants of the deceased, which includes monetary loss, expenses and loss to the estate. The purpose and Object is to mitigate hardship that has been caused to the legal heirs due to sudden death of the deceased in the accident. Compensation awarded should be adequate. Although there is no exact uniform formula for measurement of value of human life and damage, but the amount recoverable depends on broad facts and circumstances of the case.

It is apt to mention here that claim in public law for compensation for infringement of the fundamental rights has been upheld by Supreme Court in the case of *D.K. Basu* v. *State of West Bengal*, (1997) 1 SCC 416 wherein it was held that the claim in public law for compensation for unconstitutional deprivation of fundamental right to life and liberty, the protection of which is guaranteed under the Constitution, is a claim based on strict liability and is in addition to the claim available in private law for damages for tortuous acts of the public laws proceedings. Award of compensation for established infringement of the indefeasible rights guaranteed under Article 21 of the Constitution is a remedy available in public law since the purpose of public law is not only to civilise public power but also to assure the citizens that they live under a legal system wherein their rights and interests shall be protected and preserved. Grant of compensation in proceedings under Article 32 or Article 226 of the Constitution of India for the established violation of the fundamental rights guaranteed under Article 21, is an exercise of the Courts under the public law jurisdiction for penalising the wrong-doer and fixing the liability for the public wrong on the State which failed in the discharge of its public duty to protect the fundamental rights of the citizen.

Article 21 of the Constitution of India totally prohibits use of third degree methods by the police officials to extract information from a suspect for working out a crime. Article 21 bans the taking away of the life and liberty of an individual except in accordance with law. It is obligatory on the State and its functionaries to respect and protect life and liberty of an individual. Police Organisation has been formed to maintain the law and order and to curb the criminal activities. The Police Organisation has to work within the parameters of law and it cannot exceed the legal frame work. No right has been conferred upon Police to assault or disrespect any individual. Even in the name of investigation or interrogation, no torture can be made against suspect to extract the information. Sections 330 and 331 of the Indian Penal Code provide punishment for subjecting a person to torture for extracting information. These legal provisions prohibit torture, brutality and extra legal methods in extracting confession or any information from the suspect. It is necessary to change the old method of investigation by introducing scientific and upgraded mode of investigation by Police Officials, by respecting human values and the Human Rights. Recently the investigation of a crime by way of Narco test, has been declared unconstitutional and arbitrary by the Supreme Court of India in the year 2010, a Bench headed by Mr. K.G. Balakrishnan, Chief Justice particularly known as *Selvi* v. *State of Karnataka*, (2010) 7 SCC 263.

It is relevant to mention that when a suspect is subjected to third degree methods in a police station there would be no witnesses to the incident. This being the position there would be hardly any justification for delaying the grant of compensation in a writ petition or civil litigation filed against State and its functionaries. In the case of violation of Article 21 of the Constitution of India, namely death in the Police custody, rape or molestation, torture and brutality, *ex-gratia* payment or compensation should be awarded at the earliest. It should not be delayed for years together.

CHAPTER 8

HORIZON OF HUMAN RIGHTS

According to a famous jurist Jack Donnely 'Human Rights' are the new standards of civilization. All Human Rights for all is the goal of the century and the aim is to ensure that Human Rights are universally accepted and respected.

It is truly said that Human Rights are inherently available in the nature and without which no one can survive as human being. Human Rights mean the rights relating to liberty, dignity, life and equality of a man embodied in the international covenants and guaranteed by the Constitution.

Human Rights are a universal entitlement necessitating its full implementation. Undisputedly *Magna Carta* is the earliest charter of the freedom as well as certain Human Rights. It was made in the year 1216 A.D. by the King John I of England Chapter 39 of *Magna Carta* states that no man shall be arrested but by the lawful Judgment of his peers and the law of the Land. On *Magna Carta*, great John Aubery Spoken that," the Parliament intended to have him hanged and he expected no less but resolved to be hanged with bible under one arm and *Magna Carta* under the other. *Magna Carta* was re-affirmed in 1354 by King Edward III whereby it was stated that no person would be prejudiced by any State action or be harmed, except in due process of law.

After *Magna Carta*, in 1688 A.D. in England petition of rights was made repeating the faith in Human Rights thereafter Holmes and Locke declared the thought on Liberty clearly speaking that "the National liberty of man is to be free from any superior power on earth. In U.S.A., in the year 1776 the declaration of independence was made declaring that all men are created equal, endowed by the creator with creation unalienable rights such as life, liberty and pursuit of happiness. In 1789, in France declaration of Human Rights came into existence which says categorically that Human Rights are natural to mankind.

In the year 1791 in America, Bill of Rights was incorporated in the Constitution. It is to be noted that the France Declaration of Rights, 1789 and the Bill of Rights, 1791 are the main sources of development of Human Rights.

On 1-1-1942 declaration No. 26 of UN declared faith in Fundamental Human Rights in the dignity and worth of Human persons in the legal rights of man and woman.

The 20th Century has witnessed two dangerous World Wars which have created havoc and disaster to the human kind. The feeling of wellness of people disappear and hatred and animosity spread over very fastly.

The existence of world community was threatened by such grave situation and alarming condition necessitated formation of United Nations in the year 1945 and it gave rise to United Nations Charter. It says that it is necessary to save succeeding generation from scourge of war which was brought untold sorrow to mankind and Human Rights. It also declared to maintain dignity and worth of the human person.

For development and expansion of Human Rights, the Universal Declaration of Human Right, 1948 (UDHR), International Covenant and Economic, Social and Cultural Rights, 1966 and International Covenant of Civil and Political Rights, 1966 (ICPR) have played bigger role without being non-presence of those revolutionary documents, the progress of Human Rights as it is seen today would have been a dream.

Universal Declaration of Human Rights was accepted on 10-12-1948 by the General Assembly of United Nations. It is not a treaty but it enumerates the economic, political, civil, social and cultural rights of human beings. It is an instrument of protection having moral force. It is a manifesto of Fundamental Freedom of human beings. Articles 3, 6, 9 of the said UDHR are very relevant. Rule of law, requirement of fair and impartial trial, equality before the law, rights to life, are the important ingredients of Human Rights.

It is apt to mention that said UDHR is not a binding document and it is only recommendatary in nature. It contains a list of Human Rights relating to suffering of human beings, their political struggles and the understanding of standard threats to human dignity. The said UDHR has influenced the preparation of Canadian Charter of Rights, Human Rights Act, 1998 in England. According to Article 5 of Vienna declaration it treats internationally recognized Human Rights holistically as an indivisible structure in which the value of each right is augmented by the persons of many countries.

It is true that the declarations mentioned in the UDHR, 1948 are not universally accepted. For instance Indian and African society formulate their conception of Human Rights based on their understanding of human dignity. Government of China said that man exists for the State and no one can dictate to it how to govern. It is noticed that Africa has never accepted the present form of UDHR and they are opposed to applicability on them.

Article 16 of ICPR deals about right to life which recognizes no discrimination with regard to sex, religion, colour, race, birth place etc. Article 15 of ICPR says about rule of law which says no person shall be held guilty of any criminal offence on account of any act not embodied in law. Human Rights are foremost right against the society. It is the duty of the National and State Government to see that basic Human Rights are not violated and also to see that these are protected, safeguarded and maintained.

In this regard, the remarks made by Dr. Shankar Dayal Sharma, the then President of India are reproduced as under:

> "In recent times, political and constitutional developments in different countries around the world in Europe and elsewhere have led to a widening of understanding regarding the central importance of Human Rights and have, in my view, highlighted two important aspects. *First*, it appears that there is progressive increase in the realization by political scientists that recognition of Human Rights and enforcement of Human Rights leads to stability in society and also allows for upward mobility of weaker sections in society. Different political systems are now increasingly accepting the truth

that a society that is both stable and progressive can be built only i fundamental rights are recognized and enforced. *Second*, the experience of political systems wherein Human Rights were either denied or suppressed indicates that such systems, inevitably, have failed to survive and that the constitutional, legal and political thinking under which these systems functioned, proved to be both unjust and inexpedient".

The States are to maintain and protect strictly and vigorously the basic Human Rights which includes non-discrimination, equal treatment, fair and impartial trial, right to live with dignity and honour and other similar rights. In India, in the year 1993 the Protection of Human Rights Act was legislated incorporating main and substantial provisions of UDHR. The covenant on civil and political rights and cultural rights were incorporated in the said Act. Said Act constituted National Human Rights Commission, State Human Rights Commission and Human Rights Courts to check and control the violation of Human Rights and to punish the offenders.

In the Indian Constitution, the term Human Rights has not been defined but the same is defined in section 2(1)(d) of the Protection of Human Rights Act, 1993. The fundamental rights mentioned in the Indian Constitution more or less similar to the Human Rights as mentioned in UDHR, ICPR, 1966 and ICESR, 1966 for expansion of Human Rights, to check violation and infringement of Human Rights, to enlarge scope of Basic Human Rights, to punish the violators of Human Rights to direct National and State Governments to act towards protection, safeguard and enforcement of Human Rights.

Relying on Article 24 of the ICPR, 1966, Supreme Court of India in the case of *Sheela Barse* v. *Secretary, Children's Aid Society*, (1987) 3 SCC 50 directed the Government of India and State machinery to implement in proper manner to protect the rights of children who were kept in Observation Home. In the case of *Charan Lal Sahu* v. *Union of India*, (1990) 1 SCC 613 Supreme Court of India has highly appreciated the Human Right and very strongly held as under:

> "As mentioned in the Universal Declaration of Human Rights that people are born free and the dignity of the persons must be recognized and an effective remedy by competent Tribunal is one of the surest methods of effective remedy. If, therefore, as a result of this tragedy new consciousness and awareness on the part of the people of this country to be more vigilant about measures and the necessity of ensuring more strict vigilance for permitting the operations of such dangerous and poisonous gases dawn, then perhaps the tragic experience of Bhopal would not go in vain".

In *Maneka Gandhi* v. *Union of India*, (1978) 1 SCC 248 Supreme Court ruled that the scope of Article 21 of the Constitution was confined to excessive Executive action which was not in accordance with the procedure established by law.

In the case arising out of post Godhara carnage in Gujarat known as the case of *National Human Rights Commission* v. *State of Gujarat*, AIR 2009 (Supp) SC 318 Supreme Court of India entertained the petitions filed by National Human Rights Commission for transfer of the cases of the suspects arrested and charge-sheeted in those cases from Gujarat to other State and also directed to change the Investigating Officers.

CHAPTER 9

CORPORATE GOVERNANCE AND HUMAN RIGHTS

Justice Mukul Mudgal, Chief justice of Punjab and Haryana High Court in his recent article "Corporate Governance and Human Rights" published in *Human Rights Year Book*, 2009 has stated that Corporate Governance can be defined as the general set of customs, regulations, habits, laws and norms, which determine the manner in which a firm should be run. It plays a vital role in the healthy running of a corporation, as it lends a helping hand to the corporation for functioning in a moral and ethical manner. Thus, Human Rights also form an integral part of corporate governance, being a necessary ingredient for the same to result in a positive impact. The principle of 'corporate social responsibility' covers Human Rights as an integral part of corporate governance.

It is interesting to note Mahatma Gandhi's vision with regard to these principles. His perspective of ownership of capital was that of trusteeship. He believed that basically society was providing capitalists with an opportunity to manage resources, in the form of trusteeship on behalf of the society at large. At present this is the basic concept, which, has come to be articulated as the principle of social responsibility of business and industry. The broad rationale behind the entire concept is rooted in the fact that corporations derive many benefits from the society, which the corporations have an obligation to reciprocate by providing for the society as well. The system of taxation in most countries ensures that the society does benefit by way of facilities provided by the Government such as roads, transportation facilities and other services impacting its citizens. However, there exist numerous other aspects of services which are provided by the society, which have recently gained more importance than the usual traditional relationship between the government and business. The progress and welfare of the society is not merely the responsibility of governments alone, but also of all other stakeholders including the corporate sectors.

It is an admitted fact that the commercial activities and businesses are expanding from one country to another country and a continent to another continent. There is globalization of the businesses. Developed countries like America, France, England, Germany etc., have developed well-oiled system for the safeguard of Human Rights. But the developing countries and under-developed countries do not have such strong system for protection of Human Rights of their citizens. The Global Multinational Companies to earn more profits go search for cheap labour markets which they do not get in their own countries but they get in under-developed and developing countries. These big and giant companies have one point formula to capture the international market and to win competition with their rival corporations. Most of the time they do not care or bother about violation of basic Human Rights of their employees and the environmental issues. They perceive the ideas of supremacy and capitalism over the human right. These corporate bodies even ignore United Nations Declaration, International Treaties and Guidelines. Corporate sectors are using child labours and forced labours for their production activities, as they are available at cheap price.

Although in India there is total prohibition of child labours in manufacturing unit and any violation of such prohibitory law is penal. Such activities of corporate sector are clear violation of basic Human Rights of those poor and defense less employees working in their big industrial unit. Outsourcing is developing day-by-day. Even the banking, insurance and other similar activities of developed countries are being carried out in India, China and other developing and under-developed nations. It is demand of the time that before a multinational or global companies set up any factory or manufacturing unit in any other countries it must negotiate with not only the concerned government but also with local recognized non-governmental organisation, environment-friendly group, local people to access and know their needs, problems and possible environmental hazards. It is not a secret thing now that due to excessive emission of carbon di-oxide by vehicular pollution, industrial pollution and cutting of green young trees (deforestation), excessive use and misuse of electricity, covering the tanks, wells and ponds for construction activities the entire earth is facing a threat of its existence. How to get pure water and clean air for the next generation is a big question mark. Global warming is a truth and developed countries, multinational corporations and corporate bodies are major contributories to the dangerous and panicky global warming. It is well-known that the basic Human Rights are the natural rights, which are available to every individual from his birth. Due to concentrating the ideas of profit and profit only, the large number of industries take little care for violation of Human Rights. Justice K.S. Javeri, Gujarat High Court in his illustrative article "Integrity in Corporate Governance and Human Rights" has defined good corporate governance as below:

Good corporate governance means preserving core values and ethical business conduct. Lawyers and officials would often boast of ethics and integrity but recent examples of numerous corporate scandals tell a different story. Corporate governance in this context is a challenge for organisations and it is in this area that 'integrity' and 'Human Rights' play an important role. The word "integrity" literally means adherence to values. Integrity reveals that the truth about an individual or a corporation. On a personal level, integrity is measured by what an individual does and does not do when no one is looking. Does he hold to his values, beliefs, and ethics? Or does he compromise and does the opposite of what he believes are right? At the corporate level integrity does not differ. Corporate reports and communications may stage one thing when in reality the corporation is doing something else. This inconsistency can come as a result of ignorance, market/management pressure, or an outright willingness to deceive. Within corporations it may be the result of some person or group seeking to violate an organisation's governance principles, risk posture, compliance obligations, culture, and ethical practices for some personal gains. The recent Satyam Computers Scam is a shining example of violation of integrity in corporate field. The *Satyam* case is not an isolated one but similar maladies prevailed worldwide.

Integrity is violated when corporate policies and procedures are thrown out of the window in the quest for personal or corporate as two sides of the same coin. In order for a corporation to have integrity, it is important for it to have an ethical environment with employees and business partners willing to follow and enforce legal and ethical corporate culture, policies and procedures.

It is important to bear in mind that it is the people who invest in the corporate sector and therefore such investments have to be utilized for the public good. People expect ethical behaviour from public servants and corporate sectors. When things go wrong, it is the public which suffers whether it is in the form of growing non-performing assets of banks or the securities scam or the corruption scandals.

Due to advancement and expansion of global business cutting across the national boundaries, there is decline of agriculture as the biggest job provider and thereby the labour force of agriculture sector run for employment for corporate sector.

In our own country India on 2-12-1984 a biggest tragedy called Bhopal Gas Leakage occurred. When over 35 tons of toxic gases leaked from a pesticide plant in Bhopal, owned by the US based multinational Union Carbide India Limited (UCIL). In the next 2-3 days more than 7,000 people died and many more were injured. Over the last 25 years at least 15,000 more people have died from illnesses related to the gas exposure. Today, more than 100,000 people continue to suffer from chronic and debilitating illnesses, for which treatment is largely ineffective. The disaster shocked the world and raised fundamental questions about government and corporate responsibility for industrial accidents that devastate human life and local environments. Yet 25 years later, the survivors and various organisations are still fighting for justice. Issues of pestisites, toxic wastes and contaminated water have not been resolved.

It is to be kept in mind that global business companies and big corporate units are very powerful and influential in the present world. They are not only able to dominate the government but they are equally able to influence some of its international bodies. There is an urgent need to change their mind and they should rethink over the important issues of protection of basic Human Rights which has been confirmed by Universal Declaration of human right adopted by United Nations General Assembly in 1946 and other international covenants on civil and political rights and also covenants on economic and social rights both enacted in the year 1966. The big corporation, global business house and powerful manufacturer utilize land, water and air in large scale. These are the natural resources and are accessible to all human beings but now their utilization has reached a very dangerous level.

These corporations have caused very serious threats and danger to the environment by large-scale pollution. They throw chemical and dirty water in river causing havoc, killing fish and other acquatic animals and making the water undrinkable and poisonous, throwing of toxic waste from the factories. At some place in Delhi, Yamuna river looks like big drain. Although to check and prevent pollution in India, Environmental (Protection) Act, 1986, The Water Act, The Air Act, The Indian Forests Act and other similar enactments have been made. The provision for punishment for causing pollution has been provided *i.e.,* fine and jail both. It is the social responsibility of the corporation to give due care to the concept of sustainable development. It prohibits utilization of natural resource selfishly and without keeping/saving storage for future generation. Corporate sector should extend their help to provide education facilities to needy and poor children as it is undisputed that education plays an important role in shaping the country as a whole. To avoid any kind of trouble or hostilities between the society and the corporate, the growth of corporate social responsibility is must.

In this regard the article "corporate governance and relevance of the right to live in dignity," written by Justice R.C. Chavan of Gujarat High Court is quoted as under:

> In spite of what the great Mahatma Gandhi said about dignity of labour, it has been the endeavour of mankind to have plenty and to have lots of leisure, without labour, forgetting the rule of nature that nothing really comes from nowhere and nothing goes nowhere. So, if a privileged few can enjoy plenty, it can come only if somebody is deprived, denied, or forced to slog it out. Can islands of prosperity survive in oceans of poverty? Can a privileged few afford to do nothing productive, professing to be busy in creative pursuits like fine arts and literature, while multitude toils to maintain these few high comforts? Can the fundamental values of Equality and Fraternity be sacrificed at the altar of creativity? Are all men really born equal or are some more equal than others as George Orwell saw in his Animal Farm? Who slogs for whom? Can an entire nation be enslaved to produce goods and services to keep another nation in comfort, because they control strings to the purse of plundered money? These are some of the questions that torment empty minds of millions of unemployed youngsters in India.

Search for corporate response to these questions led to interesting revelations. Vision/mission statements of corporates mostly have no place for human being, or even the society. Out of about 27 vision/mission statements of leading corporates in India sampled, most underline the need to create wealth and focus on shareholders' interests. Very few, like say, Indian Oil Corporation refer to quality of life of the community and to foster a culture of participation and innovation for employee growth and contribution. Some IT companies (not the IT majors) do focus on education, creating an open and warm environment where everyone is respected, listened to and encouraged to excel. Punjab National Bank refers to high work ethos in its mission statement. Tata Motors too refers to its mission to create for employees an organisation that incubates and promotes innovation, and excellence.

Mr. P.H. Parekh, Senior Advocate and President, Supreme Court Bar Association in his thought provoking article "Integrity in Corporate Governance and Human Rights" has suggested some of the following safeguards which a corporate house must adopt before starting the business:

(a) It should assess the Human Rights protection scenario in the country in which it intends to do business.

(b) It should build up some framework which helps the company to ensure the effective implementation of the Human Rights and to ensure appropriate mechanism.

(c) It is also expected from the corporates to comply with the international guidelines and standards for the use of force for *e.g.*, the UN Basic

Principles on the Use of Force and Firearms by Law Enforcement Officials and the UN Code of Conduct for Law Enforcement Officials.

(d) In case the corporate maintains or supports any private security forces, it needs to have safeguards to ensure that such forces are not used or become instrumental in violation of Human Rights under the guise of security or on the ground of grievances against rulers of some countries.

(e) Corporates should establish contact and have effective communications with various internal and external entities or organisations to assess its impact or involvement, direct or incidental, in any Human Rights violations. It should also try to identify those activities within the company which are most likely to result into Human Rights violations.

(f) If the corporates are intending to make any large scale investments or initiate any major projects, it needs to get in touch with local residents, non-governmental organisations as well as governmental authorities to assess and analyze the impact of such proposed investment or project and needs to look into its possible violations of Human Rights due to such activities.

(g) It is well-established and recognized since long that forced labour and child labour are the enemies of the society as well as the business world. Not only it constitutes a violation of fundamental Human Rights, it is also a blot on the corporate sector to be found involved in any act, practice or policy which is exercising, promoting or covering up an act of forced labour in any disguise.

Corporates should have a clear policy not to use, be complicit in, or benefit from forced labour at any levels of the organisations. It needs to assess the laws governing or prohibiting the forced labour at national levels, if found lax or wanting in any aspect, the corporates need to adopt international standards and should not make any attempts to benefit from lax national laws. Corporates should promote greater understanding within the organisation of the laws governing forced labour in order to enable employers to avoid practicing forced labour and help employees understand laws for their own protection against any such practice.

(h) The world is said to be under an imminent and foreseeable threat of global warming. What our generation has been doing since past century, unfortunately, has turned out to be self destructive, if carried on in the same fashion for next few decades, global warming is not a distant dream but is our near future. It is the right of the coming generations to have equally clean air, water and land. We do not have any right to take these away from them and devoid them of any such basic human right to have clean and unpolluted resources. It would not be erroneous to state that industries were and still are the main contributors for this situation of global warming. We have created this we alone shall have to clean it out. Yes, it is the first responsibility of the corporate world to adopt non-polluting measures in all possible aspects. The corporates need to ensure that the future/generation enjoys their basic Human Rights by breathing cleaner air, drinking purer water and an ecology which is well-balanced.

It is relevant to mention that outsourcing of jobs resulted in cost cutting. Corporate sectors are interested only in maximum profits. They ignore the health and safety factors in manufacturing process and also in selling the product to consumers. Corporate social responsibilities are rarely followed to the issues relating to education, child labours, diversity and ethnicity. Further to protect and safeguard the basic Human Rights of the employees engaged in the manufacturing and industrial unit of corporate. Strict pro-labour laws should be enacted to allow adequate security system to move fastly to stop violation of Human Rights.

CHAPTER 10

HUMAN RIGHTS AND EDUCATION TO CHILDREN

Former Prime Minister of India Pt. Jawaharlal Nehru has said that the Indian people have to be brought together, *inter alia* through a strong education system, by a process of emotional integration which would highlight the points of unity, play down the difference, challenge the irrelevant socio-economic practice at the same time maintain the distinctive regional characteristics. He further stated that the whole idea of education is based on the co-operation of the teacher and the taught; otherwise there cannot be any education. Indian education system should improve to ensure freedom of thought, spirit and initiative among students and citizens.

Supreme Court of India in the case of *Aruna Roy* v. *Union of India*, (2002) 7 SCC 368, has defined Education as follows:

> "Education should not be for the purposes of making a child merely literate and intelligent. The real education is one in which a child gradually realizes that he is made up not only of body and mind but also some inner elemental qualities. Democracy cannot survive and Constitution cannot work unless Indian citizens are not only learned and intelligent, but they are also of moral character and imbibe the inherent virtues of human being such as truth, love and compassion."

Article 26(1) of the Universal Declaration of Human Rights declares right of education to everyone. Said Article 26(1) provides as under:

Article 26(1): Everyone has the right to education. Education shall be free, at least in the elementary and fundamental stages. Elementary education shall be compulsory. Technical and professional education shall be made generally available and higher education shall be equally accessible to all on the basis of merit.

(2) Education shall be directed to the full development of the human personality and to the strengthening of respect for Human Rights and fundamental freedoms. It shall promote understanding, tolerance and friendship among all nations, racial or religious groups, and shall further the activities of the United Nations for the maintenance of peace.

(3) Parents have a prior right to choose the kind of education that shall be given to their children.

In 1960, the UNESCO Convention against discrimination in education was held. It was expected from the States to ensure in a manner consistent with the procedures followed in the State for the application of its legislation, the religious and moral education of the children. It was also expected that no person or group of persons should be pressurized to receive religious instructions inconsistent with his conviction.

In 1966, International Covenant on Economic, Social and Cultural Rights (in short ICESCR) came in existence. Article 13 of the said Covenant says that State Parties to make primary education compulsory and free to all. Secondary education including technical and vocational shall be made general for all and accessible by progressive introduction of free education. Higher education will be made equally accessible on the basis of capacity. In 1974, UNESCO recommended to give quality education for promotion of international cooperation and peace, education and understanding relating to Human Rights and fundamental freedoms. In the said recommendation the term "Education" was defined as under:

> "The entire process of social life by means of which individual and social groups learn to develop consciously within, and for the benefit of the national and international communities, the whole of their personnel capacities, attitude, aptitudes and knowledge:"

UNESCO has advised that the education policy should promote:-

(i) an international dimension and a global perspective in education to all levels and in all its forms;

(ii) understanding and respect for all peoples, their cultures, civilizations, values and ways of life, including domestic ethnic cultures and cultures of other nations;

(iii) awareness of the increasing global interdependence between peoples and nations;

(iv) abilities to communicate with others;

(v) awareness not only of the rights but also of the duties incumbent upon individuals, social groups and nations towards each other;

(vi) understanding of the necessity for international solidarity and cooperation;

(vii) readiness on the part of the individual to participate in solving the problems of his community, his country and the world at large.

On 9-3-1993 United Nations Commission of Human Right recommended that knowledge of Human Rights, both in its theoretical dimension and practical application should be established as a priority in educational policy.

D.M. Dharmadhikari, Former Justice, Supreme Court of India in his article "Right to Education" has emphasized fulfilling the right to education as under:

> The fulfilment of the right to education can be assessed using the 4 A's framework, which asserts that for education to be a meaningful right it must be available, accessible, acceptable and adaptable.
>
> The 4 A's have been further elaborated as follows:
>
> **Availability.**—Education is free and government-funded and there is adequate infrastructure and trained teachers able to support education delivery.
>
> **Accessibility.**—The system is non-discriminatory and accessible to all, and positive steps are taken to include the most marginalized.

Acceptability.—The content of education is relevant, non-discriminatory and culturally appropriate and of quality. The school itself is safe and teachers are professional.

Adaptability.—Education can evolve with the changing needs of society and contribute to challenging inequalities, such as gender discrimination and can be adapted locally to suit specific contexts.

Right to education is instrumental in the realization of other rights. The rights of girls' education can be achieved effectively if the measures are implemented to address their right to freedom from discrimination, protection from physical violence and sexual abuse. Rights based approach to the education build respect for peace and non-violent conflict resolution. To get this aim or motto, the schools and education centers must develop learning environment and to stop all forms of physical and humiliating punishment by the teachers.

Rights based approach contributes to positive social transformation. Human Rights education empowers children and students towards social justice. Right-based approach to education highlights quality which encourages the development and progress of school environment in which children know their ideas and values. School should provide better quallity and standard of education to all the children to avoid disaffection. It also works to promote understanding and knowledge of other cultures, languages etc., and it strengthens social bindings and intra-cultural tie. A rights based approach to education is economically beneficial, sustainable and more cost effective. It is undisputed that abuse, violence, poor teaching quality are major reasons not to create the keenness in the student and to reduce drop outs. Health education should be given to all the children more particularly to the girls. Great thinkers of India, namely Mahatma Gandhi spiritual leader, Acharya Vinoba Bhave, Raja Ram Mohan Roy, Acharya Kriplani, Dr. B.R. Ambedkar, Dr. S. Radhakrishnan and several others propagated and spread the education in India.

Supreme Court of India in *Bandhua Mukti Morcha* v *Union of India*, (1997) 10 SCC 549, ruled that indeed, the democratic State may never reach its greatest potential without citizenry sufficiently educated to understand civil rights and social duties.

Article 45 of the Constitution of India provides that the State shall endeavour to provide, within a period of 10 years from the commencement of this Constitution, for free and compulsory education for all children until they complete the age of 14 years. Article 45 was repealed and in its place Article 21A was introduced by the 86th Constitutional Amendment Act, 2002 which is reproduced as under:

> "The State shall provide free and compulsory education to all children of the age of six to fourteen years in such manner as the State may, by law, determine".

Said Article 21A guarantees, free and compulsory education, which is in fact a constitutional basic Human Right. It puts an obligation on the State to provide free and compulsory education to all children of age between 6-14 years. The State must provide education which is its highest duty to the citizen.

Article 51A(k) of the Constitution of India is a fundamental duty cast upon every guardian or parent to provide opportunity for education to all children between the age of 6 and 14 years.

Supreme Court of India in *J.P. Unnikrishnan* v. *State of Andhra Pradesh,* AIR 1993 SC 2178 has specifically held that access to education is necessary for enjoyment of other-fundamental rights contained in Article 19 of Constitution of India.

India is a democratic nation and it is a multi-religious society. It is a secular country. In this context, the reference of Preamble of the Constitution of India is relevant. It resolves to constitute "Secular, Democratic, Republic to secure to all its citizens, social, economic and political justice, liberty of thoughts, expression, belief, faith and worship, equality of status and of opportunity and assuring such fraternity as to maintain the dignity of the individual and unity and integrity of the nation".

Articles 29 and 30 of the Constitution of India guarantees educational rights of the minorities to establish and manage their educational institutions subject to constitutional restriction. They can manage their institution as per their choice but educational institution funded by the State or maintained by the State is open to all the citizens irrespective of their caste, religion, language and race. In this regard, it is apt to mention that Articles 39(f) and 41 of the Constitution of India which are Directive Principles of State Policy which are reproduced as below:-

Article 39(f): "That children are given opportunities and facilities to develop in a healthy manner and in conditions of freedom and dignity and that childhood and youth are protected against exploitation and against moral and material abandonment"

Article 41: "The State shall, within the limit of its economic capacity and development, make effective provision for securing the right to work, to education and to public assistance in cases of unemployment, old age, sickness and disablement, and in other cases of underserved want".

For enforcement of the Article 21A, the right of children to free and compulsory Education Bill, 2008 was brought in Parliament. The said Bill became law and known as the Right of Children to Free and Compulsory Education Act, 2009 (in short RTE Act). It was enforced on 1-4-2010 in India. The said Act gives every child the right to a quality elementary education. According to said Act, all children aged 6-14 years shall have the right to free and compulsory elementary education at a neighbourhood school. No school fees or cost of uniform, textbooks, transportation and mid-day meals need be borne by the child or parents to obtain elementary education. All schools must comply with certain infrastructure and teacher norms. Two trained teachers will be provided for every sixty students at the primary level.

It is provided therein that schools shall constitute School Management Committees comprising parents, guardians, local officials and teachers. Said Committee will monitor utilization of government grants and the school environment. 50 per cent. women and parents of children from disadvantaged groups shall be included in the said Committee.

It is apt to mention that State Governments and local Bodies will have to establish primary schools within one kilometre of the neighbourhood. For children of class VI to VIII, the school should be within three kilometres of the neighbourhood. In the absence of a school in a small halmets, the State Government shall make adequate arrangement for free transportation and residential facilities.

It is pertinent to say that duration of compulsory education in India is 8 years like China, Cuba, and Switzerland. But duration of compulsory education in Chile is 15 years, in Germany, Paris and Italy is 12 years, in United Kingdom and Mauritius is 11 years.

It is apt to mention here that before passing of the said Act in India Sarva Siksha Abhiyan (SSA) was in operation and it was the main vehicle of spreading the education. Total requirement of RTE for five-years is worked out to be Rs. 1.71 lakhs crore. Teachers will be at the core of implementation of RTE that seeks to work toward a democratic classroom where all children participated as equal partner.

Dr. B.S. Chauhan, Judge Supreme Court of India in his judgment in the case of *State of Tamil Nadu* v. *K. Shyam Sunder*, reported in (2011) 8 SCC 737 has rightly held as follows:

> "The right of a child should not be restricted only to free and compulsory education, but should be extended to have quality education without any discrimination on the ground of its economic, social and cultural background."
>
> *
>
> "The State Government should have acted bearing in mind that destiny of a nation rests with its youths. Personality of a child is developed at the time of basic education during his formative years of life. Their career should not be left in dolorific conditions with uncertainty to such a great extent. The younger generation has to compete in global market. Education is not a consumer service nor the educational institution can be equated with shops."
>
> *
>
> "Uniform education system would achieve the code of common culture, removal of disparity and depletion of discriminatory values in human relations. It would enhance the virtues and improve the quality of human life, elevate the thoughts which advance our constitutional philosophy of equal society. In future, it may prove to be a basic preparation for the uniform civil code as it may help in dismissing opportunities to those who foment fanatic and fissiparous tendencies."

Further James Tooley, Professor of Education Policy, Newcastle University, U.K. in an article "Adding value to Education" published in *"Times of India Newspaper"* as emphasized below:

> "Something extraordinary is happening in education across rural India—that's the conclusion that stands out in Pratham's ASER, 2009 report launched recently. The extraordinary concerns private education. Pratham devotes two special sections to private schools, which shows it recognizes their importance. But it's even more significant than highlighted. True, it points to enrolment of 6-14 year old rural children in private education being stable at around 22 per cent.—that's more than one in five children who go to private school. In some States it is much higher—Haryana has 41 per cent. and Uttar Pradesh has 36 per cent. private school enrolment. In these States, two in five children go to private school. And this is about rural India, it is much higher in urban areas.

It is true that Pratham agrees children do much better in private than government schools–although it does not seem particularly excited about it. Take 'reading in children's own mother tongue'. Here, the percentage of children in government schools who can read at least a class I text is 43.6. But in private schools it is 52.2 per cent. That's an 8.6 percentage point difference, or a huge age 20 per cent. advantage in private schools. Fair enough, Pratham cautions us to hold on, it might be the brighter children who go to private schools, or the ones with more educated or wealthier parents. So the report's writers adjust the results to take this into account.

Doing so, they find the private school advantage decreases down from 8.6 percentage points to 2.9, that is, they write, "a merely 5 per cent. advantage. Perhaps it is only small. But remember, this is the children's mother tongue. Most government schools teach in the mother tongue, whereas private schools are often English medium, you'd think that for all the criticisms levelled against English medium private schools that they're damaging young children's prospects of learning that at least government schools would do better in the mother tongue". Not a bit, Private schools are doing better in the area where everyone says government schools should have the advantage."

Moreover, Mr. Karin Hulshof a UNICEF India representative in an article "follow the learning curve" published in the *Times of India* has said that:

'The coming into effect of the Right of Children to Free and Compulsory Education (RTE) Act, 2009 marks a historic movement for the children of India. This Act serves as a building block to ensure that every child has the right to guaranteed quality elementary education. The State, with the help of families and communities has a legal obligation to fulfil this duty.

Few countries in the world have such a national provision to ensure both free and child centred, child friendly education to help all children develop their fullest potential. There are an estimated eight million children and young people between the ages of six and 14 out of school. Without India, the world cannot reach the Millennium Development Goal of having every child completes primary school by 2015.

The gains in India's education system over the past few decades have been tremendous. According to India's Education for All Mid-Decade Assessment, in just five years between 2000 and 2006, the country increased primary school enrolment by 13.7 per cent. for girls, reaching close to universal enrollment in Grade I.

Even with these laudable efforts, one in four children in 2005 left school before reaching Grade 5 and almost half before reaching Grade 8. Learning assessment also shows that the children who do remain in school are not learning the basics of literacy and numeracy or the additional knowledge and skills necessary for their all round development as specified under RTE.

The RTE Act provides a ripe platform to reach the unreached, with specific provisions for disadvantaged groups, such as child labourers, migrant children, children with special needs, or those who have a "disadvantage owing to social, cultural, economical, geographical, linguistic, gender or such other factor'. In view of reducing disparities, private schools must admit at least 25 per cent. of children belonging to these groups".

The RTE Act, 2009 has some important and far-reaching features. It has banned corporal punishment to ensure the classrooms free of fear and anxiety. The said Act also provides to impart education in the mother-language of the children and focus on quality of teaching and learning. It is pertinent to add that the said Act has put burden on guardian/parents of the children to send their children to the nearest schools to get elementary education.

The School Managing Committees as mentioned above will have to make arrangement for sanitation and hygiene including providing private and separate sanitary latrine in schools to attract girls participation in large number. It is happy news that UNICEF is joining hands with the Indian Government and the State Governments to make the said Act more successful and effective.

CHAPTER 11

HUMAN RIGHTS AND CUSTODIAL CRIMES

Human Rights and torture in police custody are totally opposite terms. To curb torture in police custody is the protection of the basic Human Rights. No definition is given about the term torture in either Constitution of India or in any other penal laws. But torture means illegal or unjustified action of State police or any law enforcing bodies against a person or group of persons.

Justice Altamas Kabir, Supreme Court of India has rightly stated that, "It would take hours to cover even a miniscule portion of the world-wide transgressions of human and fundamental rights and the right to live a life of human dignity, but it is heartening and reassuring that attempts are at least being made by the world community to contain the poison that has permeated society throughout the world. In India, Courts, and in particular the High Courts and the Supreme Court, have always been the guardian of Human Rights and liberties of its citizens, and have within their jurisdiction come down heavily on their transgressions either by the police, the Executive or even by the Legislature while enacting laws, which seek to curtail such rights and liberties."

Universal Declaration of Human Rights, 1948 (In short UDHR) recognizes the inherent dignity and equal and inalienable rights of all members of the human family to be the foundation of freedom, peace and justice in the entire world. Preamble of Universal Declaration of Human Rights provides that "Whereas disregard and contempt for Human Rights have resulted in barbarous acts which have outraged the conscience of mankind, and the advent of a world in which human beings shall enjoy freedom of speech and belief and freedom from fear and want has been proclaimed as the highest aspiration of the common people."

Article 1 of Universal Declaration of Human Rights says as under:

> "Article 1 of the Universal Declaration of Human Rights also provides that all human beings are born free and equal in dignity and rights. They are endowed with reason and conscience and should act towards one another in a spirit of brotherhood."

"Living with dignity means living with the conviction that Human Rights has intrinsic worth and it possesses the potential for moral excellence and nobility".

It is universally accepted that Human Rights mean the rights relating to life, liberty, equality and dignity of the individual as embodied in the International covenants. The right to live with dignity is the basic Human Right of all. Custodial crimes are considered to be the worst crimes in a civilized society governed by the Rule of Law.

Article 3 of the Universal Declaration of Human Rights, 1948 provides that everyone has the right of life, liberty and security of person. Likewise Article 5 of the said declaration says that no one shall be subjected to torture or to cruel, inhuman or degrading treatment or punishment. Article 9 of the said Declaration speaks that no one shall be subjected to arbitrary arrest, detention or exile.

Article 10 of UDHR provides that everyone is entitled in full equality to a fair and public hearing by an independent and impartial tribunal, in the determination of his rights and obligations and of any criminal charge against him. It means that all persons deprived of the liberty shall be treated with humanity and inherent dignity. The accused persons shall generally be segregated from convicted persons and brought as early as possible for speedy trial.

Article 11(1) provides that everyone charged with a penal offence has the right to be presumed innocent until proved guilty according to law in a public trial at which he has had all the guarantees necessary for his defence. Article 11(2) says that "No one shall be held guilty of any penal offence on account of any act or omission which did not constitute a penal offence, under national or international law, at the time when it was committed. Nor shall a heavier penalty be imposed than the one that was applicable at the time the penal offence was committed". These provisions of the said declaration are safeguards to the personal liberty against the arbitrary action of the State.

Article 20 of Indian Constitution is reproduced as under:

> "20. *Protection in respect of conviction for offence.*—(1) No person shall be convicted of any offence except for violation of a law in force at the time of the commission of the act charged as an offence, nor be subjected to a penalty greater than that which might have been inflicted under the law in force at the time of the commission of the offence.
>
> (2) No person shall be prosecuted and punished for the same offence more than once.
>
> (3) No person accused of any offence shall be compelled to be a witness against himself."

Article 20 of the Constitution of India is similar to Articles 9 to 11 of the said declaration. Article 20(1) of the Constitution is concerned with the substantive law of criminal liability and penalty and prohibits against *ex post facto* penal law. This article gives constitutional recognition to the principle that there cannot be a conviction except for violation of its law in force.

Article 20(2) is concerned with the stage of procedure and incorporates a prohibition against double jeopardy (there shall not be prosecution and punishment after an earlier punishment for the same offence). This Article is inserted in the Constitution with a view to avoid unnecessary harassment which must be caused to a person for successive criminal proceedings where single crime has been committed. Article 20(3) gives protection against testimonial compulsion and is also concerned with the stage of procedure. This protection is available to accused of an offence. But there is no constitutional protection for a witness who is not the accused in the offence. Sections 132 and 148 of the Indian Evidence Act provide a limited protection against self incrimination to a witness in Criminal and Civil Courts.

Dr. B.S. Chauhan Judge Supreme Court of India in his Judgment in the case of *State of Haryana* v. *Jagdish,* (2010) 4 SCC 216 held as under:

"Liberty is one of the most precious and cherished possessions of a human being and he would resist forcefully any attempt to diminish it."

Torture in police custody is an open assault on basic Human Rights, more particularly against life and personal liberty and human dignity. It is against civilization and individual personality. Custodial torture by police was never approved by any Court of law or International Covenants or resolutions. It was always deprecated and censured and declared as inhuman and barbarous. Almost in all the International Conventions and meetings, it was resolved to ban torture of any kind. Custodial torture has no legal or statutory sanction. Custodial torture is naked violation of human dignity and it is absolutely anti-civilization.

Use of third degree methods in custody by police and other arresting agencies, custodial death and custodial rapes are the glaring examples of the violation of Human Rights. Either in Universal Declaration of Human Rights or any other International Covenants or agreements or in Indian Constitution torture in custody has been declared illegal, inhuman and naked violation of basic Human Rights. It is also contrary to human dignity and is anti-civilization.

Sometimes third degree methods are applied upon the accused to obtain confessional statement by the police or other investigating agencies. Even accused persons are not allowed to consult their lawyers while they are in custody. It is pertinent to mention here that the provisions for grant of anticipatory bail in non-bailable case had been introduced in the Code of Criminal Procedure with a view to prevent the misuse of custodial interrogation by the police as well as other investigating agencies. In custodial interrogation atmospheric pressure, psychic torture and tiring interrogative proximity are used, these facts have been taken judicial note of by the Supreme Court of India in the case of *Joginder Kumar* v. *State of Uttar Pradesh,* (1994) 4 SCC 260, wherein it was held as under:

> "The horizon of Human Rights is expanding. At the same time, the crime rate is also increasing. Of late, this Court has been receiving complaints about violation of Human Rights because of indiscriminate arrests. How are we to strike a balance between the two.
>
> A realistic approach should be made in this direction. The law of arrest is one of balancing individual rights, liberties and privileges, on the one hand, and individual duties, obligations and responsibilities on the other, of weighing and balancing the rights, liberties and privileges of the single individual and those of individuals collectively, of simply deciding what is wanted and where to put the weight and the emphasis, of deciding which comes first- the criminal or society, the law violator or the law abider; of meeting the challenge which Mr. Justice Cardozo so forthrightly met when he wrestled with a similar task of balancing individual rights against society's rights and wisely held that the exclusion rule was bad law, that society came first, and that the criminal should not go free because the constable blundered."

In Third Report describing to the quality of arrests by the police in India the National Police Commission mentioned power of arrest as one of the chief sources of corruption in the police. By and large, nearly 60% of the arrests were either unnecessary or unjustified and that such unjustified police action accounted for 43.2 per cent. of the expenditure of the jails. The said Commission in the said report specifically observed that:

"It is obvious that a major portion of the arrests were connected with very minor prosecutions and cannot, therefore, be regarded as quite necessary from the point of view of crime prevention. Continued detention in jail of the persons so arrested has also meant avoidable expenditure on their maintenance. In the above period it was estimated that 43.2 per cent. of the expenditure in the connected jails was over such prisoners only who in the ultimate analysis need not have been arrested at all."

It was further mentioned in the said report that:

"An arrest during the investigation of a cognizable case may be considered justified in one or other of the following circumstances:

(i) The case involves a grave offence like murder, dacoity, robbery, rape etc., and it is necessary to arrest the accused and bring his movements under restraint to infuse confidence among the terror-stricken victims.

(ii) Accused is likely to abscond and evade the process of law.

(iii) Accused is given to violent behaviour and is likely to commit further offences unless his movements are brought under restraint.

(iv) The accused is a habitual offender and unless kept in custody he is likely to commit similar offences again.

It would be desirable to insist through departmental instructions that a police officer making an arrest should also record in the case diary the reasons for making the arrest, thereby clarifying his conformity to the specified guidelines."

It is relevant to add here that the Royal Commission suggested restrictions on the power of arrest on the basis of the "necessity of principle". The two main objectives of this principle are that police can exercise powers only in those cases in which it was genuinely necessary to enable them to execute their duty to prevent the commission of offence, to investigate crime. The Commission was of the view that such restrictions would diminish the use of arrest and produce more uniform use of powers. At page 45 of the Royal Commission Report on Criminal Procedure, it is given as under:

"We recommended that detention upon arrest for an offence should continue only on one or more of the following criteria:

(a) the person's unwillingness to identify himself so that a summons may be served upon him;

(b) the need to prevent the continuation or repetition of that offence;

(c) the need to protect the arrested person himself or other persons or property.

(d) the need to secure or preserve evidence of or relating to that offence or to obtain such evidence from the suspect by questioning him; and

(e) the likelihood of the person failing to appear at court to answer any charge made against him".

At page 46 of the said report following are mentioned: "To help to reduce the use of arrest we would also propose the introduction here of a scheme that is used in Ontario enabling a police officer to issue what is called an appearance notice. That procedure can be used to obtain attendance at the police station without resorting to arrest provided a power to arrest exists, for example to be fingerprinted or to participate in an identification parade. It could also be extended to attendance of interview at a time convenient both to the suspect and to the police officer investigating the case..."

It is now agreed by social scientists as well as criminologists that for arrests made by police or other investigating agencies on false grounds, the arresting authorities should be proceeded according to law for making such unjustified arrests and the officer concerned will have to pay compensation to the victim from his own pocket and the Government will not be saddled with damages or compensation. It will be considered the personal accountability of the officer concerned who misused the power of arrest.

In the cases of members of Defence Forces, Army, Navy or Air Force, while making arrest intimation should be sent immediately to Officer commanding of the unit to which the member belongs. Similarly under rule 229 of the Procedure and Conduct of Business in Lok Sabha, when a member is arrested on a criminal charge or is detained under an Executive order of the Magistrate, the Executive authority must inform without delay such fact to the Speaker of the Lok Sabha. As soon as any arrest, detention, conviction or release is effected intimation should invariably be sent by telegrams and also by posts to the government concerned concurrently with the intimation sent to the Speaker/Chairman of Legislative Assembly/Council/both Houses of Parliament.

Moreover Supreme Court in the case of *Joginder Kumar* v. *State of Uttar Pradesh,* (Supra): AIR 1994 SC 1349 further held that, "No arrest can be made because it is lawful for the police officer to do so. The existence of the power to arrest is one thing. The justification for the exercise of it is quite another. The police officer must be able to justify the arrest apart from his power to do so. Arrest and detention in police lock-up of a person can cause incalculable harm to the reputation and self-esteem of a person. No arrest can be made in a routine manner on a mere allegation of commission of an offence made against a person. It would be prudent for a police officer in the interest of protection of the constitutional rights of a citizen and perhaps in his own interest that no arrest should be made without a reasonable satisfaction reached after some investigation as to the genuineness and *bona fides* of a complaint and a reasonable belief both as to the person's complicity and even so as to the need to effect arrest. Denying a person of his liberty is a serious matter. The recommendations of the Police Commission merely reflect the constitutional concomitants of the fundamental right to personal liberty and freedom. A person is not liable to arrest merely on the suspicion of complicity in an offence. There must be some reasonable justification in the opinion of the officer effecting the arrest that such arrest is necessary and justified. Except in heinous offences, an arrest must be avoided if a police officer issues notice to person to attend the Station House and not to leave the Station without permission would do."

The Supreme Court at length discussed the right against self-incrimination as provided in Article 20(3) of the Constitution and section 161(2) of Code of Criminal Procedure in the case of *Nandini Satpathy* v. *P.L. Dani,* (1978) 2 SCC 424. In the said case it was specifically held that compelled testimony is evidence procured not merely by physical threats or violence but by psychic torture, atmospheric pressure, environmental coercion, tiring interrogative prolixity, overbearing and intimidatory methods and the like. A police officer is clearly a person in authority and insistence on answering is a form of pressure especially in the atmosphere of the police station unless certain safeguards erasing duress are adherd to.

Use of third degree methods by the police and other investigating organs to extract information from an accused is clear violation of Article 21 of the Constitution as this Article categorically provides that except in accordance with law, life and liberty of a person cannot be taken away. Police or other law enforcing agencies are made to protect and safeguard the life and liberty of a person and not to misuse their powers to take away their life and liberty by arbitrary and unjustified action. Importantly sections 330 and 331 of the Indian Penal Code specifically provide punishment for subjecting a person to torture for extracting information. Therefore, assault on a body of an accused by police or other investigating organs is violative of fundamental rights guaranteed under Article 21 of the Constitution. Sometimes it is found that suspect dies in police custody due to their torture in extracting information. Such acts are very inhuman, unconstitutional, illegal and also violative of Universal Declaration on Human Rights. The wrongdoers are liable to be punished for the murder of the suspects in police custody and such wrongdoers cannot take the defence of sovereign power of the State.

One thing I want to make it clear that I cannot and should not challenge the power of the police or other investigating agencies to make arrest of a suspect and to interrogate him to find the truth. But doing such activities, police and other investigating agencies have no legal licence to use third degree methods upon the victims. More modern and scientific methods should be incorporated for making interrogation/investigation like use of lie detector, DNA test, Forensic Test, Narco test, use of electronic items like tape records, etc.

Article 5 of the Universal Declaration of Human Rights, 1948 appears to be pious hope. More or less in whole world abuse of power by police and violence in custody are seen and noted. It is true that International Organisations and Human Rights bodies are fighting with full strength to curb such misuse of power, but it will take some time and for that International Awareness are more necessary and the States are to be serious regarding protection and safeguard of basic Human Rights, namely life and personal liberty. In fact States are the main body which can curb the misuse of police power and restrict/prevent the violence in custody. Earlier in United Kingdom, torture was seen as a normal method to extract information of the crime from the suspects. But later on due to awareness of Human Rights and also publication of report of Royal Commission on Criminal Procedure, such inhuman practices were discouraged to the great extent. By custodial crimes, both body pain and mental agony are caused. Even rapes are committed on the women suspects and sometimes to the female witnesses also which is totally against the basic Human Rights. Beating, stripping, electric shocks are the normal features of torture committed in police custody.

In the case of *D.K. Basu* v. *State of West Bengal*, (1997) 1 SCC 416, Justice (Dr.) A.S. Anand, Supreme Court of India has observed "Custodial Violence" and abuse of police power is not only peculiar to this country, but it is widespread. It has been the concern of international community because the problem is universal and the challenge is almost global. The Universal Declaration of Human Rights in 1948, which marked the emergence of a worldwide trend of protection and guarantee of certain basic Human Rights, stipulates in Article 5 that: "No one shall be subjected to torture or to cruel, inhuman or degrading treatment or punishment." Despite the pious declaration the crime continues unabated, though every civilized nation shows its concern and takes steps for its eradication.

It is worthwhile to mention here that by 113th report, Law Commission has recommended inclusion of section 114B in the Indian Evidence Act. In prosecution of a police officer for an alleged offence of having caused bodily injury to a person, if there was evidence that the injury was caused during the period when the person was in the custody of the police and also while considering the question of presumption, should have regard to all relevant circumstances including the period of custody, statement made by the victim, medical evidence and the evidence which the Magistrate may have recorded. But it is very peculiar that till today the said recommendation has not been implemented, although there are continuous instances of death in custody, custodial rape, torture in custody are going on and these are the headlines of Newspapers. It is high time when Legislature should stand up immediately to legislate such law as recommended by Law Commission in the statute book to check and curb custodial crimes.

In the case of *Prem Shankar Shukla* v. *Delhi Administration,* AIR 1980 SC 1535, issue of handcuffing of suspects was discussed in detail by Supreme Court and it was very correctly held that handcuffing is *prima facie* inhuman and, therefore, unreasonable, is over-harsh and at, the first blush, arbitrary. Absent of fair procedure and objective monitoring to inflict 'irons' is to resort to zoological strategies repugnant to Article 21, surely, the competing claims of securing the prisoner from fleeing and protecting his personality from barbarity have to be harmonised. To prevent the escape of an under trial is in public interest, reasonable, just and cannot, by itself be castigated. But to bind a man hand and foot, fetter his limbs with hoops of steel, shuffle him along in the streets and stand him for hours in the courts is to torture him, defile his dignity, vulgarise society and foul the soul of our constitutional culture.

A new concept of grant of compensation has been developed by Judge-made laws (decisions delivered by Supreme Court as well as different High Courts) for illegal imprisonment, custodial death, death in false encounters. It is true that after death of suspects in police custody, the family looses bread earner. Grant of compensation to the legal heirs of the deceased are very effective and appropriate remedy. But I suggest that the amount of compensation must be recovered from the erring officials and not from the exchequer of the State. As because if the compensation is recovered from the person concerned it will give a signal to whole department not to repeat such occurrences or incidents. In the case of *R.S. Sodhi* v. *State of Uttar Pradesh,* 1994 (Supp) 1 SCC 142 wherein Supreme Court granted compensation to the heirs of the victim who died in an encounter by the Police while permitting the CBI to investigate the case. Similarly in *Rudal Sah* v. *State of Bihar,* (1983) 4 SCC 141 compensation was granted as detention was found illegal. In *SAHELI, a Women's Resources Centre* v. *Commissioner of Police Delhi,* (1990) 1 SCC 422 compensation was granted in death occurred due to police firing. In *Bhim Singh* v. *State of Jammu and Kashmir,* (1985) 4 SCC 677, compensation of Rs. 50,000 was granted due to deliberate preventing Bhim Singh from attending session of the Legislative Assembly by arresting and illegally detaining in police custody. In this case the conduct of Police Officers and even Magistrate and Sub-Judges were strongly condemned.

There are other examples also in which Courts granted compensation in the cases of death committed by police. Supreme Court had exercised such powers under Article 32 of the Constitution and High Courts have exercised under Article 226 of the Constitution.

Hon'ble Mr. K.J. Reddy, Former Judge of Supreme Court in his article "Prevention of Torture in India" has mentioned that, the dictionary meaning of the word 'torture' is

(i) "to cause extreme physical pain, especially to extract information, etc.

(ii) to give mental anguish.

(iii) to cause mental agony, etc."

Whether a given set of facts amount to torture or not, can be elusive and tricky. Torture and custodial violence are associated with the investigation of crime by the police under the domestic law. As we are all aware, the investigation commences in cognisable offences with the arrest of the culprits and criminal suspects. National Human Rights Commission issued several guidelines in respect of procedures to be followed by the police starting from the stage of arrest in consonance with the provisions of the Constitution and Cr. P.C. The greatest risk of torture and other forms of ill-treatment of individuals is in the first phase of arrest and detention before they have access to a lawyer or court, and continues as along as the investigation continues, irrespective of where a suspect is being held.

The Convention against Torture and other cruel, Inhuman or Degrading Treatment or Punishment defines the 'torture' as follows:—

"1. For the purposes of this Convention, the term "torture' means any act by which severe pain or suffering, whether physical or mental, is intentionally inflicted on a person for such purposes as obtaining from him or a third person information or a confession, punishing him or her for an act or a third person has committed or suspected of having committed, or intimidating or coercing him, or a third person, or for any reason based on discrimination of any kind, when such pain or suffering is inflicted by or at the instigation of or with the consent or acquiescence of a public official or other person acting in an official capacity. It does not include pain or suffering arising only from, inherent in or incidental to lawful sanctions.

2. This article is without prejudice to any international instrument, or national legislation which does or may contain provisions of wider application."

It is worthwhile to mention here that following the decision in the case of *Joginder Kumar* v. *State of Uttar Pradesh*, (1994) 4 SCC 260, the National Human Rights Commission has issued some guidelines regarding the arrest, namely:

(1) Except in heinous offences, an arrest must be avoided if a police officer issues notice to the person to attend the police station and not to leave the station without the permission and that the power to arrest must be avoided where the offence is bailable unless there is a strong apprehension of the suspect absconding.

(2) As a rule use of force should be avoided while effecting arrest. However, in case of forceful resistance to arrest, minimum force to overcome the resistance may be used.

(3) As far as is practicable, woman police officers should be associated where the person or persons being arrested are women and arrest of woman between sun-set and sun-rise should be avoided. There are several other guidelines also in respect of their arrest.

Supreme Court of India in *D.K. Basu* v. *State of West Bengal*, (1997) 1 SCC 416 has ruled that "No violation of any of the Human Rights has been the subject of so many Conventions and Declarations as 'torture' – all aiming at total banning of it in all forms, but in spite of the commitments made to eliminate torture, the fact remains that torture is more widespread now than ever before "Custodial torture" is a naked violation of human dignity an degradation which destroys, to a very large extent, the individual personality. It is a calculated assault on human dignity and whenever human dignity is wounded, civilisation takes a step backward—flag of humanity must on each occasion fly half-mast."

National Police Commission in its 3rd report has mentioned that about 60 per cent. of the arrests were unjustified and unnecessary. Innocent persons are sent to jail although they have not committed any crime. The relevant portions of the said report are set out below:—"It is obvious that a major portion of the arrests were connected with very minor prosecutions and cannot, therefore, be regarded as quite necessary from the point of view of crime prevention. Continued detention in jail of the persons so arrested has also meant unvoidable expenditure on their maintenance. In the above period it was estimated that 43.2 per cent. of the expenditure in the connected jails was over such prisoners only who in the ultimate analysis need not have been arrested at all."

The Royal Commission in its report on criminal procedure stated that police can exercise power only in those cases in which it was necessary to enable them to execute their duty for prevention of the commission of crime and to investigate the offence. It was mentioned in the said report as under:

> "To help to reduce the use of arrest we would also propose the introduction here of a scheme that is used in Ontario enabling a police officer to issue what is called an appearance notice. That procedure can be used to obtain attendance at the police station without resorting to arrest provided a power to arrest exists, for example to be fingerprinted or to participate in an identification parade. It could also be extended to attendance of interview at a time convenient both to the suspect and to the police officer investigating the case..."

It is apt to mention that when a member of Parliament is arrested in a criminal case or is detained under an order of Magistrate, under provision of rule 229 of the procedure and conduct business in Lok Sabha, the arresting authority must inform to the speaker of Parliament without any delay. Further while making arrest of the member of Defence Force namely Army, Navy or Air Force, intimation of such arrest should be sent immediately to the Officer Commanding of the unit to which the arrestee belongs. One thing I want to make it clear that I cannot and should not challenge the power of the police or other investigating agencies to make arrest of a suspect and to interrogate him to find the truth. But doing such activities, police and other investigating agencies have no legal licence to use third degree methods upon the victims. More modern and scientific methods should be incorporated for making interrogation/investigation like use of lie detector, DNA test, Forensic Test, Narco test, use of electronic items like tape records, etc.

Article 5 of the Universal Declaration of Human Rights, 1948 appears to be pious hope. It is true that International Organisations and Human Rights bodies are fighting with full strength to curb such misuse of power, but it will take some time and for that International Awareness is more necessary and States are to be serious regarding protection and safeguard of basic Human Rights, namely life and personal liberty.

Custodial violence like torture was never alien to Indian crimes from the pre-independence period. However, after Constitution came into force the State Authorities and law enforcing agencies are expected to ensure to its citizens the charter of fundamental rights mentioned in Articles 14, 19 and 21 of the Constitution of India. But the question is, despite all the provisions in Constitution, Criminal laws, Police Manuals and Regulations which require the police to act in a restrained and restricted way whether the police have shown that restraint or continued to take recourse to short cuts and used excessive force to extract confessional statements.

Torture in police custody is an assault against life and personal liberty and custodial torture is blatant violation of human dignity and the same is contrary to the International Convention and civilization and Universal Declaration of Human Rights. Often police makes arrest of a person without valid cause and arrestees are given physical and mental torture in the custody. Victims are not allowed to consult their lawyer while they are in custody. To obtain confession third degree methods are applied by the police upon the arrestees.

In the Code of Criminal Procedure, the Parliament of India has inserted section 438 to grant anticipatory bail in a non-bailable case to a person who is apprehending his arrest. The Sessions Judge of a District and the High Court of the State are authorised to grant or refuse anticipatory bail. The provisions of section 438 of the said Code are reproduced as under:

"*438. Direction for grant of bail to person apprehending arrest.*—(1) Where any person has reason to believe that he may be arrested on accusation of having committed a non-bailable offence, he may apply to the High Court or the Court of Session for a direction under this section that in the event of such arrest he shall be released on bail; and that Court may, after taking into consideration, *inter alia*, the following factors, namely:—

(i) the nature and gravity of the accusation;

(ii) the antecedents of the applicant including the fact as to whether he has previously undergone imprisonment on conviction by a Court in respect of any cognizable offence;

(iii) the possibility of the applicant to flee from justice; and

(iv) where the accusation has been made with the object of injuring or humiliating the applicant by having him so arrested,

either reject the application forthwith or issue an interim order for the grant of anticipatory bail:

Provided that, where the High Court or, as the case may be, the Court of Sessions, has not passed any interim order under this sub-section or has rejected the application for grant of anticipatory bail, it shall be open to an officer in-charge of a police station to arrest, without warrant the applicant on the basis of the accusation apprehended in such application.

(1A) Where the Court grants an interim order under sub-section (1), it shall forthwith cause a notice being not less than seven days' notice, together with a copy of such order to be served on the Public Prosecutor and the Superintendent of Police, with a view to give the Public Prosecutor a reasonable opportunity of being heard when the application shall be finally heard by the Court.

(1B) The presence of the applicant seeking anticipatory bail shall be obligatory at the time of final hearing of the application and passing of final order by the Court, if on an application made to it by the Public Prosecutor, the Court considers such presence necessary in the interest of justice.

(2) When the High Court or the Court of Sessions makes a direction under sub-section (1), it may include such conditions in such directions in the light of the facts of the particular case, as it may thinks fit, including:—

(i) a condition that the person shall make himself available for interrogation by a police officer as and when required;

(ii) a condition that the person shall not, directly or indirectly, make any inducement, threat or promise to any person acquainted with the facts of the case so as to dissuade him from disclosing such facts to the Court or to any police officer;

(iii) a condition that the person shall not leave India without the previous permission of the Court;

(iv) such other conditions as may be imposed under sub-section (3) of section 437, as if the bail were granted under that section.

(3) If such person is thereafter arrested without warrant by an officer in-charge of a police station on such accusation, and is prepared either at the time of arrest or at any time while in the custody of such officer to give bail, he shall be released on bail, and if a Magistrate taking cognisance of such offence decides that a warrant should issue in the first instance against that person, he shall issue a bailable warrant in conformity with the direction of the Court under sub-section (1).

The Supreme Court also in the case of *D.K. Basu* v. *State of West Bengal*, AIR 1997 SC 610 has observed as follows:

"Custodial death is perhaps one of the worst crimes in a civilised society governed by the Rule of Law. The rights inherent in Articles 21 and 22(1) of the Constitution are required to be zealously and scrupulously protected. We cannot whisk away the problem. Any form of torture or cruel, inhuman or degrading treatment would fall within the inhibition of Article 21 of the Constitution, whether it occurs during investigation, interrogation or otherwise. If the functionaries of the Government become law-breakers, it is bound to breed contempt for law and would encourage lawlessness and every man would have the tendency to become law unto himself thereby leading to anarchism."

Indian Constitution incorporates several provisions to safeguard the life and liberty and protection against custodial crimes and connected matters. Articles 20, 21 and 22 are available in the Indian Constitution as fundamental rights, which guarantees the right to life and personal liberty, human dignity and protection from illegal action of the State.

Supreme Court of India in the case of *A.K. Gopalan* v *State of Madras,* AIR 1950 SC 27 has specifically held that the object of Article 21 is to prevent encroachment upon personal liberty by the Executive save accordance with law and in conformity with the provisions thereof. Personal liberty means freedom from physical restraint of person by incarceration or otherwise. The protection of this article extends to all the persons and not only to the citizens. Persons who are imprisoned are also protected by the said article. In the case of *Makhan Singh Tarsikka* v. *State of Punjab,* AIR 1952 SC 27, it was declared by Supreme Court that before a person is deprived of his life or personal liberty, the procedure established by law must be strictly followed and must not be departed from to the disadvantage of the person affected.

Article 21 of the Constitution of India provides that, "No one shall be deprived of his life or personal liberty except according to the procedure established by law".

In Article 21 the term law means State-made law and not as an equivalent of law. Law will not include mere departmental instructions or Executive Orders as they are not statutory and procedure established by law means the law prescribed by Parliament. It is important to mention here that constitutionality of a law, which deprives a person of his life or personal liberty can be challenged in Court of law on the grounds that the law suffers from the vice of excessive delegation, it was not enacted by a competent Legislature, it contravenes fundamental rights, it constitutes a colourable exercise of the Legislative powers. Speedy trial is one of the requirements of Article 21. Supreme Court in the case of *State of Rajasthan* v. *Sukhpal,* (1983) 1 SCC 393 has clearly observed that inordinate delay by the State in bringing an accused for trial or for preferring an appeal against an acquittal is violative of Article 21 of the Constitution, if there is no fault by the accused. Further in the case of *Kartar Singh* v. *State of Punjab,* (1994) 3 SCC 569, it was held that speedy trial is a component of personal liberty.

Here reference of Article 22 of the Constitution of India is very relevant, which provides for protection against arrest and detention in certain cases. It is reproduced as under:

> "22. *Protection against arrest and detention in certain cases.*—(1) No person who is arrested shall be detained in custody without being informed, as soon as may be, of the grounds for such arrest nor shall he be denied the right to consult, and to be defended by, a legal practitioner of his choice.
>
> (2) Every person who is arrested and detained in custody shall be produced before the nearest Magistrate within a period of twenty-four hours of such arrest excluding the time necessary for the journey from the place of arrest to the Court of the Magistrate and no such person shall be detained in custody beyond the said period without the authority of a Magistrate."

Article 22 as aforesaid has two parts:—Articles 22(1) and (2) are applicable to persons arrested under a law. Supreme Court in the case of *A.K. Gopalan* v. *State of Madras* (Supra): has observed that information about grounds of arrest is mandatory and it is also mandatory to consult and to be defended by a legal practitioner of his choice under Article 22 (1). But Article 22(4) to (7) are applicable to persons detained under Preventive Detention law.

Sections 330 and 331 of Indian Penal Code forbids torture. Section 330 of Indian Penal Code provides as under:

> "330. *Voluntarily causing hurt to extort confession, or to compel restoration of property*:—Whoever voluntarily causes hurt for the purpose of extorting from the sufferer or from any person interested in the sufferer, any confession or any information which may lead to the detection of an offence or misconduct, or for the purpose of constraining the sufferer or any person interested in the sufferer to restore or to cause the restoration of any property or valuable security or to satisfy any claim or demand, or to give information which may lead to the restoration of any property or valuable security, shall be punished with imprisonment of either description for a term which may extend to seven years, and shall also be liable to fine."

Supreme Court in the case of *D.K. Basu* v. *State of West Bengal*, (1997) 1 SCC 416 has held that Police is, no doubt, under a legal duty and has legitimate right to arrest a criminal and to interrogate him during the investigation of an offence but the law does not permit use of third- degree methods or torture of accused in custody during interrogation and investigation with a view to solve the crime. End cannot justify the means. The interrogation and investigation into a crime should be in true sense purposeful to make the investigation effective. By torturing a person and using third degree methods, the police would be accomplishing behind the closed doors what the demands of our legal order forbid. No society can permit it. Further, in the case of *Sham Khan* v. *State of Maharashtra*, 1992 Supp (2) SCC 521 it was observed that where Police Officers subjected the suspect to ill treatment to extort confession, without any reliable information, they would be guilty of offence under section 330, I.P.C.

Section 331 of Indian Penal Code says as below:

> "331. *Voluntarily causing grievous hurt to extort confession, or to compel restoration of property*:—Whoever voluntarily causes grievous hurt for the purpose of extorting from the sufferer or from any person interested in the sufferer any confession or any information which may lead to the detection of an offence or misconduct, or for the purpose of constraining the sufferer or any person interested in the sufferer to restore or to cause the restoration of any property or valuable security, or to satisfy any claim or demand or to give information which may lead to the restoration of any property or valuable security, shall be punished with imprisonment of either description for a term which may extend to ten years, and shall also be liable to fine."

While analysing and examining the custodial violence, I think the condition of police force in which they work all through ought to have taken note of. It is true that police force is subjected to enormous pressure and comments for increase in crime rate. Every one knows that the ability of the Police to check and control the criminal activities is limited. No proper training of Human Rights are given to them. They are taken to work for *sometimes* more than 14 to 18 hours in a day.

The politicians used the police force for their own purposes when they are in power. Many times, Supreme Court and also other High Courts of India have issued guidelines to have reform in police force regarding their working condition, job security, health, hike in salary, restriction of the government in their working, etc. but none of the governments are serious to implement the reforms so suggested so as to improve and upgrade the conditions of police force in India.

Moreover, it is to be mentioned that proper scientific and methodological system of investigation are not provided to the subordinate police force, in fact which are the backbone of the criminal investigation system. They need periodical training regarding the applicability of modern investigation pattern with a view to reduce the 3rd degree methods for collection of the information and confessional statements. Not only this, there is always acute shortage of transport, essential equipment and sufficient strength. In India, the population is more than 110 crore whereas the percentage of police force is not appropriate considering such high rate of population. Well-trained police force are deputed for VIP duties and they are required to perform a large number of other jobs which are not at all related to the basic work or investigation. Further, it is often seen that the police officer uses illegal methods in some cases because of inadequacies in the law, and the law is not reformed on the ground that the behaviour of policemen does not justify reposing trust in them. Therefore, it is proper time that sufficient police force be recruited and a separate unit of police force be recruited for VIP duties without taking away from the strength of police forces meant to check the crimes and engaged in investigation.

Besides the Constitution of India, Code of Criminal Procedure contains many provisions to check and control the illegal and arbitrary arrest and detention by the police in the course of investigation. Section 41 of the said Code deals with arrest without warrant, section 46 says about how arrest is made. Section 49 of the Code says that the person arrested shall not be subjected to more restraint than is necessary to prevent his escape. More importantly section 50 of the said Code specifically provides that the person arrested to be informed of grounds of arrest and of right to bail. Section 57 of the said Code contemplates that person arrested shall not be detained for more than 24 hours.

Section 300 of Criminal Procedure Code speaks about double jeopardy as under:—(1) A person who has once been tried by a Court of competent jurisdiction for an offence and convicted or acquitted of such offence shall, while such conviction or acquittal remains in force, not be liable to be tried again for the same offence, nor on the same facts for any other offence for which a different charge from the one made against him might have been made under sub-section (1) of section 221, or for which he might have been convicted under sub-section (2) thereof.

(2) A person acquitted or convicted of any offence may be afterwards tried, with the consent of the State Government for any distinct offence for which a separate charge might have been made against him at the former trial under sub-section (1) of section 220.

(3) A person convicted of any offence constituted by any act causing consequences which, together with such act, constituted by a different offence from that of which he was convicted, may be afterwards tried for such last mentioned offence, if the consequences had not happened, or were not known to the Court to have happened, at the time when he was convicted.

(4) A person acquitted or convicted of any offence constituted by any acts may, notwithstanding such acquittal or conviction, be subsequently charged with and tried for any other offence constituted by the same acts which he may have committed if the Court by which he was first, tried was not competent to try the offence with which he is subsequently charged.

(5) A person discharged under section 258 shall not be tried again for the same offence except with the consent of the Court by which he was discharged or of any other Court to which the first mentioned Court is subordinate.

(6) Nothing in this section shall affect the provisions of section 26 of the General Clauses Act, 1897 (10 of 1897) or of section 188 of this Code.

It is very relevant to mention that to prevent and check the custodial crimes which is blatant violation and infringement of basic Human Rights and denial of human dignity, it is absolutely necessary to provide adequate training and refresher courses to the policemen and other law enforcing agencies regarding protection of Human Rights and respect for life and liberty. Moreover, their service conditions will have to be improved and upgraded substantially. Their strength to be enhanced and they should be provided adequate numbers of transport, necessary equipments and they should also be trained for scientific and modern investigation.

CHAPTER 12

HUMAN RIGHTS AND THE DETAINEE

Dignity of human being is an essential concept in the society as well as in the morality, because through it, the quality and honour of the people can be determined, and from the sense of dignity the concept of Human Rights can be measured. The quality of human life is a very complex phenomenon. It touches the various spheres of the people *i.e.*, health, food, education, liberty, equality, franchise of the citizens. Supreme Court in *Sunil Batra* v. *Delhi Administration*, reported in (1980) 2 SCR 557 has held that even a convict of capital sentence has got some fundamental rights as provided in Indian Constitution. Various International and Regional treaties and even the decision in the case of *D.K. Basu* v. *State of West Bengal*, (1997) 1 SCC 416 has issued guidelines to follow in all cases of detention and arrest, till law is made in that behalf, as a preventive measure.

Indian Constitution, Code of Criminal Procedure and other statutes have taken care of the Human Rights aspects of accused as well as victims. Article 20(1) of Indian Constitution provides for protection against conviction or enhanced punishment under *Ex-post facto* Law. Article 20(3) gives right not to be a witness against himself. Article 21(2) of the Constitution contemplates protection against double jeopardy. Article 22 says about protection against arbitrary and unlawful arrest and also right to consult a lawyer of his own choice. It also speaks about right to be produced before a Magistrate within 24 hours of his arrest.

Sections 93, 94, 97, 100(4) to (8) and 165 Code of Criminal Procedure provide Protection against arbitrary or unlawful searches. Sections 50, 55 and 75 of the said Code provides right to be informed of the grounds immediately after the arrest. Sections 436, 437 and 439 of Cr. P.C. and sections 50(2) and 167 provide right to be released on bail, if arrested. Sections 173(7), 208 and 238 provide right to get copies of the documents and statements of witnesses on which the prosecution relies. Sections 273 and also 317 of the said Code provide right to insist that evidence be recorded in his presence except in some special circumstances. Sections 218 and 240(2) of the said code provide right to have due notice for the charge. Section 313 provides right to have opportunity for explaining the circumstances appearing in evidence against him at the trial. Section 54 provides right to have himself medically examined for evidence to disprove the commission of offence by him or for establishing commission of offence against his body by any other person. Section 243 provides right to produce defence witnesses. Sections 479, 327, 191 provide right to be tried by an independent and impartial Judge. Sections 235(2) and 248(2) provide right to be heard about the sentence upon conviction.

It is correctly defined that Human Rights are those minimal rights which every individual must have against the State or other public authority by virtue of his being a member of the human family irrespective of any other consideration.

Dr. B.S. Chauhan, Judge Supreme Court of India in his Judgment in the case of *Mohd. Yunus Khan* v. *State of Uttar Pradesh*, reported in (2010) 10 SCC 539 has held as follows:

"Our Constitution protects not only life and liberty but also the dignity of every person. Life convicts and hardcore criminals deprived of personal liberty are also not wholly denuded of their constitutional rights."

On 9-12-1988 U.N. General Assembly, by its resolutions 43/173 has adopted "body of Principles for the Protection of all persons under any Form of detention or Imprisonment' for the protection of imprisoned and detained persons. It has adopted 39 principles namely:—

Principle 1:—All persons under any form of detention or imprisonment shall be treated in a humane manner and with respect for the inherent dignity of the human person.

Principle 2:—Arrest, detention or imprisonment shall only be carried out strictly in accordance with the provisions of the law and by competent officials or persons authorised for that purpose.

Principle 3:—There shall be no restriction upon or derogation from any of the Human Rights of persons under any form of detention or imprisonment recognized or existing in any State pursuant to law, conventions, regulations or custom on the pretext that this body of Principles does not recognize such rights or that it recognizes that it recognizes them to a lesser extent.

Principle 4:—Any form of detention or imprisonment and all measures affecting the Human Rights of a person under any form of detention or imprisonment shall be ordered by, or be subject to the effective control of, a judicial or other authority.

Principle 5.1:—These principles shall be applied to all persons within the territory of any given State, without distinction of any kind, such as race, colour, sex, language, religion or religious belief, political or other opinion, national, ethnic or social origin, property, birth or other status.

Principle 5.2:—Measures applied under the law and designed solely to protect the rights and special status of women, especially pregnant women and nursing mothers, children and juveniles, aged, sick or handicapped persons shall not be deemed to be discriminatory. The need for, and the application of, such measures shall always be subject to review by a judicial or other authority.

Principle 6:—No person under any form of detention or imprisonment shall be subjected to torture or to cruel, inhuman or degrading treatment or punishment. No circumstance whatever may be invoked as a justification for torture or other cruel, inhuman or degrading treatment or punishment.

Principle 7.1:—States should prohibit by law any act contrary to the rights and duties contained in these principles, make any such act subject to appropriate sanctions and conduct impartial investigations upon complaints. The term "cruel, inhuman or degrading treatment or punishment" should be interpreted so as to extend the widest possible protection against abuses, whether physical or mental, including the holding of a detained or imprisoned person in conditions which deprive him, temporarily or permanently, of the use of any of his natural senses, such as sight or hearing, or of his awareness of place and the passing of time.

Principle 7.2:—Officials who have reason to believe that a violation of this Body of Principles has occurred or is about to occur shall report the matter to their superior authorities and, where necessary, to other appropriate authorities or organs vested with reviewing or remedial powers.

Principle 7.3:—Any other person who has ground to believe that a violation of this Body of Principles has occurred or is about to occur shall have the right to report the matter to the superiors or the officials involved as well as to other appropriate authorities or organs vested with reviewing or remedial powers.

Principle 8:—Persons in detention shall be subject to treatment appropriate to their unconvicted status. Accordingly, they shall, whenever possible, be kept separate from imprisoned persons.

Principle 9:—The authorities which arrest a person, keep him under detention or investigate the case shall exercise only the powers granted to them under the law and the exercise of these powers shall be subject to recourse to a judicial or other authority.

Principle 10:—Anyone who is arrested shall be informed at the time of his arrest of the reason for his arrest and shall be promptly informed of any charges against him.

Principle 11.1:—A person shall not be kept in detention without being given an effective opportunity to be heard promptly by a judicial or other authority. A detained person shall have the right to defend himself or to be assisted by counsel as prescribed by law.

Principle 11.2:—A detained person and his counsel, if any, shall receive prompt and full communication of any order of detention, together with the reasons therefor.

Principle 11.3:—A judicial or other authority shall be empowered to review as appropriate the continuance of detention.

Principle 12.1:—There shall be duly recorded:

(a) The reasons for the arrest;

(b) The time of the arrest and the taking of the arrested person to a place of custody as well as that of his first appearance before a judicial or other authority;

(c) The identity of the law enforcement officials concerned;

(d) Precise information concerning the place of custody.

Principle 12.2:—Such records shall be communicated to the detained person, or his counsel, if any, in the form prescribed by law.

Principle 13:—Any person shall, at the moment of arrest and at the commencement of detention or imprisonment, or promptly thereafter, be provided by the authority responsible for his arrest, detention or imprisonment, respectively with information on and an explanation of his rights and how to avail himself of such rights.

Principle 14:—A person who does not adequately understand or speak the language used by the authorities responsible for his arrest, detention or imprisonment is entitled to receive promptly in a language which he understands the information referred to in Principle 10, Principle 11, paragraph 2, principle 12, paragraph 1, and principle 13 and to have the assistance, free of charge, if necessary, of an interpreter in connection with legal proceedings subsequent to his arrest.

Principle 15:—Notwithstanding the exceptions contained in principle 16, paragraph 4, and Principle 18, paragraph 3, communication of the detained or imprisoned person with the outside world and in particular, his family or counsel, shall not be denied for more than one month.

Principle 16.1:—Promptly after arrest and after each transfer from one place of detention or imprisonment to another, a detained or imprisoned person shall be entitled to notify or to require the competent authority to notify members of his family or other appropriate persons of his choice of his arrest, detention or imprisonment or of the transfer and of the place where he is kept in custody.

Principle 16.2:—If a detained or imprisoned person is a foreigner, he shall also be promptly informed of his right to communicate by appropriate means with a consular post or the diplomatic mission of the State of which he is a national or which is otherwise entitled to receive such communication in accordance with international law or with the representative of the competent international organisation, if he is a refugee or is otherwise under the protection of an inter-governmental organisation.

Principle 16.3:—If a detained or imprisoned person is a juvenile or is incapable of understanding his entitlement, the competent authority shall on its own initiative undertake the notification referred to in the present principle. Special attention shall be given to notifying parents or guardians.

Principle 16.4:—Any notification referred to in the present principle shall be made or permitted to be made without delay. The competent authority may, however, delay a notification for a reasonable period where exceptional needs of the investigation is required.

Principle 17.1:—A detained person shall be entitled to have the assistance of a legal counsel. He shall be informed of his right by the competent authority promptly after arrest and shall be provided with reasonable facilities for exercising it.

Principle 17.2:—If a detained person does not have a legal counsel of his own choice, he shall be entitled to have a legal counsel assigned to him by a judicial or other authority in all cases where the interests of justice so require and without payment by him if he does not have sufficient means to pay.

Principle 18.1:—A detained or imprisoned person shall be entitled to communicate and consult with his legal counsel.

Principle 18.2: A detained or imprisoned person shall be allowed adequate time and facilities for consultation with his legal counsel.

Principle 18.3: The right of a detained or imprisoned person to be visited by and to consult and communicate, without delay or censorship and in full confidentiality, with his legal counsel may not be suspended or restricted save in exceptional circumstances, to be specified by law or lawful regulations, when it is considered indispensable by a judicial or other authority in order to maintain security and good order.

Principle 18.4: Interviews between a detained or imprisoned person and his legal counsel may be within sight, but not within the hearing, of a law enforcement official.

Principle 19: A detained or imprisoned person shall have the right to be visited by and to correspond with, in particular, members of his family and shall be given adequate opportunity to communicate with the outside world, subject to reasonable conditions and restrictions as specified by law or lawful regulations.

Principle 20: If a detained or imprisoned person so requests, he shall, if possible, be kept in a place of detention or imprisonment reasonably near his usual place of residence.

Principle 21.1:—It shall be prohibited to take undue advantage of the situation of a detained or imprisoned person for the purpose of compelling him to confess, to incriminate himself otherwise or to testify against any other person.

Principle 21.2: No detained person while being interrogated shall be subject to violence, threats or methods of interrogation which impair his capacity of decision or his judgment.

Principle 22: No detained or imprisoned person shall, even with his consent, be subjected to any medical or scientific experimentation which may be detrimental to his health.

Principle 23.1: The duration of any interrogation of a detained or imprisoned person and of the intervals between interrogations as well as the identity of the officials who conducted the interrogations and other persons present shall be recorded and certified in such form as may be prescribed by law.

Principle 23.2: A detained or imprisoned person, or his counsel when provided by law, shall have access to the information described in paragraph 1 of the present principle.

Principle 24: A proper medical examination shall be offered to a detained or imprisoned person as promptly as possible after his admission to the place of detention or imprisonment, and thereafter medical care and treatment shall be provided whenever necessary. This care and treatment shall be provided free of charge.

Principle 25: A detained or imprisoned person or his counsel shall, subject only to reasonable conditions to ensure security and good order in the place of detention or imprisonment, have the right to request or petition a judicial or other authority for a second medical examination or opinion.

Principle 26: The fact that a detained or imprisoned person underwent a medical examination, the name of the physician and the results of such an examination shall be duly recorded. Access to such records shall be ensured. Modalities therefore shall be in accordance with relevant rules of domestic law.

Principle 27:—Non-compliance with these principles in obtaining evidence shall be taken into account in determining the admissibility of such evidence against a detained or imprisoned person.

Principle 28:—A detained or imprisoned person shall have the right to obtain within the limits of available resources, if from public sources, reasonable quantities of educational, cultural and informational material, subject to reasonable conditions to ensure security and good order in the place of detention or imprisonment.

Principle 29.1:—In order to supervise the strict observance of relevant laws and regulations, places of detention shall be visited regularly by qualified and experienced persons appointed by, and responsible to, a competent authority distinct from the authority directly in-charge of the administration of the place of detention or imprisonment.

Principle 29.2:—A detained or imprisoned person shall have the right to communicate freely and in full confidentiality with the persons who visit the places of detention or imprisonment in accordance with paragraph 1 of the present principle, subject to reasonable conditions to ensure security and good order in such places.

Principle 30.1:—The types of conduct of the detained or imprisoned person that constitute disciplinary offences during detention or imprisonment, the description and duration of disciplinary punishment that may be inflicted and the authorities competent to impose such punishment shall be specified by law or lawful regulations and duly published.

Principle 30.2:—A detained or imprisoned person shall have the right to be heard before disciplinary action is taken. He shall have the right to bring such action to higher authorities for review.

Principle 31:—The appropriate authorities shall endeavour to ensure, according to domestic law, assistance when needed, to dependent and in particular, minor members of the families of detained or imprisoned persons and shall devote a particular measure of care to the appropriate custody of children left without supervision.

Principle 32.1:—A detained person or his counsel shall be entitled at any time to take proceedings according to domestic law before a judicial or other authority to challenge the lawfulness of his detention in order to obtain his release without delay, if it is unlawful.

Principle 31.2:—The proceedings referred to in paragraph 1 of the present principle shall be simple and expeditious and at no cost for detained persons without adequate means. The detaining authority shall produce without unreasonable delay the detained person before the reviewing authority.

Principle 33.1:—A detained or imprisoned person or his counsel shall have the right to make a request or complaint regarding his treatment, in particular in case of torture or other cruel, inhuman or degrading treatment, to the authorities responsible for the administration of the place of detention and to higher authorities and when necessary, to appropriate authorities vested with reviewing or remedial powers.

Principle 33.2:—In those cases where neither the detained or imprisoned person nor his counsel has the possibility to exercise his rights under paragraph 1 of the present principle, a member of the family of the detained or imprisoned person or any other person who has knowledge of the case may exercise such rights.

Principle 33.3:—Confidentiality concerning the request or complaint shall be maintained if so requested by the complainant.

Principle 33.4:—Every request or complaint shall be promptly dealt with and replied to without undue delay. If the request or complaint is rejected or, in case of inordinate delay, the complainant shall be entitled to bring it before a judicial or other authority. Neither the detained or imprisoned person nor any complainant under paragraph 1 of the present principle shall suffer prejudice for making a request or complaint.

Principle 34:—Whenever the death or disappearance of a detained or imprisoned person occurs during his detention or imprisonment, an inquiry into the cause of death or disappearance shall be held by a judicial or other authority, either on its own motion or at the instance of a member of the family of such a person or any person who has knowledge of the case. When circumstances so warrant, such an inquiry shall be held on the same procedural basis whenever the death or disappearance occurs shortly after the termination of the detention or imprisonment. The findings of such inquiry or a report thereon shall be made available upon request, unless doing so would jeopardize an ongoing criminal investigation.

Principle 35.1:—Damage incurred because of acts or omissions by a public official contrary to the rights contained in these principles shall be compensated according to the applicable rules or liability provided by domestic law.

Principle 35.2:—Information required to be recorded under these principles shall be available in accordance with procedures provided by domestic law for use in claiming compensation under the present principle.

Principle 36.1:—A detained person suspected of or charged with a criminal offence shall be presumed innocent and shall be treated as such until proved guilty according to law in a public trial at which he has had all the guarantees necessary for his defence.

Principle 36.2:—The arrest or detention of such a person pending investigation and trial shall be carried out only for the purposes of the administration of justice on grounds and under conditions and procedures specified by law. The imposition of restrictions upon such a person which are not strictly required for the purpose of the detention or to prevent hindrance to the process of investigation or the administration of justice, or for the maintenance of security and good order in the place of detention shall be forbidden.

Principle 37:—A person detained on a criminal charge shall be brought before a judicial or other authority provided by law promptly after his arrest. Such authority shall decide without delay upon the lawfulness and necessity of detention. No person may be kept under detention pending investigation or trial except upon the written order of such an authority. A detained person shall, when brought before such an authority, have the right to make a statement on the treatment received by him, while in custody.

Principle 38:—A person detained on a criminal charge shall be entitled to trail within a reasonable time or to release pending trial.

Principle 39:—Except in special cases provided for by law, a person detained on a criminal charge shall be entitled, unless a judicial or other authority decides otherwise in the interest of the administration of justice, to release pending trial subject to the conditions that may be imposed in accordance with the law. Such authority shall keep the necessity of detention under review.

To protect the Human Rights, in England, Human Rights Act, 2000 (U.K.) was legislated. English law now recognizes a whole host of constitutional rights namely right of access to the Courts, right to personal liberty, right to fair trial and right to trial by jury. Moreover, Universal Declaration of Human Rights which was adopted and proclaimed by General Assembly on 10-12-1948 has incorporated Thirty articles. Out of which Articles 5, 7, 8, 9 and 11 provide protection to the accused/detainees. Said declarations have been also recognized and ratified by India. In my opinion, the said declarations are very similar to the ideology of Mahatma Gandhi which says hate the sin and not the sinners.

CHAPTER 13

PUBLIC INTEREST LITIGATION AS AID TO THE PROTECTION OF HUMAN RIGHTS

Former Chief Justice of India, Dr. Justice A.S. Anand while addressing M.C. Bhandari Memorial Lecture quoted the *Bhagwat Geeta* saying that "Whatever a great man thinks and does, other men follow: whatever standards he sets up, the generality of men observe the same.".

Ordinarily, Public Interest Litigation (in short PIL) means the right of a member of the public having sufficient interest to maintain an action for redressal of public injury arising from breach of legal duty or infringement of provisions of the Constitution of India. Rationale of class action in PIL is necessity, effective access to justice to poor and weaker persons, enforcement of fundamental rights. PIL is the new device by which public participation in judicial review of administrative action is being assured. PIL is a new chapter in the Indian Legal system and has come to stay. It has opened gate for entry to the apex Court as well as Hon'ble High Courts by relaxation of *locus standi* so that people of weaker sections, women, labour class, social activists and journalists could make grievances regarding infringement of law, Constitution and Human Rights.

In United States, legal aid is in part supported by private sources, Government's financial aid is the backbone of delivery of legal services to the needy people. In 1970s, Legal Service Corporation offered legal services for indigent persons. In US and England rule of *locus standi* were also relaxed.

In India, Judicial system achieved more credibility and showed public accountability and as necessary consequences law of pleadings and also law of evidence underwent changes significantly. PIL shows that Courts are no longer satisfied with their traditional role and they are willing and interested to participate in reconstruction of the country. But on some occasions, Courts are blamed for judicial activitism and it brings direct clash with Executive and Legislature. However one thing cannot be forgotten that PIL has shown ray of hope to people who had no financial resources or strength to approach courts of law for vindication of their grievances like child labour exploitation, *Bandhua Mazdoor* Problems, persons languishing in jails even after completing the tenure of punishment, sexual harassment of women, etc. By PIL cases, considerable amount of favourtism, nepotism, corruption, arbitrariness in discharge of public duties by Executive Authorities and Administrative Officers has been curbed and their actions were made transparent, reasonable and accountable.

For filing Public Interest Litigation, one can approach under Article 32 of the Constitution directly before Hon'ble Supreme Court or by filing writ petition under

Article 226 of the Constitution to the concerned High Court. The District Courts are not conferred with the jurisdiction to entertain the PIL. But I am of the view that it is high time to confer jurisdiction to entertain PIL cases to District Courts, so that access to judicial forum could be made at the door steps and one should not come to the Hon'ble High Court or Supreme Court for simply filing PIL. It is undisputed that the access to the Court of law should be less expensive, easier, non- cumbersome and speedy. The legal philosophy is not to close the doors of justice, but to allow as many grievances as possible to be brought for redressal. I would also like to suggest that for filing PIL cases either before Supreme Court or before High Court, the required Court-fee at the time of filing should be exempted, but if ultimately it is found by the courts that the case was bogus and frivolous then order could be passed against the petitioner to deposit the required Court-fee.

Whole purpose of entertaining PIL is for the benefit of the public and enforcement of fundamental rights and Human Rights. The law has shifted emphasis from person aggrieved to the person having sufficient interest and now it is not necessary that the seeker of justice should be only a person aggrieved.

According to Hon'ble Dr. Justice Arijit Pasayat of Supreme Court of India, Human Rights are those minimal rights, which every individual must have against the State or other public authority by virtue of his being a member of the human family, irrespective of any other consideration. The concept of Human Rights embodies the minimum rights of an individual versus his own State and it is as old as political philosophy. Human Rights are those rights, which are inherent in nature and without which one cannot live as a human being.

The first documentary use of expression "Human Rights" is found in the Charter of the United Nations, which was adopted after the Second World War at San Francisco on 25-6-1945 and was ratified by the majority of its signatories in October that year. The Preamble of the charter declared its object 'to reaffirm faith in fundamental Human Rights'. The first concrete step of formulating various Human Rights was taken by the United Nations General Assembly by adopting the Universal Declaration of Human Rights in December, 1948.

It is pertinent to mention here that violation and non-compliance with the standards of Human Rights norms were rampant. Sub-human living conditions, illiteracy, usurpation of natural resources by vested interests, exploitation, bonded labour and the like problems were present all around. Plural justice, breaking of shackles of technicalities of law was the only need of the hour, which was realized by the Courts, Courts did not even hesitate to spring into action on mere letter petition or information through any other source including PIL in connection with atrocities by State force, regarding living conditions in prisons, custodial deaths and the like or to render plural justice for the masses.

India has a written Constitution. The Preamble of the Constitution of India provides as under:

We, the people of India, having solemnly resolved to constitute India into a SOVEREIGN SOCIALIST SECULAR DEMOCRATIC REPUBLIC and to secure to all its citizens. Justice, social, economic and political. Liberty of thought, expression, belief, faith and worship; Equality of status and of opportunity; and to promote among them all, Fraternity assuring the dignity of the individual and the unity and integrity of the Nation.

It is worthwhile to mention here that in *Paschim Bangal Khet Mazdoor Samity* v. *State of West Bengal,* AIR 1996 SC 2426, the Supreme Court recognized the need for providing medical treatment to a person, denial of such treatment, it was held, results in violation of "right to life" guaranteed under Article 21 of the Constitution of India.

In *Bodhisatwa Gautam* v. *Subhra Chakraborty,* (1996) 1 SCC 49 the Supreme Court awarded an interim compensation of Rs. 1000 per month to the victim of rape. The logic behind this order appears to be that the complainant's most cherished fundamental right to live with human dignity is violated by the accused. Every human being is a divine being entitled to dignity, liberty, equality and other basic rights.

Preamble of Universal Declaration of Human Rights (1948) says as under: "Whereas recognition of the inherent dignity and of equal inalienable rights of all members of the human family is the foundation of freedom, justice and peace in the world..." and the 1st article saying "All human beings are born free and equal in dignity and rights. They are endowed with reason and conscience and should act towards one another in a spirit of brotherhood."

Articles 3 and 4 provide for right to life, liberty and security of person, and slavery or servitude is prohibited. Article 8 provides effective remedy by the Courts for violation of fundamental rights granted by the Constitution or law."

The Charter describes about many other rights too, most of them are covered under Part III of the Constitution of India as fundamental rights including Article 21 which is fountain head for dignified human existence with opportunities for self-development. Enforcement of such rights is also ensured more particularly by Articles 32 and 226 of Constitution. Matters relating to Human Rights would be covered under Article 32, whereas matters falling outside the scope of fundamental rights may seek shelter under Public Interest Litigation. It is pertinent to mention here that Articles 226 and 32 of the Constitution fulfill the object as mentioned under the Article 8 of the said Charter.

It is to be noted that the model of Public Interest Litigation available in India is different from the Public Interest Litigation model applicable in America. Indian model is a judiciary fashioned tool which deals with issues like consumer protection, prevention of environmental pollution and ecological destruction as in the United States and perhaps in other jurisdictions, but it does much more. Its primary focus is on exploitation of disadvantaged groups, denial of their Human Rights and entitlements and repression by agencies of the State. The Public Interest Litigation model, applicable in America, it is concerned with immediate as well as long-term resolution of the problems of the disadvantaged. It also seeks to ensure that the authorities of the State fulfil the statutory obligations and also to prevent and check violations of Human Rights as also fundamental rights. It is said that Public Interest Litigation is a collaborative effort on the part of the petitioner, the Court and the Government or the public official to see that basic Human Rights become meaningful for large masses of people. It also tries to see that the State authorities should adhere to their constitutional and legal obligations and to enforce them so that the rule of law be prevailed in all sides.

It is necessary to mention here that Supreme Court has recognized the *locus standi* of the other persons and not only the injured or affected persons in approaching for violation of fundamental rights and basic Human Rights of other aggrieved persons. Human Rights are necessary to promote the personality development of human beings, which also include healthy environment. Public Interest Litigation has come to provide benefit and help to the poor people, farmers, Mazdoors, women, disadvantaged and unprivileged persons, with a view to protect their Human Rights.

CHAPTER 14

SOCIAL JUSTICE AND HUMAN RIGHTS UNDER THE INDIAN CONSTITUTION

Dr. Justice Arijit Pasayat, Judge, Supreme Court of India in a lecture held on 10-12-2006 at India International Centre, New Delhi rightly stated that "Appalled by the barbarism of the Second World War, the United Nations General Assembly adopted the Universal Declaration of Human Rights in 1948. While not legally binding, it urged member nations to promote a number of human, civil, economic and social rights, asserting these rights are part of the "foundation of freedom, justice and peace in the world". The declaration was the first international legal effort to limit the behaviour of States and press upon them duties to their citizens following the model of the rights-duty quality.

Many States wanted to go beyond the declaration of rights and create legal covenants, which would put greater pressure on States to follow Human Rights norms. Because some States disagreed over whether this international Covenant should contain economic and social rights (which usually require a greater effort to fulfil on the part of individual States), two treaties were prepared.

In 1966 and 1976 respectively, the International Covenant on Civil and Political Rights and the International Covenant on Economic, Social and Cultural Rights came into force with the Universal Declaration of Human Rights these documents form the International Bill of Rights.

"Recognition of the inherent dignity and of the equal and inalienable rights of all members of the human family is the foundation of freedom, justice and peace in the world."

Social Justice is based upon the principle/theory of a society, which provides just and fair treatment to every human being.

Social Justice is defined as under:

> According to Universal Declaration of Human Rights, 1948 human dignity is an unalienable right which is foundation of peace, freedom and justice in the world. The said declaration has protected the social, economic, political, Civil and also culture rights. It is relevant to mention that Articles 23 and 24 of the Indian Constitution Protects the rights of children and women from forced labour declaring that traffic in human beings is totally prohibited and banned and the same is punishable in law also.

It is apt to say that the scope of Article 21 of the Constitution of India expanded with the Directives Principles of State Policy and consistently proved the principle of Convention. Indian Supreme Court in the case of *Consumer Education and Research Centre* v. *Union of India*, (1995) 3 SCC 42 has held as under:—

"20. The Preamble and Article 38 of the Constitution of India—the supreme law envisions social justice as its arch to ensure life to be meaningful and liveable with human dignity, jurisprudence is the eye of the law giving as insight into the environment of which it is the expression. It relates the law to the spirit of the time and makes it richer. Law is the ultimate aim of every civilized society as a key system in a given era, to meet the needs and demands of its time. Justice, according to law, comprehends social urge and commitment. The Constitution commands justice, liberty, equality and fraternity as supreme values to usher in the egalitarian social, economic and political democracy. Social Justice, equality and dignity of person are corner stones of social democracy. The concept 'social justice' which the Constitution of India engrafted, consists of diverse principles essential for the orderly growth and development of personality of every citizen. "Social Justice" is thus an integral part of "justice" in generic sense. Justice is the genus, of which social justice is one of its species. Social justice is a dynamic device to mitigate the sufferings of the poor, weak, Dalits Tribals and deprived sections of the society and to elevate them to the level of equality to live a life with dignity of person. Social justice is not a simple or single idea of a society but is an essential part of complex of social change to relieve the poor etc., from handicaps, penury to ward off distress, and to make their life liveable, for greater good of the society at large. In other words, the aim of social justice is to attain substantial degree of social, economic and political equality, which is the legitimate expectation. Social security, just and humane conditions of work and leisure to workman are part of his meaningful right to life and to achieve self-expression of his personality and to enjoy the life with dignity, the State should provide facilities and opportunities to them to reach at least minimum standard of health, economic security and civilized living while sharing according to the capacity, social and cultural heritage."

It was held in the case of *CESC Ltd.* v. *S.C. Bose*, 1991 Supp (2) SCR 267 that the right to social justice is a fundamental rights it is to be mentioned that social justice was treated at par with fundamental rights which is guaranteed under part (iii) of the Constitution of India.

Eminent Jurist Blaise Pascal rightly said: "Justice without power is inefficient, power without justice a tyranny. Justice without power is opposed, because there are always wicked men. Power without justice is soon questioned. Justice and power must therefore be brought together, so that whatsoever is just may be powerful and whatever is powerful may be just."

It is judicially settled in India that right to life is regarded as basic Human Right under Article 21 of the Constitution of India and it has recognized right to live with dignity. Declaration of Human Rights was largely discussed in the Vienna Declaration and in World Conference on Human Rights in the year 1993, programme action was adopted. The United Nations had constituted number of bodies to monitor and study Human Rights, under the leadership of the U.N. High Commissioner for Human Rights.

In the case of *Chameli Singh* v. *State of Uttar Pradesh*, (1996) 2 SCC 549, Supreme Court has observed that the right to shelter is a fundamental right. It was further held as under:—

"8. In any organised society, right to live as a human being is not ensured by meeting only the animal needs of man. It is secured only when he is assured of all facilities to develop himself and is freed from restrictions which inhibit his growth. All Human Rights are designed to achieve this object. Right to live guaranteed in any civilized society implies the right to food, water, decent environment education, medial care and shelter. These are basic Human Rights known to any civilized society. All civil, political, social and cultural rights enshrined in the Universal Declaration of Human Rights and Convention or under the Constitution of India cannot be exercised without these basic Human Rights. Shelter for a human being, therefore, is not a mere protection of his life and limb. It is home where he has opportunities to grow physically, mentally, intellectually and spiritually. Right to shelter, therefore, includes adequate living space, safe and decent structure, clean and decent surroundings, sufficient light, pure air and water, electricity, sanitation and other civic amenities like roads etc., so as to have easy access to his daily avocation. The right to shelter, therefore, does not mean a mere right to a roof over one's head but right to all the infrastructure necessary to enable them to live and develop as a human being. Right to shelter when used as an essential requisite to the right to live, should be deemed to have been guaranteed as a fundamental right. As is enjoined in the Directive Principles, the State should be deemed to be under an obligation to secure it for its citizens, of course subject to its economic budgeting. In a democratic society as a member of the organised civic community one should have permanent shelter so as to physically, mentally and intellectually equip to improve his excellence as a useful citizen as enjoined in the fundamental duties and to be useful citizen and equal participant in democracy. The ultimate object of making a man equipped with a right to dignity of person and equality of status is to enable him to develop himself into a cultured being. Want of decent residence, therefore, frustrates the very object of the Constitutional animation of right to equality, economic justice, fundamental right to residence, dignity of person and right to live itself. To bring the Dalits and Tribes into the mainstream of national life providing these facilities and opportunities to them is the duty of the State as fundamental to their basic human and constitutional rights."

It is to be noted that life, liberty, equality and dignity are the main pillars of Human Rights.

It is apt to mention here that social justice is an integral part of the justice of generic sense. Social justice is people's justice where the tyranny of power is transformed into the democracy of social good under Article 32 of the Constitution of India, any citizen can approach for violation of fundamental rights directly before the Supreme Court has held by a Constitution Bench of 5 Judges in the case of *Romesh Thaper* v. *State of Madras*, AIR 1950 SC 124.

The Human Rights Committee has been constituted by International covenant on civil and political rights with 18 members in total. The said Committee has powers to decide as to whether a particular practice is a violation of fundamental rights. Said Committee also works to promote compliance of norms and from time- to-time makes recommendations regarding the major Conventions. The reports of the said Committee are only suggestive in nature and the same is not binding in law.

CHAPTER 15

HUMAN RIGHTS OF PHYSICALLY DISABLED AND AIDS/HIV-AFFECTED PERSONS

According to the survey made in the year 2009, about 10 per cent. of the world's population, live with disabilities. Eighty per cent. of persons with disabilities live in poor countries. Survey also points out that in the developing countries 80 per cent. – 90 per cent. of persons with disabilities of working age are jobless.

Physically handicapped and mentally retarded persons are not physically fit like able bodied persons. They are also entitled to avail Human Rights. On the ground of principle of equality they are entitled to be treated at par.

The meeting to launch the Asian and Pacific decade of the disabled persons 1993-2002 convened by the Economic and Social Commission for Asian and Pacific held on 1-12-1992 to 5-12-1992 in China adopted the proclamation on the full participation and equality of people with disabilities. In India in the year 1995 the Persons with Disabilities (Equal Opportunities, Protection of Rights, and Full Participation) Act was enacted.

Section 2(i) of the said Act define disability as under:—

(i) blindness, (ii) low vision, (iii) leprosy cured, (iv) hearing impairment, (v) locomotor disability, (vi) mental retardation, and (vii) mental illness.

Section 25 of the said Act directs the appropriate Governments and local authorities to take steps for the prevention of occurrence of disabilities by undertaking survey, investigation and research concerning the cause of occurrence of disabilities, promote various methods of preventing disabilities, screen all the children at lest once in a year for the purpose of identifying 'at risk' cases to sponsor awareness campaigns, take measures for pre-natal and post-natal care of mother and child, educate the public, etc.

Similarly section 26 of the said Act directs the appropriate Governments and local authorities to provide children with disabilities free education. Section 33 of the said Act provides that every appropriate Government shall appoint in every Government Establishment such percentage of vacancies not less than three per cent. for persons or class of persons with disability of which one per cent. each shall be reserved for persons suffering from:

(i) blindness or low vision, (ii) hearing impairment, (iii) locomotor disability or cerebral palsy in the posts identified for each disability.

The Preamble of Constitution of India provides as under:—

We, the People of India, having solemnly resolved to constitute India into a (SOVEREIGN, SOCIALIST, SECULAR, DEMOCRATIC, republic) and to secure to all its citizens.

Justice, social, economic and political;

Liberty of thought, expression, belief, faith and worship;

Equality of status and of opportunity; and to promote among them all.

Fraternity assuring the dignity of the individual and the unity and integrity of the Nation.

The said Preamble speaks to secure to citizens of India Justice, economic and political, equality of a status and opportunity and to promote among them fraternity, assuring the dignity of the individual and unity and integrity of the country. Although in the Constitution of India there is no distinction between disabled and physical person but in fact in India disabled persons are never treated at par with the physically fit person. The disabled persons are considered inferior type of citizen. They are rarely considered for selection in their own quota of disabled persons. Although under Article 14 of Indian Constitution, it was specifically provided that every person is equal in the eyes of law and they are equally protected. Such constitutional guarantee is still a dream. In other constitutional provisions namely Article 41 of the Constitution of India which says that the State shall within the limit of economic capacity and development, make effective provisions of securing the right to work, to education and to public assistance in the cases of old age, sickness, disablement and unemployment.

Declaration of Rights of mentally retarded person proclaimed by General Assembly resolution dated 20-12-1971 requested all the International Organizations/bodies in all the States to take steps for protection of the right of mentally related person.

(i) The mentally retarded person has a right to proper medical care and physical therapy and to such education, training, rehabilitation and guidance as will enable him to develop his ability and maximum potential.

(ii) Whenever possible, the mentally retarded person should live with his own family or with foster parents and participate in different forms of community life. The family with which he lives should receive assistance. In case if an institution becomes necessary, it should be provided, in surroundings and other circumstances as close as possible to those of normal life.

(iii) The mentally retarded person has a right to protection from exploitation, abuse and degrading treatment. If prosecuted for any offence, he shall have a right to due process of law with full recognition being given to his degree of mental responsibility.

In view of the said declaration, it is bounden duty of the State/Govt. to treat the disable persons at par with the physically fit person in all respects namely Education, Employment, Security, medical care etc.

The Declaration on the rights of disabled person proclaimed by General Assembly resolution dated 9-12-1975 contemplates that:

(a) Disabled persons have the inherent right to respect for their human dignity. Disabled persons, whatever the origin, nature and seriousness of their handicaps and disabilities, have the same fundamental rights as their fellow citizens of the same age, which implies first and foremost the right to enjoy a decent life, as normal and full as possible, (b) Disabled persons have the same civil and political rights as other human beings; paragraph 7 of the Declaration on the rights of Mentally retarded persons applies to any possible limitation or suppression of those right for mentally disabled persons; (c) Disabled persons have the right to medical, psychological and functional treatment, including prosthetic and orthetic appliances, to medical and social rehabilitation, education, vocational training and rehabilitation, aid, counselling, placement services and other services which will enable them to develop their capabilities and skills to the maximum and will hasten the process of their social integration or re-integration, (d) Disabled persons have the right to economic and social security and to a decent level of living. They have the right, according to their capabilities, to secure and retain employment or to engage in a useful, productive and remunerative occupation and to join trade unions, (e) Disabled persons have the right to live with their families or with foster parents and to participate in all social, creative or recreational activities. No disabled person shall be subjected, as far as his or her residence is concerned, to differential treatment other than that required by his or her condition or by the improvement which he or she may derive therefrom. If the stay of a disabled person in a specialized establishment is indispensable, the environment and living conditions therein shall be as close as possible to those of the normal life of a person of his or her age, (f) Disabled persons shall be able to avail themselves of qualified legal aid when such aid proves indispensable for the protection of their persons and property. If judicial proceedings are instituted against them, the legal procedure applied shall take their physical and mental condition fully into account.

General Assembly on 17-12-1991 declared principles for the protection of mentally retarded persons and improvement of their mental health.

On 17-12-1991 General Assembly has evolved principles for the protection of persons with mental illness and the improvement of mental health care. Principle No. 1 of the said resolution are (a) all persons with a mental illness, or who are being treated as such persons, shall be treated with humanity and respect for the inherent dignity of the human person. (b) All persons with a mental illness, or who are being treated as such persons, have the right to protection from economic, sexual and other forms of exploitation, physical or other abuse and degrading treatment, (c) Every person with a mental illness shall have the right to exercise all civil, political, economic, social and cultural rights as recognized in the Universal Declaration of Human Rights, the International Covenant on Economic, Social and Cultural Rights, the International Covenant on Civil and Political Rights and in other relevant instruments, such as the Declaration on the Rights of Disabled persons and the Body of Principles for the Protection of all persons under any forms of Detention or Imprisonment, (d) Any decision that, by reason of his or her mental illness, a person lacks legal capacity, and any decision that, in consequence of such incapacity, a personal representative shall be appointed, shall be made only after a fair hearing by an independent and impartial tribunal established by domestic law. The person whose capacity is at issue shall be entitled to be represented by a counsel. If the person whose capacity is at issue does not himself or herself secure such representation, it shall be made available without payment by that person to the extent that he or she does not have sufficient means to pay for it.

Supreme Court of India in the case of *Javed Abidi* v. *Union of India*, AIR 1999 SC 512 has deeply considered the problems of disabled people and directed Indian Airlines to grant concessions for passengers suffering from locomotor disability to the extent of 80 per cent. Orissa High Court in the case of *Ramchandra Tandai* v. *State of Orissa*, AIR 1994 Ori 228 directed the State Government to accord recognition and financial assistance to a school for the deaf and dumb (disabled persons) This decision is in right spirit of Article 25 of the Universal Declaration on Human Rights, which provides that each person has the right to security in the event of unemployment, sickness, disability, widowhood, old age, or other lack of livelihood in circumstances beyond his control.

It is apt to mention here that in the year 1993, Supreme Court delivered a landmark judgment in the case of *National Federation of Blind* v. *Union Public Service Commission*, AIR 1993 SC 1916, wherein directions were issued to the Commission to permit the blind candidates to appear in the Civil Service Examination.

With regard to protection of Human Rights in respect of AIDS/HIV patient, it is stated that AIDS (Acquired Immune Deficiency Syndrome)/HIV (Human Immune Deficiency Virus) patients are discarded and neglected from the Society and educational institutes without their any fault.

According to an estimate about more than 25 million persons have expired due to AIDS and more than 50 million persons are suffering from said diseases. Although it is medically proved in the whole world that the AIDS/HIV are not spread by touching the person or by talking or sitting with them. In fact, it spreads by having sex with HIV/AIDS persons, use of syringe which has already used by infected persons, shaving of beard by used blade, transfusion of blood of the affected persons and birth of child from affected persons.

It is high time that entire Executive capitals of the world sit together and deliberate to get a way to curb the menace of the HIV/AIDS diseases. It is undisputed that medical treatment of such disease is very costly and it is not affordable by poor patient. Essential drugs are not available in large quantity and due to their non-production at larger scale. Cost factor is very material in their non-production of the drugs. There is acute shortage of trained and qualified medical and paramedical staff to treat such patients. Although, National AIDS Control Organization in India is working as in a bigger way to check and control. The other way to prevent the said disease is to a spread awareness about the cause/root of the said disease among the persons. Patients are shy about disclosing their suffering of such diseases because of re-action of the society of treating them untouchable.

In developing countries of the world the spread of AIDS/HIV is at large scale. Reason is costly medical treatment and lack of proper awareness of prevention of the said disease.

What I mean to say very clearly that even disabled persons either physically handicapped or mentally retarded or patients of AIDS/HIV are all human beings and they are entitled to enjoy the basic Human Rights. To treat them as untouchables or to discard or neglect them from society is the violation of Human Rights.

In 2001, UN General Assembly has issued declaration of commitment of HIV/AIDS. Said declaration says about leadership which involved personal commitment and concrete action for prevention, care, treatment of the affected persons and also planning for poverty eradication and increase in national budget to tackle the spreading of disease like AIDS/HIV.

The said declaration of 2001 gives much more stress to ensure non-discrimination and full and equal enjoyment of Human Rights by the affected patients of HIV/AIDS, including their access to education, inheritance, employment and health care, legal protection and social boycott or social exclusion. The said declaration also emphasizes for elimination of all sorts of discrimination and to promote shared responsibility of men and women to ensure safe sex and to empower woman to decide responsibility on subject relating their sexuality to increase their ability to protect themselves from infections of HIV. International communities and civil societies are required to take appropriate measures to help to alleviate the social and economic impact on such disease in the most affected developing countries by giving financial aids for promotion and medical treatment of AIDS/HIV.

CHAPTER 16

HUMAN RIGHTS AND THE FUNDAMENTAL RIGHTS OF INDIAN CONSTITUTION

It is very much true that the makers of the Indian Constitution were influenced by Bill of Rights of the American Constitution, Irish Constitution and French Declaration of the Rights of Men, Constitution of Japan adopted after World War II, Universal Declaration of Human Rights, 1948. Further the Human Rights Act, 1998 was legislated in United Kingdom to give further effect to the rights and freedoms guaranteed under the European Convention on Human Rights. It made the Convention rights enforceable in the United Kingdom Law Courts. Fundamental rights are mentioned in Part III of the Constitution of India starting from Articles 12 to 35 and these fundamental rights conform Human Rights. Directive Principles of State Policy are mentioned in Part IV of the Indian Constitution. The term Human Rights has not been defined in the Indian Constitution. But Part III of Indian Constitution covers more or less complete basic Human Rights.

It is pertinent to mention here that Article 1 of the Universal Declaration of Human Rights provides that all human beings are born free and equal in dignity and rights. They are endowed with reason and conscience and should act towards one another in a spirit of brotherhood. Article 2 of the said Declaration contemplates that everyone is entitled to all the rights and freedoms set forth in this declaration, without distinction of any kind, such as race, colour, sex, language, religion, political or other opinion, national or social origin, property, birth or other status. Furthermore, no distinction shall be made on the basis of the political, jurisdictional or international status of the country or territory to which a person belongs, whether it is independent, trust, non self-governing or under any other limitation of sovereignty.

Article 14 of the Constitution of India provides that "the State shall not deny to any person equality before the law or the equal protection of the laws within the territory of India."

The source of Article 14 is the English Common Law and American Constitution. This article gives effect to the preamble of the Indian Constitution. Article 14 of the Indian Constitution corresponds to Article 7 of the Declaration of Human Rights, which is reproduced as under:—

Article 7—All are equal before the law and are entitled without any discrimination to equal protection of law. All are entitled to equal protection against any discrimination in violation of this declaration and against any incitement to such discrimination.

Article 14 of the Indian Constitution can be divided into 2 parts, *firstly* equality before law and *secondly*, equal protection of the laws. Equality before law means every person is equal in the eye of law and no person whatever post he holds is above the law. Equal protection of laws means similarly situated persons shall be protected equally. It is important to mention here that Article 14 is a safeguard to an important Human Right namely every person is equal before the law and equal protection of laws is provided to all persons within the territory of India. Article 14 corresponds to Article 21.2 of Universal Declaration of Human Rights, 1948, which provides as under: "Everyone has the right to equal access to public services in his country." But it is sad that inspite of lapse of 55 years after getting independence, India could not fulfil the pious hope as mentioned in Article 23(1)-(3) of Universal Declaration of Human Rights, which is quoted as under:—

Article 23(1) everyone has the right to work, to free choice of employment, to just and favourable conditions of work and to protection against un-employment.

(2) Everyone, without any discrimination, has the right to equal pay for equal work.

(3) Everyone who works has the right to just and favourable remuneration ensuring for himself and his family an existence worthy of human dignity, and supplemented, if necessary, by other means of social protection.

Article 15 of the Indian Constitution is set out as under:

> "15. *Prohibition of discrimination on grounds of religion, race, caste, sex or place of birth.*—(1) The State shall not discriminate against any citizen on the grounds only of religion, race, caste, sex, place of birth or any of them.
>
> (2) No citizen shall, on grounds only of religion, race, caste, sex, place of birth or any of them, be subject to any disability, liability, restriction or condition with regard to:—
>
> (a) access to shops, public restaurants, hotels and places of public entertainment; or
>
> (b) the use of wells, tanks, bathing ghats, roads and places of public resort maintained wholly or partly out of State funds or dedicated to the use of general public.
>
> (3) Nothing in this article shall prevent the State from making any special provision for women and children.
>
> (4) Nothing in this article or in clause (2) of Article 29 shall prevent the State from making any special provision for the advancement of any socially and educationally backward classes of citizens or for the Scheduled Castes and the Scheduled Tribes."

Article 16 of the Indian Constitution guarantees equality of opportunity in matters of public employment, which is reproduced as under:

> "16. *Equality of opportunity in matters of public employment.*—(1) There shall be equality of opportunity for all citizens in matters relating to employment or appointment to any office under the State.
>
> (2) No citizen shall, on grounds only of religion, race, caste, sex, descent, place of birth, residence or any of them, be ineligible for, or discriminated against in respect of, any employment or office under the State.

(3) Nothing in this article shall prevent Parliament from making any law prescribing, in regard to a class or classes of employment or appointment to an office under the Government of, or any local or other authority within, a State or Union territory, any requirement as to residence within that State or Union Territory prior to such employment or appointment.

(4) Nothing in this article shall prevent the State from making any provision for the reservation of appointments or posts in favour of any backward class of citizens which, in the opinion of the State, is not adequately represented in the services under the State.

(4A) Nothing in this article shall prevent the State from making any provision for reservation in matters of promotion with consequential seniority, to any class or classes of posts in the services under the State in favour of the Scheduled Castes and the Scheduled Tribes which, in the opinion of the States, are not adequately represented in the services under the State.

(4B) Nothing in this article shall prevent the State from considering any unfilled vacancies of a year which are reserved for being filled-up in that year in accordance with any provision for reservation made under clause (4) or clause (4A) as a separate class of vacancies to be filled up in any succeeding year or years and such class of vacancies shall not be considered together with the vacancies of the year in which they are being filled-up for determining the ceiling of fifty per cent. reservation of total number of vacancies of that year.

(5) Nothing in this article shall affect the operation of any law which provides that the incumbent of an office in connection with the affairs of any religious or denominational institution or any member of the governing body thereof shall be a person professing a particular religion or belonging to a particular denomination."

Article 16(3) permits the State to prescribe a requirement of residence within the State or Union territory by legislation made by Parliament. Article 16(4) contemplates providing reservation of posts in favour of backward class of citizens which, in the opinion of the State is not adequately represented in the services under the State.

Article 16(5) provides that offices connected with religious or denominational institutions may be reserved for members professing any particular religion and belonging to any particular denomination. Here two issues regarding reservation has been settled by judicial pronouncements, *firstly*, Supreme Court in the case *Trilokinath* v. *State of Jammu and Kashmir*, reported in AIR 1967 SC 1283 and *Indra Sawhney* v. *Union of India*, 1992 Supp (3) SCC 217 has held that in no case reservation should exceed more than 50%. *Secondly*, in the case of *PGI Chandigarh* v. *Faculty Association*, (1998) 4 SCC 1 Constitution Bench of Supreme Court has upheld that there cannot be 100% reservation, which means if there is only one post in the cadre, it cannot be reserved and earlier decision in the case of *Chakradhar Paswan* v. *State of Bihar*, (1988) 2 SCC 214 was affirmed.

Article 17 was brought in the Constitution to abolish the untouchability. The main purpose of this article is to ban the practice of untouchability in any form. Article 17 has been implemented by the protection of Civil Rights Act, 1955. Untouchability was a social disability. It was forcibly imposed by people of higher caste in India upon people of lower caste by reason of their birth. Article 17 of Constitution is set out as under:

"17. *Abolition of untouchability.*—'Untouchability' is abolished and its practice in any form is forbidden. The enforcement of any disability arising out of 'Untouchability' shall be an offence punishable in accordance with law."

This Article more or less corresponds to Article 5 of the Universal Declaration of Human Rights which reads as under:—

"No one shall be subject to torture or to cruel, inhuman or degrading treatment or punishment."

Article 19 is reproduced as under:

"19. *Protection of certain rights regarding freedom of speech, etc.*—(1) All citizens shall have the right—

(a) to freedom of speech and expression;

(b) to assemble peacefully and without arms;

(c) to form associations or unions or co-operative societies;

(d) to move freely throughout the territory of India;

(e) to reside and settle in any part of the territory of India;

(f) ****

(g) to practise any profession, or to carry on any occupation, trade or business.

(2) Nothing in sub-clause (a) of clause (1) shall affect the operation of any existing law, or prevent the State from making any law, in so far as such law imposes reasonable restrictions on the exercise of the right conferred by the said sub-clause in the interest of the sovereignty and integrity of India, the security of the State, friendly relations with foreign States, public order, decency or morality, or in relation to contempt of Court, defamation or incitement to an offence.

(3) Nothing in sub-clause (b) of the said clause shall affect the operation of any existing law in so far as it imposed, or prevents the State from making any law imposing, in the interests of the sovereignty and integrity of India or public order, reasonable restrictions on the exercise of the right conferred by the said sub-clause.

(4) Nothing in sub-clause (c) of the said clause shall affect the operation of any existing law in so far as it imposes, or prevents the State from making any law imposing, in the interest of the sovereignty and integrity of India or public order or morality, reasonable restrictions on the exercise of the right conferred by the said sub-clause.

(5) Nothing in sub-clauses (d) and (e) of the said clause shall affect the operation of any existing law in so far as it imposes, or prevents the State from making any law imposing, reasonable restrictions on the exercise of any of the rights conferred by the said sub-clauses either in the interests of the general public or for the protection of the interests of any Scheduled Tribe.

(6) Nothing in sub-clause (g) of the said clause shall affect the operation of any existing law in so far as it imposes, or prevents the State from making any law imposing, in the interests of the general public, reasonable restrictions on the exercise of the right conferred by the said sub-clause, and, in particular,

nothing in the said sub-clause shall affect the operation of any existing law in so far as it relates to, or prevent the State from making any law relating to:—

(i) the professional or technical qualifications necessary for practising any profession or carrying on any occupation, trade or business, or

(ii) the carrying on by the State, or by a corporation owned or controlled by the State, of any trade, business, industry or service, whether to the exclusion, complete or partial, of citizens or otherwise.

Article 19(1)(a) of the Indian Constitution is similar to Article 19 of the Declaration of Human Rights, 1948. Article 19(1)(b) and (c) of the Indian Constitution corresponds to Article 20 of the said Declaration. Article 19(1)(d) and (e) corresponds to Article 13(1) of the said Declaration. For convenience the relevant provisions of said declaration are given below:

"Article 13(1): Everyone has the right to freedom of movement and residence within the borders of each State.

Article 19: Everyone has the right to freedom of opinion and expression; this right includes freedom to hold opinions without interference and to seek, receive and impart information and ideas through any media and regardless of frontiers.

In the case of *Babu Lal* v. *State of Maharashtra*, AIR 1961 SC 884, it was held that Article 19(1)(b) guarantees the freedom of citizens to meet with each other in any number provided the assembly is peaceful and unarmed. But Article 19 is not an absolute right and it is always subject to reasonable restrictions in the interest of public order. Article 19(1)(c) guarantees to form an association or unions by the citizens. Article 19(1)(b) guarantees its citizens to move freely through the country. But restrictions can be imposed upon free movement in the interest of general public. In the case of *Kharak Singh* v. *State of Madhya Pradesh*, (1964) 1 SCR 352 surveillance by the police upon the movement of a person was found a restriction upon such guaranteed right. In the case of *State of Madhya Pradesh* v. *Thakur Bharat Singh*, AIR 1967 SC 1170, order requiring a person not to leave his place of residence or to reside at a specified place other than his place of ordinary residence are held to be restriction upon the guaranteed right of free movement.

Article 20 provides protection in respect of conviction for offences, which is set out as under:

"20. *Protection in respect of conviction for offence*—(1) No person shall be convicted of any offence except for violation of a law in force at the time of the commission of the act charged as an offence, nor be subjected to a penalty greater than that which might have been inflicted under the law in force at the time of the commission of the offence.

(2) No person shall be prosecuted and punished for the same offence more than once.

(3) No person accused of any offence shall be compelled to be a witness against himself."

Article 20 of the Constitution corresponds Articles 9 to 11 of the said Declaration. For ready reference Articles 9 to 11 of the said declaration are reproduced as under:—

Article 9 of the said Declaration speaks that no one shall be subjected to arbitrary arrest, detention or exile. Article 10 of the said declaration provides that Everyone is entitled to full equality to a fair and public hearing by an independent and impartial tribunal, in the determination of his rights, and obligations and of any criminal charge against him and Article 11(1) provides that everyone charged with a penal offence has the right to be presumed innocent until proved guilty according to law in a public trial at which he has had all the guarantees necessary for his defence. Article 11(2) says that No one shall be held guilty of any penal offence on account of any act or omission which did not constitute a penal offence, under national or international law, at the time when it was committed. Nor shall a heavier penalty be imposed than the one that was applicable at the time the penal offence was committed.

Article 20(2) is concerned with the stage of procedure and incorporates a prohibition against double jeopardy (there shall not be prosecution and punishment after an earlier punishment for the same offence). This article is inserted in the Constitution with a view to avoid unnecessary harassment which must be caused to a person for successive criminal proceedings where single crime has been committed. Article 20 (3) gives protection against testimonial compulsion and is also concerned with the stage of procedure. This protection is available to accused of an offence. But there is no constitutional protection for a witness who is not the accused in the offence.

Article 21 of the Constitution is reproduced as under:—

"21. *Protection of life and personal liberty.*—No person shall be deprived of his life or personal liberty except according to procedure established by law."

The Article 21 of the Constitution of India can be divided in 2 Parts. *First* part provides that no person shall be deprived of his life or personal liberty and the *second* part says that if a person is deprived of his life and liberty it shall be made according to the procedure established by law.

Supreme Court of India in the case of *A.K. Gopalan* v. *State of Madras,* reported in 1950 SCR 88 specifically held that the object of Article 21 is to prevent encroachment upon personal liberty by the Executive save in accordance with law and in conformity with the provisions thereof. Personal liberty means freedom from physical restraint of person by incarceration or otherwise. Protection of this article extends to all the persons and not only to the citizens. Persons who are in the imprisonment are also protected by Article 21 of the Indian Constitution. Speedy trial is one of the requirement of Article 21 of the Indian Constitution.

Article 22 of the Constitution of India is mentioned as under:

"22. *Protection against arrest and detention in certain cases.*—(1) No person who is arrested shall be detained in custody without being informed, as soon as may be, of the grounds for such arrest nor shall he be denied the right to consult, and to be defended by, a legal practitioner of his choice.

(2) Every person who is arrested and detained in custody shall be produced before the nearest Magistrate within a period of twenty-four hours of such arrest excluding the time necessary for the journey from the place of arrest to court of the Magistrate and no such person shall be detained in custody beyond the said period without the authority of a Magistrate.

(3) Nothing in clauses (1) and (2) shall apply—

(a) to any person who for the time being is an enemy, alien; or

(b) to any person who is arrested or detained under any law providing for preventive detention.

(4) No law providing for preventive detention shall authorise the detention of a person for a longer period than three months unless:—

(a) an Advisory Board consisting of persons who are, or have been , or are qualified to be appointed as, Judges of a High Court has reported before the expiration of the said period of three months that there is in its opinion sufficient cause for such detention:

Provided that nothing in this sub-clause shall authorise the detention of any person beyond the maximum period prescribed by any law made by Parliament under sub-clause (b) of clause (7); or

(b) such person is detained in accordance with the provisions of any law made by Parliament under sub-clauses (a) and (b) of clause (7).

(5) When any person is detained in pursuance of an order made under any law providing for preventive detention, the authority making the order shall, as soon as may be, communicate to such person the grounds on which the order has been made and shall afford him the earliest opportunity of making a representation against the order.

(6) Nothing in clause (5) shall enquire the authority making any such order as is referred to in that clause to disclose facts which such authority considers to be against the public interest to disclose.

(7) Parliament may by law prescribe—

(a) the circumstances under which, and the class or classes of cases in which, a person may be detained for a period longer than three months under any law providing for preventive detention without obtaining the opinion of an Advisory Board in accordance with the provisions of sub-clause (a) of clause (4);

(b) the maximum period for which any person may in any class or classes of cases be detained under any law providing for preventive detention; and

(c) the procedure to be followed by an Advisory Board in an inquiry under sub-clause (a) of clause (4).

Article 22(1) and (2) are applicable to persons arrested under a law. But Article 22(4) to (7) are applicable to persons detained under Preventive Detention Law.

Torture in police custody is an open assault on basic Human Rights, more particularly against life, personal liberty and human dignity. It is against civilization and individual personality. Custodial torture by police was never approved by any Court of Law or International Covenants or resolutions. It was always deprecated, censured and declared as inhuman and barbarous. Almost in all the International Conventions and meetings, it was resolved to ban torture of any kind. Custodial torture has no legal or statutory sanction. It is totally arbitrary and highhanded actions of the arresting authorities. Custodial torture is naked violation of human dignity and honour.

Use of third degree methods in custody by police and other arresting agencies, custodial death and custodial rapes are the glaring examples of the violation of Human Rights. Either in Universal Declaration of Human Rights or any other International Covenants or agreements or in Indian Constitution torture in custody has been declared illegal, inhuman and naked violation of basic Human Rights. It is also contrary to human dignity and anti-civilization. Supreme Court has defined custodial death in *Union Carbide Corporation* v. *Union of India,* (1989) 1 SCR 730 and held as under:

"Custodial death is perhaps one of the worst crimes in a civilised society governed by the Rule of Law. The rights inherent in Articles 21 and 22(1) of the Constitution are required to be zealously and scrupulously protected. We cannot whisk away the problem. Any form of torture or cruel, inhuman or degrading treatment would fall within the inhibition of Article 21 of the Constitution, whether it occurs during investigation, interrogation or otherwise. If the functionaries of the Government become law breakers, it is bound to breed contempt for law and would encourage lawlessness and every man would have the tendency to become law unto himself thereby leading to anarchism."

The object of giving constitutional status to preventive detention was to prevent subversive and anti-social element from imperilling the welfare of the country, but certain safeguards were provided to mitigate the harshness by placing fetters on legislative powers conferred under Articles 21 and 22 of the Constitution. By reason of Article 21, preventive detention cannot be ordered by Executive without the authority of a valid law and unless conformity with the procedure mentioned therein. Article 22 imposes hard restrictions making it obligatory to constitute advisory to recommend confirmation of the detention where it is sought to continue for more than 2 months. Parliament cannot make a law authorize detention beyond 2 months without the intervention of Advisory Board unless conforms to the provisions mentioned in Article 22(7) and a State law cannot authorize detention beyond the maximum period prescribed by parliament. In the case of *Samir* v. *State of West Bengal,* AIR 1975 SC 1165, it is held that a person detained under a law of preventive detention has a right to obtain information as to the grounds of his detention and has also the right to make a representation protesting against an order of preventive detention.

The law of preventive detention is very harsh to the detenuee and so it should be strictly construed. Article 22(3) provides that the safeguard provided under Article 22 (1) and (2) are not available to any person who for the time being is an enemy alien and to any person who is arrested or detained under any law providing for preventive detention. Article 22(4) contemplates that no law providing for preventive detention shall authorize the detention of a person for a longer period than three months unless an Advisory Board has reported before the expiry of the period of three months that there is in its opinion sufficient cause for detention. Article 22(5) of the Constitution confers rights to the detained person to make a representation against his detention.

Article 23 says about prohibition of traffic in human being and forced labour which is reproduced as under:—

"23. *Prohibition of traffic in human beings and forced labour.*—Traffic in human beings and begar and other similar forms of forced labour are prohibited and any contravention of this provision shall be an offence punishable in accordance with law.

(2) Nothing in this article shall prevent the State from imposing compulsory service for public purposes, and in imposing such service the State shall not make any discrimination on grounds only of religion, race, caste, class or any of them."

Article 23 aforesaid specifically makes prohibition of traffic in human beings and forced labour, but authorizes the State to impose compulsory service on the ground of public purposes.

Article 23 of the Indian Constitution is similar to Article 23(1)(2)(3) of Universal Declaration of Human Rights, 1948, which are reproduced as under:

Article 23(1) Everyone has the right to work, to free choice of employment, to just and favourable conditions of work to protection against unemployment.

(2) Everyone, without any discrimination, has the right to equal pay for equal work.

(3) Everyone who works has the right to just and favourable remuneration ensuring for himself and his family an existence worthy of human dignity, and supplemented, if necessary, by other means of social protection.

Moreover Article 8(1) of the International Covenant on Civil and Political Rights, 1966 also provides that:—

> "No one shall be held in slavery, and the slave trade in all their forms shall be prohibited." Article 8(1)(3a) further contemplates that "no one shall be required to perform, forced or compulsory labour".

Supreme Court of India in the case of *M.C. Mehta* v. *State of Tamil Nadu*, (1996) 6 SCC 756 has framed guidelines regarding child labour, wherein it was categorically specified that child shall not be engaged in hazardous employment and there shall be set-up child labour rehabilitation welfare fund in which erred employer should make deposit of Rs. 20,000. Moreover in the case of *Bandhua Mukti Morcha* v. *Union of India*, AIR 1997 SC 2218, Supreme Court issued suitable direction regarding health, nutrition and education of child labour.

Article 24 of the Constitution of India provides as under:

> "24. *Prohibition of employment of children in factories, etc.*—No child below the age of fourteen years shall be employed to work in any factory or mine or engaged in any other hazardous employment."

Article 24 of the Constitution of India prohibits the employment of child below the age of 14 years in factories, mines or other hazardous employments. Reason behind this is that till that age child is not physically fit to perform hard duties in those organisations and also child should be engaged in study in schools in place of earning money by getting employed in the factories, mines or other hazardous employments, namely construction work, rickshaw pulling, etc.

Articles 25 to 30 of the Constitution of India relates to freedom of all religions in the country:

> "25. *Freedom of conscience and free profession, practice and propagation of religion.*—(1) Subject to public order, morality and health and to the other provisions of this part, all persons are equally entitled to freedom of conscience and the right freely to profess, practise and propagate religion.

(2) Nothing in this article shall affect the operation of any existing law or prevent the State from making any law—

(a) regulating or restricting any economic, financial, political or other secular activity which may be associated with religious practise;

(b) providing for social welfare and reform or the throwing open of Hindu religious institutions of a public character to all castes and sections of Hindus.

Explanation I.—The wearing and carrying of *Kirpans* shall be deemed to be included in the profession of the Sikh religion.

Explanation II.— In sub-clause (b) of clause (2), the reference to Hindus shall be construed as including a reference to persons professing the Sikh, Jain or Buddhist religion, and the reference to Hindu religious institutions shall be construed accordingly."

Article 25 is very clear in this regard that all persons are equally entitled to freedom of conscience and the right freely to profess, practise and propagate religion, but the same is subject to public order, morality and health. Therefore, such freedom is not unrestricted or unfettered. Government can impose necessary and suitable ban or restrictions on the ground of public order, morality and health and other provisions of Part III of the Constitution of India. State can put reasonable restrictions to check forcible conversion of religion as held by Supreme Court in the case of *Stainislaus* v. *State of Madhya Pradesh,* (1977) 1 SCC 677.

It is relevant to mention here that Article 18 of Universal Declaration of Human Rights, 1948 also provides that:—

"Everyone has the right to freedom of thought, conscience and religion; this right includes freedom to change his religion or belief; and freedom, either alone or in community with others and in public or private, to manifest his religion or belief in teaching, practice, worship and observance."

Article 18(1)(2)(3) of the International Covenant on Civil and Political Rights, 1966 also provides similar provisions, which are reproduced as below:

"Article 18(1): Everyone shall have the right to freedom of thought, conscience and religion. This right shall include freedom to have or adopt a religion or belief of his choice and freedom, either individually or in community with others and in public or private, to manifest his religion or belief in worship, observance, practice and teaching.

(2) No one shall be subject to coercion, which would impair his freedom to have or to adopt a religion or belief of his choice.

(3) Freedom to manifest one's religion or belief may be subject only to such limitations as are prescribed by law and are necessary to protect public safety, order, health or morals or the fundamental rights and freedoms of others."

It is worthwhile to mention here that Article 25(1) of the Constitution gives guarantee to freedom of conscience to every citizen and not to a particular religion. It permits transmission or spread one's own religion or an exposition of its tenets.

Article 26 of the Constitution of India is mentioned as below:

"26. *Freedom to manage religious affairs.*—Subject to public order, morality and health, every religious denomination or any section thereof shall have the right—

(a) to establish and maintain institutions for religious and charitable purposes;
(b) to manage its own affairs in matters of religion;
(c) to own and acquire movable and immovable property; and
(d) to administer such property in accordance with law."

Article 26 of the Constitution of India provides protection to every religious denominations or any section thereof to establish and maintain institutions for religious and charitable purposes, to manage its own affairs in matters of religion, to own and acquire movable and immovable property; and to administer such property in accordance with law. But these rights are subject to public order, morality and health, but it is not subject to other provisions of Part III of the Indian Constitution. In the case of *Mahant Ram Kishan Dass* v. *State of Punjab*, AIR 1981 SC 1576 it was held that law made by State can certainly regulate the administration of religious endowment's property, but it cannot take away the right of administration altogether. Similar view was earlier taken by Supreme Court in the case of *Rati Lal Panachand Gandhi* v. *State of Bombay*, 1954 SCR 1055.

Article 27 of the Constitution of India contemplates as under:

"27. *Freedom as to payment of taxes for promotion of any particular religion.*—No person shall be compelled to pay any taxes, the proceeds of which are specifically appropriated in payment of expenses for the promotion or maintenance of any particular religion or religious denomination."

Article 28 of the Constitution of India provides as under:

"28. *Freedom as to attendance at religious instruction or religious worship in certain educational institutions.*—(1) No religious instruction shall be provided in any educational institution wholly maintained out of State funds:"

(2) Nothing in clause (1) shall apply to an educational institution which is administered by the State but has been established under any endowment or trust which requires that religious instruction shall be imparted in such institution.

(3) No person attending any educational institution recognised by the State or receiving aid out of State funds shall be required to take part in any religious instruction that may be imparted in such institution or to attend any religious worship that may be conducted in such institution or in any premises attached thereto unless such person or, if such person is a minor, his guardian has given his consent thereto.

Article 29 of the Constitution of India contemplates as under:

"29. *Protection of interests of minorities.*—(1) Any section of the citizens residing in the territory of India or any part thereof having a distinct language, script or culture of its own shall have the right to conserve the same.

(2) No citizen shall be denied admission into any educational institution maintained by the State or receiving aid out of State funds on grounds only of religion, race, caste, language or any of them."

An institution established by minority may claim to impart education in keeping with its religious faith and belief but cannot insist in imparting such education to members of its own community only. No religion, however, dogmatic is narrow in its outlook. Therefore, both on general approach and constitutional prohibition under Article 29(2) the reservation policy of the institution cannot be sustained. Neither Government is entitled to interfere with right of minority and direct it to admit a student as it may contravene the choice of minority under Article 30 nor the institution can deny admission to any student because he is not a member of any community nor it can reserve seats for members of its community so as to preclude others as it shall be in violation of Article 29(2) of the Constitution of India.

Article 29(2) applies to minorities as well as to non-minorities. When other qualifications being equal, the religion, race, caste, language of a citizen shall not be a ground of preference or disability. Similarly, the words "any of them" as used in Article 29(2) are intended to give further emphasis that none of the grounds mentioned in the article can be made the sole basis of discrimination.

Article 30 of the Constitution of India provides as under:

> "30. *Right of minorities to establish and administer educational institutions.*—(1) All minorities, whether based on religion or language, shall have the right to establish and administer educational institutions of their choice.
>
> (1A) In making any law providing for the compulsory acquisition of any property of an educational institution established and administered by a minority, referred to in clause (1) the State shall ensure that the amount fixed by or determined under such law for the acquisition of such property is such as would not restrict or abrogate the right guaranteed under that clause.
>
> (2) The State shall not, in granting aid to educational institutions, discriminate against any educational institution on the ground that it is under the management of a minority, whether based on religion or language."

In view of the law laid down by the Supreme Court in *A.P. Christian Medical Educational Society* v. *Government of Andhra Pradesh*, (1986) 2 SCR 749 it is clear that the right under Article 30(1) of the Constitution can be claimed only in respect of such institution, which can be identified as an educational institution by reference to some real positive index.

The right to establish and administer an institution under Article 30 even though absolute is not above regulation and control. The right of admission which vests in an institution by virtue of the power of Administration enjoyed by it under Article 30(1) cannot be in violation of Article 29(2).

The Government order dated 20th July, 1982, insofar as it relates to the making of study of Kannada as a compulsory subject to children belonging to linguistic minority groups from the first year of the primary school and compelling the primary schools established by linguistic minorities to introduce it as a compulsory subject from the first year of the primary school and also insofar it compels the students joining high schools to take Kannada as the sole first language and compelling the high schools established by linguistic minorities to introduce Kannada as the sole first language in the secondary schools, is violative of Articles 29(1) and 30(1) of the Constitution.

By not releasing the funds for payment of salaries to the teachers, the State is not carrying out its constitutional and statutory obligation under Article 30(1) of the Constitution of India. From a bare perusal of the provision, it is evident that the State cannot discriminate in making grant only on the ground that the institution in question is under the Management of a minority community, whether based on religion or language.

Minority institutions cannot be allowed to fall below the standard of excellence on the pretext of their exclusive right of management but at the same time their constitutional right to administer their institutions cannot be completely taken away by superseding or dissolving Managing Committee or by appointing *ad hoc* Committees in place thereof. Section 7(2)(n) of the Bihar State Madarsa Education Board Act, 1982 (32 of 1982) is clearly violative of constitutional right of minorities under Article 30(1) of the Constitution insofar as it provides for dissolution of Managing Committee of a Madarsa. Article 30(1) protects the minorities right to manage and administer institutions established by them according to their choice, but while seeking aid and recognition for their institutions there is no constitutional obligation that the Board granting aid or recognition or regulating efficiency in minority institution should consist of members exclusively belonging to minority communities.

India is undoubtedly, a secular State though the words 'secular or secularism' have not been defined anywhere in the Constitution. It, however, finds mention in the Preamble of the Constitution. In a secular State, the balance of the State should not tilt in favour of or against any section, group or individual on the basis of any religion how much so ever pressing the situation may be. In *Ahmedabad St. Xavier's College Society* v. *State of Gujarat*, (1974) 1 SCC 717 it was held:—

> "There is no mysticism in the secular character of the State. Secularism is neither anti-God, not pro-God. It treats alike the devout, the agnostic and atheist. It eliminates God from the matters of the State and ensures that no one shall be discriminated against on the ground of religion."

In this context the provisions of Article 32 and 226 of the Constitution of India are given below:—

> "32. *Remedies for enforcement of rights conferred by this Part.*—(1) The right to move the Supreme Court by appropriate proceedings for the enforcement of the rights conferred by this part is guaranteed.
>
> (2) The Supreme Court shall have power to issue directions or orders or writs, including writs in the nature of *habeas corpus, mandamus*, prohibition, *quo warranto* and *certiorari*, whichever may be appropriate, for the enforcement of any of the rights conferred by this part.
>
> (3) Without prejudice to the powers conferred on the Supreme Court by clauses (1) and (2), Parliament may by law empower any other Court to exercise within the local limits of its jurisdiction all or any of the powers exercisable by the Supreme Court under clause (2).
>
> (4) The right guaranteed by this article shall not be suspended except as otherwise provided for by this Constitution."
>
> "226. *Power of High Courts to issue certain writs.*—(1) Notwithstanding anything in article 32, every High Court shall have power. Throughout the territories in relation to which it exercises jurisdiction, to issue to any person or authority, including in appropriate cases, any government, within those territories, directions, orders or writs, including writs in the nature of *habeas corpus, mandamus*, prohibition, *quo warranto* and *certiorari*, or any of them, for the enforcement of any of the rights conferred by Part III and for any other purpose.

(2) The power conferred by clause (1) to issue directions, orders or writs to any Government, authority or person may also be exercised by any High Court exercising jurisdiction in relation to the territories within which the cause of action, wholly or in part, arises for the exercise of such power, notwithstanding that the seat of such government or authority or the residence of such person is not within those territories.

(3) Where any party against whom an interim order, whether by way of injunction or stay or in any other manner, is made on , or in any proceedings relating to, a petition under clause (1), without—

(a) furnishing to such party copies of such petition and all documents in support of the plea for such interim order, and

(b) giving such party an opportunity of being heard,

makes an application to the High Court for the vacation of such order and furnishes a copy of such application to the party in whose favour such order has been made or the counsel of such party, the High Court shall dispose of the application within a period of two weeks from the date on which it is received or from the date on which the copy of such application is so furnished, whichever is later, or where the High Court is closed on the last day of that period, before the expiry of the next day afterwards on which the High Court is open; and if the application is not so disposed of, the interim order shall, on the expiry of that period, or, as the case may be, the expiry of the said next day, stand vacated.

(4) The power conferred on a High Court by this article shall not be in derogation of the power conferred on the Supreme Court by clause (2) of Article 32."

It is rightly said that Indian Constitution is a complete charter of Human Rights.

CHAPTER 17

HUMAN RIGHTS AND DIRECTIVE PRINCIPLES OF STATE POLICY OF INDIAN CONSTITUTION

Articles 37 to 51 of the Indian Constitution deal with the Directive Principles of State Policy. The principles have inspired the ideal of socialistic pattern of society and a welfare State. In *Air India, Statutory Corporation* v. *United Labour Union*, (1997) 9 SCC 377 it has been observed that Directive Principles are the forerunners of the U.N. Convention on Right to Development, 1986.

Article 1 of this Declaration provides that the right to development is an inalienable Human Right by virtue of which every person and all people are entitled to participate in, contribute to, and enjoy economic, social, cultural and political development in which all Human Rights and fundamental freedoms can be fully realised. Directive Principles, not being justiciable have been criticised time and again but in some of the cases, Directive Principles have been enforced like fundamental rights for the reason that Article 14 or Article 16 were also violated in those cases. There can be a writ to get the principle of equal pay for equal work enforced if Article 14 is infringed. Supreme Court of India in the case of *Randhir Singh* v. *Union of India*, (1982) 1 SCC 618 has held that "Equal pay for equal work for both men and women' means equal pay for equal work for everyone and as between the sexes. Directive Principles, as has been pointed out in some of the judgments of this Court have to be read into the fundamental rights as a matter of interpretation."

Article 37 of the Indian Constitution says as under:

> "37. *Application of the principles contained in this Part*.—The provisions contained in this Part shall not be enforceable by any Court, but the principles therein laid down are nevertheless fundamental in the governance of the country and it shall be the duty of the State to apply these principles in making laws."

According to Article 37 the provisions of Directive Principles of State Policy shall not be enforced by any Court. But it shall be the duty of the State to apply these principles while making the law and the said Principle are fundamental in the governance of the Country.

Article 38 of the Constitution of India reads as under:

> 38. *State to secure a social order for the promotion of welfare of the people*.—(1) The State shall strive to promote the welfare of the people by securing and protecting as effectively as it may a social order in which justice, social, economic and political, shall inform all the institutions of the national life.

(2) the State shall, in particular, strive to minimise the inequalities in income, and endeavour to eliminate in equalities in status, facilities and opportunities, not only amongst individuals but also amongst groups of people residing in different areas or engaged in different vocations."

Article 39 reads as under:—

39. *Certain principles of a policy to be followed by the State.*—The State shall, in particular, direct its policy towards securing:—

(a) that the citizens, men and women equally, have the right to an adequate means of livelihood;

(b) that the ownership and control of the material resources of the community are so distributed as best to subserve the common good;

(c) that the operation of the economic system does not result in the concentration of wealth and means of production to the common detriment;

(d) that there is equal pay for equal work for both men and women;

(e) that the health and strength of workers, men and women, and the tender age of children are not abused and that citizens are not forced by economic necessity to enter avocations unsuited to their age or strength;

(f) that children are given opportunities and facilities to develop in a healthy manner and in conditions of freedom and dignity and that childhood and youth are protected against exploitation and against moral and material abandonment."

Supreme Court in *Srinivasa* v. *State of Karnataka*, (1987) 2 SCC 692 has ruled that Article 39 of the Constitution of India has been described as having the object to secure a Welfare State and may be utilized for construing provisions as to fundamental rights. Similar view had been taken earlier in the case of *State of Tamil Nadu* v. *L. Abu Kavur Bai*, AIR 1984 SC 326 and *Sanjeev Coke* v. *Bharat Coaking Coal*, AIR 1983 SC 239.

In the case of *Grih Kalyan Kendra Workers' Union* v. *Union of India*, (1991) 1 SCC 619 it was held that the denial of equal pay for equal work becomes irrational classification within Article 14 of the Indian Constitution.

Though right to employment cannot, as a right, be claimed but after the appointment to a post be it under the State, its instrumentality or private entrepreneur it is required to be dealt with as per public element and to act in public interest assuring equality, which is a genus of Article 14 of the Constitution of India. Supreme Court in the case of *M.C. Mehta* v. *State of Tamil Nadu*, (1996) 6 SCC 756 has ruled that State should see that an adult member of the family whose child is in employment in the factory, mine or hazardous employment get employment anywhere, in lieu of the child.

Article 39A reads as below:

"39A. *Equal justice and free legal aid.*—The State shall secure that the operation of the legal system promotes justice, on a basis of equal opportunity, and shall, in particular, provide free legal aid, by suitable legislation or schemes or in any other way, to ensure that opportunities for securing justice are not denied to any citizen by reason of economic or other disabilities."

Article 39A has been brought by Constitution (Forty-second Amendment) Act, 1976. In the case of *Kishore* v. *State of Himachal Pradesh*, (1991) 1 SCC 286, Supreme Court while interpreting Article 39A of the Constitution of India has held that legal aid is to be treated as a part of the right created under Article 21 of the Constitution of India. Further, Article 39A has been used for interpretation of the right conferred by section 304 of the Code of Criminal Procedure, reliance is placed on the decision of the Supreme Court in the case of *Hussainara* v. *Home Secretary, State of Bihar*, (1980) 1 SCC 98.

Article 40 reads as under:

> 40. *Organisation of village panchayats.*—The State shall take steps to organise village panchayats and endow them with such powers and authority as may be necessary to enable them to function as units of self-government.

Article 40 of the Constitution of India confers power upon the State to take steps to organise village panchayats and to grant powers and authorities to function as units of self-government. It is based on the principle of decentralization of power and to grant stability to the Gram Panchayats.

> "41. *Right to work, to education and to public assistance in certain cases.*—The State shall, within the limits of its economic capacity and development, make effective provision for securing the right to work, to education and to public assistance in cases of unemployment, old age, sickness and disablement, and in other cases of undeserved want."

The Directive Principles as contained in Chapter IV of the Constitution deals with the question of education and other subjects. Article 41 directs the State for making effective provision for securing right to education and Article 45 require the State to provide free and compulsory education within a period of 10 years from commencement of the Constitution to the children until they complete age of 14 years. Even though these rights are not fundamental and are judicially enforceable as such, once the State by Legislature or administrative action provides facility for education its action must conform to the standard of equality and rationality underlying Article 14 of the Constitution. After 42nd Amendment of Constitution the subject of education has been inserted in List III of 7th Schedule attached to the Constitution.

Article 42 reads as under:

> "42. *Provision for just and humane conditions of work and maternity relief.*—The State shall make provision for securing just and humane conditions of work and for maternity relief."

Article 43 reads as under:

> "43. *Living wage, etc., for workers.*—The State shall endeavour to secure, by suitable legislation or economic organisation or in any other way, to all workers agricultural, industrial or otherwise, work, a living wage, conditions of work ensuring a decent standard of life and full enjoyment of leisure and social and cultural opportunities and, in particular, the State shall endeavour to promote cottage industries on an individual or co-operative basis in rural areas."

The right to live like a human being which confirms to much lesser degree the State's obligation to ensure a decent standard of life and full enjoyment of leisure to all its workmen as provided by Article 43 of the Constitution. To convert human existence into animal existence no doubt amounts to taking away human life, because a man lives not by his mere physical existence or by bread alone but by his human existence. It can hardly be disputed that securing of living wages to Mazdoors which ensure not only bare physical substance, but also maintenance of health and decency, is conducive to the general interest of the public.

"43A. *Participation of workers in management of industries.*—The State shall take steps, by suitable legislation or in any other way, to secure the participation of workers in the management of undertakings, establishment or other organisations engaged in any industry."

"44. *Uniform civil Code for the citizens.*—The State shall endeavour to secure for the citizens a Uniform Civil Code throughout the territory of India."

While interpreting Article 44 of the Constitution of India Supreme Court in the case of *Mohd. Ahmed Khan* v. *Shah Bano Begum*, (1985) 2 SCC 556 has held that a common Civil Code will help the cause of national integration by removing disparate loyalties to laws which have conflicting ideologies but in *Maharishi Avdhesh* v. *Union of India*, 1994 Supp (1) SCC 713 the Supreme Court had held that introduction of common Civil Code was matter for the Legislature and the Court cannot legislate on these matters.

Article 45 reads as under:

> "45. *Provision for early childhood care and education to children below the age of six years.*—The State shall endeavour to provide early childhood care and education for all children until they complete the age of six years.

Directive Principles as contained in Chapter IV of the Constitution under Articles 41 and 45 deal with the question of education and other subjects. Article 41 directs the State for making effective provision for securing right to education and Article 45 requires the State to provide free and compulsory education within a period of 10 years from commencement of the Constitution to the children until they complete age of 14 years. In 2009, the Parliament has enacted Right to Education Act, which grants every child to a quality elementary education. All children aged 6-14 years shall have the right to free and compulsory elementary education at a neighbourhood school.

Article 46 reads as under:

> "46. *Promotion of educational and economic interests of Scheduled Castes, Scheduled Tribes and other weaker sections.*—The State shall promote with special care the educational and economic interests of the weaker sections of the people, and, in particular of the Scheduled Castes and the Schedule Tribes, and shall protect them from social injustice and all forms of exploitation."

Article 47 reads as under:

> "47. *Duty of the State to raise the level of nutrition and the standard of living and to improve public health.*—The State shall regard the raising of the level of nutrition and the standard of living of its people and the improvement of public health as among its primary duties and, in particular, the State shall endeavour to bring about prohibition of the consumption except for medicinal purposes of intoxicating drinks and of drugs which are injurious to health."

Article 48 reads as under:

"48. *Organisation of agriculture and animal husbandry.*—The State shall endeavour to organise agriculture and animal husbandry on modern and scientific lines and shall, in particular, take steps for preserving and improving the breeds, and prohibiting the slaughter of cows and calves and other milch and draught cattle."

Article 48A reads as under:

"48A. *Protection and improvement of environment and safeguarding of forest and wild life.*—The State shall endeavour to protect and improve the environment and to safeguard the forest and wild life of the country."

Article 48A was brought by Constitution (42nd Amendment) Act, 1976.

Supreme Court in the case of *Satish* v. *State of Uttar Pradesh*, 1992 Supp (2) SCC 94 has ruled that through a PIL brought by an institution in the area on the basis of Article 21 of the Constitution, the duty under Article 48A can be enforced.

Article 49 reads as under:

"49. *Protection of monuments and places and objects of national importance.*—It shall be the obligation of the State to protect every monument or place or object of artistic or historic interest, declared by or under law made by Parliament to be of national importance, from spoilation, disfigurement, destruction, removal disposal or export, as the case may be."

Article 50 reads as under:—

"50. *Separation of judiciary from executive.*—The State shall take steps to separate the judiciary from the executive in the public services of the State."

Article 51 reads as under:

"51. *Promotion of international peace and security.*—The state shall endeavour to:—

(a) promote international peace and security;

(b) maintain just and honourable relations between nations;

(c) foster respect for international law and treaty obligation in the dealings of organised peoples with one another; and

(d) encourage settlement of international disputes by arbitration."

This Article clearly states that the State shall endeavour to foster respect for International Law and Treaty Obligations. Therefore, the provisions of the Universal Declaration of Human Rights, I.C.C.P.R., I.C.E.S.C.R and several Declarations, Covenants, Conventions and Resolutions should be implemented for protection of Human Rights.

"51A. *Fundamental duties.*—It shall be the duty of every citizen of India:

(a) to abide by the Constitution and respect its ideals and institutions, the National Flag and the National Anthem.

(b) to cherish and follow the noble ideals which inspired our national struggle for freedom;

(c) to uphold and protect the sovereignty, unity and integrity of India.

(d) to defend the country and render national service when called upon to do so;

(e) to promote harmony and the spirit of common brotherhood amongst all the people of India transcending religious, linguistic and regional or sectional diversities; to renounce practices derogatory to the dignity of women;

(f) to value and preserve the rich heritage of our composite culture;

(g) to protect and improve the natural environment including forests, lakes, rivers, and wild life, and to have compassion for living creatures,

(h) to develop the scientific temper, humanism and the spirit of inquiry and reform;

(i) to safeguard public property and to abjure violence;

(j) to strive towards excellence in all spheres of individual and collective activity so that the nation constantly rises to higher levels of endeavour and achievement."

(k) who is a parent or guardian to provide opportunities for education to his child or, as the case may be, ward between the age of six and fourteen years.

Supreme Court in the case of *Mumbai Kamgar Sabha* v. *Abdul Bhai Faizullabhai,* (1976) 3 SCC 832 has held that the fundamental duties as mentioned in Article 51A of the Constitution of India cannot be enforced by Courts of law. No writ petition is maintainable to enforce the fundamental duties. In the case of *Mohan* v. *Union of India*, 1992 Supp (1) SCC 594, it has been ruled that where the constitutionality of a law is challenged, the Court may look at Article 51 of the Constitution to uphold the said law. In the case of *Rural Litigation and Entitlement Kendra* v. *State of Uttar Pradesh,* AIR 1987 SC 359, fundamental duties have been invoked in the environmental cases.

Having regard to the grave consequences of the pollution of water and air and the need for protecting and improving the natural environment which is considered to be one of the fundamental duties under the Constitution, the Court is of the view that it is the duty of the Central Government to direct all the educational institutions throughout India to teach at least for one hour in a week lessons relating to the protection and the improvement of the natural environment including forests, lakes, rivers and wild life.

Article 51A of the Constitution speaks of citizens duty to strive towards excellence in all spheres of individual and collective activity so that the nation constantly rises to higher levels of endeavour and achievement. University Ordinances, Regulations and other statutory provisions fulfilling the mandate of Article 51A(i) are to be construed liberally and enforced strictly to sub-serve their purpose effectively. Unless University's decision is *mala fide,* or so arbitrary and discriminatory as is voided by Article 14 of the Constitution, a candidate adopting unfair means may be rendered defenceless by the University's Ordinances by excluding expressly also the right of personal hearing.

CHAPTER 18

ROLE OF NATIONAL HUMAN RIGHTS COMMISSION IN PROTECTION OF HUMAN RIGHTS IN INDIA

United Nations sponsored meeting of representatives of National Institutions in Paris held in 1991 wherein a set of principles on the status/scope of National Human Rights Institutions were developed. It is called as 'Paris principles'. These principles were subsequently endorsed by the United Nations Commission on Human Rights and the United Nations General Assembly. Six criterias of National Human Rights Institutions under Paris principles are mentioned as under:

(a) Independence guaranteed by the Statute or Constitution.

(b) Autonomy from Government.

(c) Pluralism in membership.

(d) Board mandate based on Human Rights standards.

(e) Adequate power of State.

(f) Sufficient resources.

In respect of composition and guarantees of independence and pluralism, it provides that the composition of the national institution and the appointment of its members, whether by means of an election or otherwise, shall be established in accordance with a procedure which affords all necessary guarantees to ensure the pluralist representation of the social forces (of civilian society) involved in the protection and promotion of Human Rights, particularly by powers which will enable effective cooperation to be established with, or through the presence of, representatives of Non-governmental organisations responsible for Human Rights and efforts to combat racial discrimination, trade unions, concerned social and professional organisations, for example, Associations of Journalists, Lawyers, Doctors and social activists. India is a party to said covenant and has established the National Human Rights Commission by legislating the Protection of Human Rights Act, 1993. Section 2(1)(d) of the said Act defines Human Rights as under:

Human Rights means the rights relating to life, liberty, equality and dignity of the individual guaranteed by the Constitution or embodied in the International Covenants and enforceable by Courts in India.

Section 3 of the said Act provides that the Central Government shall constitute a body to be known as National Human Rights Commission to exercise the power conferred upon, and to perform the functions assigned to, it under this Act. The said Commission shall be headed by a Former Chief Justice of Supreme Court, who shall be known as Chairperson of the said Commission shall be appointed on the basis of recommendation of a Committee consisting of Prime Minister as Chairperson and Speaker of House of People, and Home Minister, Leader of Opposition of Lok Sabha and Rajya Sabha and Deputy Chairman of Rajya Sabha as its member. It is apt to mention that the Chairperson of the Commission has no control or say over the appointment of members of the Commission.

According to section 5 of the said Act, the Chairperson or any Member of Commission can be relieved from his office by the order of the President on the ground of proved misbehaviour or incapacity. The President will make a reference to the Supreme Court of India to hold an enquiry and only on the basis of enquiry report the President will pass appropriate order under section 5(2) of the said Act. The President can pass order of removal of the Chairperson or any member of Commission on the following grounds:

(a) is adjudged an insolvent; or

(b) engages during his term of office in any paid employment outside the duties of his office; or

(c) is unfit to continue in office by reason of infirmity of mind or body; or

(d) is of unsound mind and stands so declared by a competent Court; or

(e) is convicted and sentenced to imprisonment for an offence which in the opinion of the President involves moral turpitude.

The term of the office of the Chairperson and members of the said Commission is for 5 years or until he attains the age of 70 years whichever is earlier. Section 11 of the said Act provides that the Government of India shall make available an officer of the rank of Secretary to the Government of India to occupy the post of Secretary-General of the Commission and a police officer not below the rank of Director-General of Police as Chief of the investigation team. The Commission has say over the appointment of Secretary-General as well as Director-General of Investigation. Section 12 of the said Act provides the functions of Commission which are set out as under:

(a) inquire, *suo-motu* or on a petition presented to it by a victim or any person on his behalf or on a direction or order of any court, into complaint of—

  (i) violation of human rights or abetment thereof; or

  (ii) negligence in the prevention of such violation, by a public servant;

(b) intervene in any proceeding involving any allegation of violation of human rights pending before a court with the approval of such court;

(c) visit, notwithstanding anything contained in any other law for the time being in force, any jail or other institution under the control of the State Government, where persons are detained or lodged for purposes of treatment, reformation or protection, for the study of the living conditions of the inmates thereof and make recommendations thereon to the Government;

(d) review the safeguards provided by or under the Constitution or any law for the time being in force for the protection of human rights and recommend measures for their effective implementation;

(e) review the factors, including acts of terrorism, that inhibit the enjoyment of human rights and recommend appropriate remedial measures;

(f) study treaties and other international instruments on human rights and make recommendations for their effective implementation;

(g) undertake and promote research in the field of human rights;

(h) spread human rights literacy among various sections of society and promote awareness of the safeguards available for the protection of these rights through publications, the media, seminars and other available means;

(i) encourage the efforts of non-governmental organisation and institutions working in the field of human rights;

(j) such other functions as it may consider necessary for the promotion of human rights.

It is apt to mention that violators of the Human Rights are mainly public servants, members of police and para-military force, landlords, factory owners, terrorists and contractors.

Section 13 of the said Act mentions the power relating to the enquiry conferred to the said Commission which is given as under:

1. The Commission shall, while inquiring into complaints under this Act, have all the powers of a Civil Court trying a suit under the Code of Civil Procedure, 1908, and in particular in respect of the following matters namely:—

(a) Summoning and enforcing the attendance of witnesses and examining them on oath;

(b) discovery and production of any document;

(c) receiving evidence on affidavits;

(d) requisitioning any public record or copy thereof from any Court or office;

(e) issuing Commissions for the examination of witnesses or documents;

(f) any other matter which may be prescribed.

2. The Commission shall have the power to require any person, subject to any privilege which may be claimed by that person under any law for the time being in force to furnish information on such points or matters as in the opinion of the Commission, may be useful for, or relevant to, the subject-matter of the inquiry and any person so required shall be deemed to be legally bound to furnish such information within the meaning of sections 176 and 177 of the Indian Penal Code.

3. The Commission or any other officer, not below the rank of a Gazetted Officer, specially authorized in this behalf by the Commission may enter any building or place where the Commission has reason to believe that any document relating to the subject-matter of the inquiry may be found, and may seize any such document or take extracts or copies therefrom subject to the provisions of section 100 of the Code of Criminal Procedure, 1973, insofar as it may be applicable.

4. The Commission shall be deemed to be a civil Court and when any offence as described in sections 175, 178, 179, 180 or 228 of the Indian Penal Code is committed in the view or presence of the Commission, the Commission may, after recording the facts constituting the offence and the statement of the accused as provided for in the Code of Criminal Procedure, 1973, forward the case to a Magistrate to whom any such case is forwarded shall proceed to hear the complaint against the accused as if the case has been forwarded to him under section 346 of the Code of Criminal Procedure, 1973.

5. Every proceeding before the Commission shall be deemed to be a judicial proceeding within the meaning of sections 193 and 228 and for the purpose of section 196 of the Indian Penal Code, and the Commission shall be deemed to be a Civil Court for all the purpose of section 195 and the Chapter XXVI of the Code of Criminal Procedure, 1973.

6. Where the Commission considers it necessary or expedient so to do, it may, by order, transfer any complaint filed or pending before it to the State Commission of the State from which the complaint arises, for disposal in accordance with the provisions of this Act:

Provided that no such complaint shall be transferred unless the same is one respecting which the State Commission has jurisdiction to entertain the same.

7. Every complaint transferred under sub-section (6) shall be dealt with and disposed of by the State Commission as if it were a complaint initially filed before it.

In this regard, it is apt to mention here that the said Commission is competent to take cognizance of a report published in Newspaper, Magazine or electronics media regarding violation of Human Rights and can initiate enquiry to bring the truth. Cases of custodial death, illegal detention by police, *lathi* charge by the police upon the agitators etc.

Section 17 of the said Act authorises the said Commission to call for information or report from the Central Government or any State Government or any organisation or authority subordinate thereto which enquires into the complaints of violation of Human Rights. The said section 17 has a proviso which says that:

(a) If the information or the report is not received within the time stipulated by the Commission, it may proceed to enquire into the complaint on its own,

(b) If on the receipt of the information or the report, the Commission is satisfied either that no further enquiry is required or that the required action has been initiated or taken by the concerned government or authority, it may not proceed with the complaint and inform the complainant accordingly

Section 17(II) contemplates that without prejudice to anything contained in section 17(I) of the said Act, if it considers necessary, having regard to the nature of the complaint, initiate an enquiry.

Section 18 of the said Act provides that the Commission may take following steps during or upon the completion of the enquiry held under the said Act, namely:—

(a) where the inquiry discloses the commission of violation of human rights or negligence in the prevention of violation of human rights or abetment thereof by a public servant, it may recommend to the concerned Government or authority—

   (i) to make payment of compensation or damages to the complainant or to the victim or the members of his family as the Commission may consider necessary;

   (ii) to initiate proceedings for prosecution or such other suitable action as the Commission may deem fit against the concerned person or persons;

   (iii) to take such further action as it may think fit;

(b) approach the Supreme Court or the High Court concerned for such directions, orders or writs as that Court may deem necessary;

(c) recommend to the concerned Government or authority at any stage of the inquiry for the grant of such immediate interim relief to the victim or the members of his family as the Commission may consider necessary;

(d) subject to the provisions of clause (e), provide a copy of the inquiry report to the petitioner or his representative;

(e) the Commission shall send a copy of its inquiry report together with its recommendations to the concerned Government or authority and the concerned Government or authority shall, within a period of one month, or such further time as the Commission may allow, forward its comments on the report, including the action taken or proposed to be taken thereon, to the Commission;

(f) the Commission shall publish its inquiry report together with the comments of the concerned Government or authority, if any, and the action taken or proposed to be taken by the concerned Government or authority on the recommendations of the Commission.

Section 21 of the said Act empowers the State Government to constitute a State Human Rights Commission. The State Commission may enquire into enforcement of Human Rights in respect of matter related to entries of Lists II and III in the Seventh Schedule to the Indian Constitution.

Section 30 of the said Act provides for setting up of Human Rights Courts for the purpose of providing speedy trial of offences arising out of infringement of Human Rights, the State Government may with the concurrence of Chief Justice of High Court, by a notification, specify for each district a Court of Sessions to be a Human Rights Court to try the said offences.

In India, National Human Rights Commission and other State Human Rights Commissions have been performing excellent job regarding protection of basic Human Rights to initiate action against the violators of Human Rights. After post-Godhra incident in the State of Gujarat large-scale alleged riotous activities occurred. National Human Rights Commission brought the matter before the Supreme Court of India for its intervention and wanted an impartial enquiry into the entire incident and to punish the wrongdoers. On the initiative of the Commission, the Supreme Court ordered to transfer of criminal cases pending against accused persons from State of Gujarat to other States and also directed to restart of the disposed of criminal cases and further directed for fresh investigation of the criminal cases by independent investigating agency like CBI and Task Force. On the basis of such fresh inquiry, several high police officials were arrested and charge sheeted. Further, in the cases of unprovoked assault and torture of North Indian people residing in Maharashtra by the activists of a regional political party, the said Commission issued notice to the State of Maharashtra and suggested to take immediate measures to stop lawlessness in the State.

In Delhi, in the past several terrorists grouped at Batala house at Jamia Nagar and they attacked police officials in which one Police Inspector was killed and several police men were injured. The said Commission initiated enquiry to ascertain violation of Human Rights and after thorough enquiry, the Commission found that there was no violation of Human Rights.

CHAPTER 19

ROLE OF JUDICIARY IN PROTECTION OF HUMAN RIGHTS

Justice Altamas Kabir, Supreme Court of India in an article "Basic and Fundamental Human Rights and the Indian Response" published in *Human Rights Year Book*, 2009 has stated as under:

> "The question of basic and fundamental Human Rights has been relevant ever since the rudimentary structure of human society came to be established. Those were the days when human needs were simple and basic in nature and uncomplicated. In comparison, as society developed, complexity increased, and in today's society human problems have acquired new dimensions which have to be addressed in conditions which are relevant today. In simplified terms basic and fundamental Human Rights can be said to comprise basic needs of human beings such as the right to food, the right to breathe fresh air, the right to shelter, the right to clothing, the right to a decent environment, all of which are essential for human beings to at least live and survive, as against natural rights which all living beings enjoy and which no human agency can give or take away."

It is true that in the Indian Constitution, the term Human Rights has not been defined but the same is defined in section 2(1)(d) of the Protection of Human Rights Act, 1993 as under:

> "Human Rights" means the rights relating to life, liberty, equality and dignity of the individual guaranteed by the Constitution or embodied in the international covenant and enforceable by Courts in India".

The Preamble of the Indian Constitution, Articles 14, 15, 16, 19 and 21 other provisions of Part III of Indian Constitution including Article 32 and Directive Principles of State Policy are related to Human Rights.

It is a fact that the fundamental rights mentioned in the Indian Constitution are more or less similar to the Human Rights as mentioned in UDHR, ICPR 1966 and ICESR 1966 for expansion of Human Rights, to check violation and infringement of Human Rights, to enlarge scope of Basic Human Rights, to punish the violators of Human Rights to direct National and State Government to act towards protection, safeguard and enforcement of Human Rights. In the case of *Union Carbide Corporation* v. *Union of India* commonly known as *Bhopal Gas Leak Disaster* case, (1989) 1 SCR 730 Supreme Court of India has highly appreciated the Human Rights and held as under:

> "As mentioned in the Universal Declaration of Human Rights that people are born free and the dignity of the persons must be recognized and effective

remedy by competent tribunal is one of the surest methods of effective remedy. If, therefore, as a result of this tragedy new consciousness and awareness on the part of the people of this country to be more vigilant about measures and the necessity of ensuring more strict vigilance for permitting the operation of such dangerous and poisonous gases dawn, then perhaps the tragic experience of Bhopal would not go in vain."

There are three wings of Constitution of India *firstly* Legislature, *secondly* Executive and *thirdly* Judiciary. Legislature makes the law either through Parliament or by State Legislature. Executive enforces the laws and the role of Judiciary is to interpret the law and to check the action and role of Legislature and Executive both and to dispense justice to the aggrieved persons. Judiciary starts from Lower Court to the Supreme Court. The Supreme Court and the High Courts have played very vital and important role in protection of Human Rights and also to punish the violators of Human Rights of the citizens of India.

Remedy of protection of Human Rights is achieved from Supreme Court and High Courts by filing Public Interest Litigation/Social Interest Litigation, writ petition, *suo motto* intervention by Supreme Court and High Courts in the cases of violation of Human Rights by reading the media report *viz., Yamuna River Cleaning Case*, initiation of proceedings on the basis of petition filed by National Human Rights Commission, like post-*Godhara Carnage case* in Gujarat.

Supreme Court in the case of *Consumer Education and Research Centre* v. *Union of India*, (1995) 3 SCC 42 has discussed the Social Justice and Human Rights and more particularly Article 21 of the Indian Constitution and Directive Principle of State Policy. Social justice has been treated at par with fundamental rights of the Constitution of India and a part of Human Rights. Supreme Court has recognized right to shelter is a fundamental right in the case of *Chameli Singh* v. *State of Uttar Pradesh*, (1996) 2 SCC 549.

It is apt to mention here that life, liberty, equality and dignity are the main pillars of Human Rights. Social justice is a people's justice where the tyranny of power is transformed into the democracy of social goods. Under Article 32 of Constitution of India any citizen can approach for violation of any one of the fundamental rights before the Supreme Court of India as held by a Constitution Bench of 5 Hon'ble Judges in the case of *Romesh Thappar* v. *State of Madras*, 1950 SCR 594.

Great Jurist A.V. Dicey has said that British Constitution, though unwritten, is founded on rule of law and contains three conceptions, that is the law is supreme and there is no scope for arbitrariness, nobody is above law and that general rules of Constitutional Law are the result of ordinary law. Rule of law is a concept which is dear to all men of law, who cherish freedom. It is the concept which man has evolved to eschew the rule of man and the arbitrariness in official and public conduct. It is to ensure the rule of reason. Golden principles of rule of law controls/checks the Government and its other organs from acting arbitrarily and against the due procedure of law. Arbitrary action of such authorities can be challenged before Court of law on the ground of violation of principle of rule of law.

The rule of law forms part of the basic structure of the Constitution of India. Supreme Court of India in a landmark decision in the case of *S.G. Jaisinghani* v.

Union of India, AIR 1967 SC 1427 has held that in a system governed by rule of law, discretion when conferred upon executive authorities, must be confined within clearly defined limits. The rule of law from this point of view means that decisions should be made by the application of known principles and rules, in general, such decisions should be predictable and citizen should know where he is. If a decision is taken without any principle or without any rule it is unpredictable and such a decision is the anti-thesis of a decision taken in accordance with the rule of law.

Similarly in the case of *Bachan Singh* v. *State of Punjab,* (1982) 3 SCC 24, Supreme Court has held that the rule of law has really three basic and fundamental assumptions, one is that law making must be essentially in the hands of a democratically elected Legislature. *Second* is that even in the hands of democratically elected Legislature, there should not be unfettered legislative power and *Third,* there must be an independent Judiciary to protect the citizens against excesses of Executive and Legislative power.

Former Chief Justice of India Mr. Sabyasachi Mukharji while delivering speech on Human Rights Day Celebrations at New Delhi said that, "Long time ago, Plato proclaimed: "I proclaim that might is right, justice is the interest of the stronger." Human nature has since changed, in natural state perhaps, a man will and perhaps should take whatever he can. But with civilisation we should change. But still we have apartheid in practice. Apartheid is denial of Human Rights. Slavery has a long history and abolition of slavery is not possible by proclamations. Indeed, the abolition of slavery has gone for a long time. Rome abolished slavery. America abolished it and Russia did it but only the words were abolished not the thing. Harijans in India are still prosecuted. The social discrimination against Harijans is decried in its name. Not perhaps much has been done about the cry of poverty stricken people who are unable to get food, education and medical aid for their children. Refusal of immigration is an offence against Human Rights."

Judiciary plays very significant role in dispensing justice to the needy people, who come to Court being harassed by Executive and other Governmental organs. Judiciary also interpretates the law of the Parliament and the Assembly and ordinances issued by President of India or the Governors of the State. Independence of Judiciary must be absolute and there should not be any kind of interference in its functioning by Executive. In India, even today Judiciary is not given financial autonomy. For their budget, Judiciary has to seek sanction of the Executive Authorities. According to me this is not good for Independence of Indian Judiciary. There should be complete financial Autonomy so that there should not be any slightest control over the Judiciary by the Executive. Justice delivery system should be more simple and easy, less expensive less time consuming.

In India, Judicial system achieved more credibility and showed public accountability and as necessary consequences law of pleadings and also law of evidence underwent changes significantly. PIL shows that courts are no longer satisfied with their traditional role and they are willing and interested to participate in reconstruction of the country. But on some occasions, courts are blamed for judicial activitism and it brings direct clash with Executive and Legislature. However one thing cannot be forgotten that PIL has shown ray of hope to people who had no financial resources or strength to approach courts of law for vindication of their grievances like child labour exploitation, *Bandhua* Mazdoor

Problems, persons languishing in jails even after completing the tenure of punishment, sexual harassment of women, etc. By PIL cases, considerable amount of favouritism, nepotism, corruption, arbitrariness in discharge of public duties by Executive Authorities and Administrative Officers has been curbed and their actions were made transparent, reasonable and accountable.

For filing Public Interest Litigation, one can approach under Article 32 of the Constitution directly before Hon'ble Supreme Court or by filing Writ Petition under Article 226 of the Constitution to the concerned High Court. The District Courts are not conferred with the jurisdiction to entertain the PIL. But I am of the view that it is high time to confer jurisdiction to entertain PIL cases by District Courts, so that access to judicial forum could be made at the door steps and one should not come to the High Court or Supreme Court for simply filing PIL. It is undisputed that the access to the Court of law should be less expensive, easier, non-cumbersome and speedy. The legal philosophy is not to close the doors of justice, but to allow as many as grievances as possible to be brought for redressal. I would also like to suggest that for filing PIL Cases either before Supreme Court or before High Court, the required Court-fee at the time of filing should be exempted, but if ultimately it is found by the courts that the case was bogus and frivolous then, order could be passed against the petitioner to deposit the required Court-fee.

According to Dr. Justice Arijit Pasayat, former Judge of Supreme Court of India, Human Rights are those minimal rights, which every individual must have against the State or other public authority by virtue of his being a member of the human family, irrespective of any other consideration. The concept of Human Rights embodies the minimum rights of an individual *versus* his own State and it is as old as political philosophy. Human Rights are those rights, which are inherent in nature and without which one cannot live as a human being.

It is pertinent to mention here that violation and non-compliance with the standards of Human Rights norms are rampant. Sub-standard living conditions, illiteracy, usurpation of natural resources by vested interests, exploitation, bonded labour and the like problems were present all around. Plural justice, breaking of shackles of technicalities of law was the only need of the hour, which was realized by the Courts, Courts did not even hesitate to spring into action on mere letter petition or information through any other source including PIL in connection with atrocities by State force, regarding living conditions in prisons, custodial deaths and the like or to render plural justice for the masses.

The Constitution of India specifically provides that every organ of the State, the Executive, the Legislature and the Judiciary, working harmoniously to strive to realize the objectives concretized in the fundamental rights and the Directive Principles of the State Policy. Since the last 30-35 years, the Supreme Court is increasingly invoking the Directive Principles of the State Policy in interpreting the fundamental rights. The Constitution of India has assigned the task of enforcing fundamental rights to the Supreme Court and right to move Supreme Court for enforcement of fundamental rights is itself a fundamental right as provided under Article 32 of the Constitution.

A Constitution Bench of Five Hon'ble Judges of Supreme Court in the case of *Romesh Thappar* v. *State of Madras,* supra has held that "Advocate-General of Madras appearing on behalf of the respondents raised a preliminary objection, not indeed to the jurisdiction of this Court to entertain the application under Article

32, but to the petitioner resorting to this Court directly for such relief in the first instance. He contended that, as a matter of orderly procedure, the petitioner should first resort to the High Court at Madras which under Article 226 of the Constitution has concurrent jurisdiction to deal with the matter. He cited criminal revision petitions under section 435 of the Criminal Procedure Code, applications for bail and applications for transfer under section 24 of the Civil Procedure Code as instances where, concurrent jurisdiction having been given in certain maters to the High Court and the Court of a lower grade, a rule of practice has been established that a party should proceed first to the latter Court for relief before resorting to the High Court. He referred to *Emperor* v. *Bisheswer Prasad Sinha,* AIR 1933 All 678 (FB) where such a rule of practice was enforced in a criminal revision case, and called our attention also to certain American decisions *Urquhart* v. *Brown* and *Hooney* v. *Kolohan,* as showing that the Supreme Court of the United States ordinarily required that whatever judicial remedies remained open to the applicant in Federal and State Courts should be exhausted before the remedy in the Supreme Court be it *habeas corpus* or *certiorari* would be allowed. We are of opinion that neither the instances mentioned by the learned Advocate-General nor the American decisions referred to by him are really analogous to the remedy afforded by Article 32 of the Indian Constitution. That article does not merely confer power on this Court, as Article 226 does on the High Courts. It is also empowered to issue certain writs for the enforcement of the rights conferred by Part III or for any other purpose, as part of its general jurisdiction. In that case it would have been more appropriately placed among Articles 131 to 139 which define that jurisdiction. Article 32 provides a "guaranteed" remedy for the enforcement of those rights, and this remedial right is itself made a fundamental right by being included in Part III. This Court is thus constituted the protector and guarantor of fundamental rights, and it cannot, consistently with the responsibility so laid upon it, refuse to entertain applications seeking protection against infringements of such rights. No similar provision is to be found in the Constitution of the United States and we do not consider that the American decisions are in point."

It is apt to say that Public Interest Litigation in the true sense of its term is integrally linked with protection of Human Rights. By several landmark judgments, this aspect has been highlighted by the Apex Court and several High Courts. Public interest lawyers have done a lot in certain areas of Human Rights jurisprudence. They have demonstrated that the common man can raise voice, impress and when the need arises, fight against wrongful political and Executive actions. The resultant effect that emerged is that destitute got the benefits to which they are entitled.

The Judiciary regarded it as its duty to come to the rescue of the under-privileged to help them to reap the benefits of economic and social entitlements. The Supreme Court realized that one of the drawbacks of the justice delivery system has been the denial to the common man, access to justice. It realized that it was necessary to depart from the traditional rule of *locus standi* and to broaden access to justice by providing that where a legal wrong or a legal injury is caused to a person or to a class of persons, who by reason of their poverty or disability or socially or economically disadvantaged position, cannot approach the court for relief, any member of the public or social action group or a concerned citizen, acting *bona fide* can move Supreme Court or the High Court, seeking judicial remedy for redressal of such legal wrong caused to them and therefore, through Judicial creativity, representative standing was expanded to the disadvantaged groups of persons who were not "free" to approach the courts due to financial and social factors rather than physical restraint.

There is always a scope of some criticism of one or the other aspect of PIL, *e.g.*, where it may relate to Human Rights aspect of terrorists or where it is thought that Courts sometimes exceed the limits and so on and so forth. It is also true that misuse of the tool of the PIL and too much of interference is a matter of continued debate. But criticism on that ground would not deter the Courts nor the Courts would desist from acting in a PIL where ends of justice require to do so on the basis of accepted parameters as laid down time and again in several decisions.

In India, Public Interest Litigation is one of the most effective ways for enforcement of Human Rights and for redressal of violation thereof and to provide dignified human existence to large number of people with opportunity for self-development as a human being. It is a simple and easiest tool for redressal of grievances relating to Human Rights and violation of fundamental rights besides some other matters of general importance without sticking to the question of *locus standi* or in granting relief for the benefit of masses for enforcement of fundamental rights and Human Rights.

Supreme Court of India in the case of *A.K. Gopalan* v. *State of Madras,* AIR 1950 SC 27 has categorically ruled that the object of Article 21 is to prevent encroachment upon personal liberty by the Executive save accordance with law and in conformity with the provisions thereof. Personal liberty means freedom from physical restraint of person by incarceration or otherwise. Protection of this article extends to all the persons and not only to the citizens. Persons who are undergoing imprisonment are also protected by Article 21 of the Constitution of India.

It is pertinent to state that torture in police custody is an open assault on basic Human Rights, more particularly against life, personal liberty and human dignity. It is against civilization and individual personality. Custodial torture by police was never approved by any Court of law or International Covenants or resolutions. It was always deprecated, censured and declared as inhuman and barbarous. Almost in all the International Conventions and meetings, it was resolved to ban torture of any kind. Custodial torture is totally arbitrary and highhanded actions of the arresting authorities. Custodial torture is naked violation of human dignity and honour. Use of third degree methods in custody by police and other arresting agencies, custodial death and custodial rapes are the glaring examples of the violation of Human Rights. Supreme Court has held in *D.K. Basu* v. *State of West Bengal* as under: "Custodial death is perhaps one of the worst crimes in a civilised society governed by the rule of law. The rights inherent in Articles 21 and 22(1) of the Constitution are required to be zealously and scrupulously protected. We cannot whisk away the problem. Any form of torture or cruel, inhuman or degrading treatment would fall within the inhibition of Article 21 of the Constitution, whether it occurs during investigation, interrogation or otherwise. If the functionaries of the Government become law-breakers, it is bound to breed contempt for law and would encourage lawlessness and every man would have the tendency to become law unto himself thereby leading to anarchism."

Article 25 of the Constitution of India is very clear in this regard that all persons are equally entitled to freedom of conscience and the right freely to profess, practise and propagate religion, but the same is subject to public order, morality and health. Therefore, such freedom is not unrestricted or unfettered. Government can impose necessary and suitable ban or restrictions on the ground of public order, morality and health and other provisions of Part III of the Constitution of India. India is undoubtedly, a secular State though the words 'secular or secularism' have not been defined anywhere in the Constitution. It, however, finds mention in the Preamble to the Constitution. In a secular State, the balance of the State should not tilt in favour of or against any section, group or individual on the basis of any religion how much so ever pressing the situation may be.

Supreme Court of India in the case of *D.K. Basu* v. *State of West Bengal*, (1997) 1 SCC 416, has issued guidelines to follow in all cases of detention and arrest, till law is made in that behalf, as a preventive measure.

1. The police personnel carrying out the arrest and handling the interrogations of the arrestee should bear accurate, visible and clear identification and name tags with their designations. The particulars of all such police personnel who handle interrogation of the arrestee must be recorded in a register.
2. That the police officer carrying out the arrest of the arrestee shall prepare a memo of arrest at the time of arrest and such memo shall be attested by at least one witness, who may be either a member of the family of the arrestee or a responsible person of the locality from where the arrest is made. It shall also be counter-signed by the arrestee and shall contain the time and date of arrest.
3. A person who has been arrested or detained and is being held in the custody in a police station or interrogation centre or other lock- up, shall be entitled to have one friend or relative or other person known to him or having interest in his welfare being informed, as soon as practicable, that he has been arrested and is being detained at the particular place, unless the arresting witness of the memo of arrest is himself such a friend or a relative of the arrestee.
4. The time, place of arrest and venue of custody of an arrestee must be notified by the police where the next friend or relative of the arrestee lives outside the district or town through the Legal Aid Organisation in the District and the police station of the area concerned telegraphically within a period of 8 to 12 hours after the arrest.
5. The person arrested must be made aware of the right to have someone informed of his arrest or detention as soon as he is put under arrest or is detained.
6. An entry must be made in the diary at the place of detention regarding the arrest of the person, the person who has been informed of the arrest and the names and particulars of the police officials in whose custody the arrestee is.
7. The arrestee should, where he so requests, be also examined at the time of his arrest and major and minor injuries, if any, present on his/her body, must be recorded at that time. The "Inspection Memo" must be

signed both by the arrestee and the police officer effecting the arrest and its copy provided to the arrestee.

8. The arrestee should be subjected to medical examination by a trained Doctor every 48 hours of his detention in custody by a Doctor on the panel of approved Doctors appointed by Director Health Services of the Concerned State or Union territory. Director, Health Services should prepare such a panel for all Tehsils and Districts as well.
9. Copies of all the documents including the memo of arrest referred to above, should be sent to the concerned Magistrate for his record.
10. The arrestee may be permitted to meet his lawyer during interrogation, though not throughout the interrogation.
11. A police control room should be provided at all district and State headquarters, where information regarding the arrest and the place of custody of the arrestee shall be communicated by the officer causing the arrest, within 12 hours of effecting the arrest and at the police control room it should be displayed at a conspicuous notice board.

With a view to create a special and speedy machinery, to punish, and thereby deter, the violators the Court has in para 37 of the judgement provided: "mentioned shall, apart from rendering the concerned official liable for departmental action, also render him liable to be punished for contempt of Court, and the proceedings for contempt may be instituted in any High Court of country having territorial jurisdiction over the matter."

On 9-12-1988 U.N. General Assembly, by its resolution 43/173 has adopted "body of Principles for the Protection of all persons under any form of detention or Imprisonment' for the protection of Imprisonment and detained persons. It has adopted 39 principles of which Principle Nos. 1-3 are very important which are reproduced as under:

Principle 1:—All persons under any form of detention or imprisonment shall be treated in a humane manner and with respect for the inherent dignity of the human person. Principle 2:—Arrest, detention or imprisonment shall only be carried out strictly in accordance with the provisions of the law and by competent officials or persons authorised for that purpose. Principle 3:—There shall be no restriction upon or derogation from any of the Human Rights of persons under any form of detention or imprisonment recognized or existing in any State pursuant to law, conventions, regulations or custom on the pretext that this body of Principles does not recognize such rights or that it recognizes them to a lesser extent.

Further, Supreme Court in the case of *Bhim Singh MLA* v. *State of Jammu and Kashmir*, (1985) 4 SCC 677 considering the seriousness and gravity of the situation, has observed as under:—"We do not wish to use stronger words to condemn the authoritarian acts of the police. If the personal liberty of a member of the Legislative Assembly is to be played with in this fashion, one can only wonder what may happen to lesser mortals. Police Officers who are the custodians of law and order should have the greatest respect for the personal liberty of citizens and should not flout the laws by stooping to such bizarre acts of lawlessness. Custodians of law and order should not become depredators of civil liberties. Their duty is to protect and not to abduct."

Also in the case of *Prem Shankar Shukla* v. *Delhi Administration,* AIR 1980 SC 1535 Supreme Court of India has held that "If today freedom of one forlorn person falls to the police somewhere, tomorrow the freedom of many may fall, else where, with none to whimper unless the Court process invigilates in time and polices, the police before it is too late."

In *State of Rajasthan* v. *Vidyawati,* AIR 1962 SC 933 Supreme Court expressly rejected the maxim "the king can do no wrong". Observing that there is no corresponding provision in the Indian law and has ruled that the doctrine of Sovereign immunity, in the absence of any express legislation to the contrary, does not apply.

It is true that the role of Judiciary in protection of Human Rights is very vital and important. In the whole world, whenever and wherever the Human Rights of the people are violated/infringed, the Judiciary takes immediate action to grant all possible reliefs to the victims.

APPENDIX 1

THE MAGNA CARTA (THE GREAT CHARTER)

Preamble: John, by the grace of God, king of England, lord of Ireland, duke of Normandy and Aquitaine, and count of Anjou, to the archbishop, bishops, abbots, earls, barons, justiciaries, foresters, sheriffs, stewards, servants, and to all his bailiffs and liege subjects, greetings. Know that, having regard to God and for the salvation of our soul, and those of all our ancestors and heirs, and unto the honor of God and the advancement of his holy Church and for the rectifying of our realm, we have granted as underwritten by advice of our venerable fathers, Stephen, archbishop of Canterbury, primate of all England and cardinal of the holy Roman Church, Henry, archbishop of Dublin, William of London, Peter of Winchester, Jocelyn of Bath and Glastonbury, Hugh of Lincoln, Walter of Worcester, William of Coventry, Benedict of Rochester, bishops; of Master Pandulf, subdeacon and member of the household of our lord the Pope, of brother Aymeric (master of the Knights of the Temple in England), and of the illustrious men William Marshal, earl of Pembroke, William, earl of Salisbury, William, earl of Warenne, William, earl of Arundel, Alan of Galloway (constable of Scotland), Waren Fitz Gerold, Peter Fitz Herbert, Hubert De Burgh (seneschal of Poitou), Hugh de Neville, Matthew Fitz Herbert, Thomas Basset, Alan Basset, Philip d'Aubigny, Robert of Roppesley, John Marshal, John Fitz Hugh, and others, our liegemen.

1. In the first place we have granted to God, and by this our present charter confirmed for us and our heirs forever that the English Church shall be free, and shall have her rights entire, and her liberties inviolate; and we will that it be thus observed; which is apparent from this that the freedom of elections, which is reckoned most important and very essential to the English Church, we, of our pure and unconstrained will, did grant, and did by our charter confirm and did obtain the ratification of the same from our lord, Pope Innocent III, before the quarrel arose between us and our barons: and this we will observe, and our will is that it be observed in good faith by our heirs forever. We have also granted to all freemen of our kingdom, for us and our heirs forever, all the underwritten liberties, to be had and held by them and their heirs, of us and our heirs forever.

2. If any of our earls or barons, or others holding of us in chief by military service shall have died, and at the time of his death his heir shall be full of age and owe "relief", he shall have his inheritance by the old relief, to wit, the heir or heirs of an earl, for the whole barony of an earl by £100; the heir or heirs of a baron, £100 for a whole barony; the heir or heirs of a knight, 100s, at most, and whoever owes less let him give less, according to the ancient custom of fees.

3. If, however, the heir of any one of the aforesaid has been under age and in wardship, let him have his inheritance without relief and without fine when he comes of age.

4. The guardian of the land of an heir who is thus under age, shall take from the land of the heir nothing but reasonable produce, reasonable customs, and reasonable services, and that without destruction or waste of men or goods; and if we have committed the wardship of the lands of any such minor to the sheriff, or to any other who is responsible to us for its issues, and he has made destruction or waster of what he holds in wardship, we will take of him amends, and the land shall be committed to two lawful and discreet men of that fee, who shall be responsible for the issues to us or to him to whom we shall assign them; and if we have given or sold the wardship of any such land to anyone and he has therein made destruction or waste, he shall lose that wardship, and it shall be transferred to two lawful and discreet men of that fief, who shall be responsible to us in like manner as aforesaid.

5. The guardian, moreover, so long as he has the wardship of the land, shall keep up the houses, parks, fishponds, stanks, mills, and other things pertaining to the land, out of the issues of the same land; and he shall restore to the heir, when he has come to full age, all his land, stocked with ploughs and wainage, according as the season of husbandry shall require, and the issues of the land can reasonable bear.

6. Heirs shall be married without disparagement, yet so that before the marriage takes place the nearest in blood to that heir shall have notice.

7. A widow, after the death of her husband, shall forthwith and without difficulty have her marriage portion and inheritance; nor shall she give anything for her dower, or for her marriage portion, or for the inheritance which her husband and she held on the day of the death of that husband; and she may remain in the house of her husband for forty days after his death, within which time her dower shall be assigned to her.

8. No widow shall be compelled to marry, so long as she prefers to live without a husband; provided always that she gives security not to marry without our consent, if she holds of us, or without the consent of the lord of whom she holds, if she holds of another.

9. Neither we nor our bailiffs will seize any land or rent for any debt, as long as the chattels of the debtor are sufficient to repay the debt; nor shall the sureties of the debtor be distrained so long as the principal debtor is able to satisfy the debt; and if the principal debtor shall fail to pay the debt, having nothing wherewith to pay it, then the sureties shall answer for the debt; and let them have the lands and rents of the debtor, if they desire them, until they are indemnified for the debt which they have paid for him, unless the principal debtor can show proof that he is discharged thereof as against the said sureties.

10. If one who has borrowed from the Jews any sum, great or small, die before that loan be repaid, the debt shall not bear interest while the heir is under age, of whomsoever he may hold; and if the debt fall into our hands, we will not take anything except the principal sum contained in the bond.

11. And if anyone die indebted to the Jews, his wife shall have her dower and pay nothing of that debt; and if any children of the deceased are left under age, necessaries shall be provided for them in keeping with the holding of the deceased; and out of the residue the debt shall be paid, reserving, however, service due to feudal lords; in like manner let it be done touching debts due to others than Jews.

12. No scutage not aid shall be imposed on our kingdom, unless by common counsel of our kingdom, except for ransoming our person, for making our eldest son a knight, and for once marrying our eldest daughter; and for these there shall not be levied more than a reasonable aid. In like manner it shall be done concerning aids from the city of London.

13. And the city of London shall have all it ancient liberties and free customs, as well by land as by water; furthermore, we decree and grant that all other cities, boroughs, towns, and ports shall have all their liberties and free customs.

14. And for obtaining the common counsel of the kingdom anent the assessing of an aid (except in the three cases aforesaid) or of a scutage, we will cause to be summoned the archbishops, bishops, abbots, earls, and greater barons, severally by our letters; and we will moveover cause to be summoned generally, through our sheriffs and bailiffs, and others who hold of us in chief, for a fixed date, namely, after the expiry of at least forty days, and at a fixed place; and in all letters of such summons we will specify the reason of the summons. And when the summons has thus been made, the business shall proceed on the day appointed, according to the counsel of such as are present, although not all who were summoned have come.

15. We will not for the future grant to anyone license to take an aid from his own free tenants, except to ransom his person, to make his eldest son a knight, and once to marry his eldest daughter; and on each of these occasions there shall be levied only a reasonable aid.

16. No one shall be distrained for performance of greater service for a knight's fee, or for any other free tenement, than is due therefrom.

17. Common pleas shall not follow our court, but shall be held in some fixed place.

18. Inquests of novel disseisin, of mort d'ancestor, and of darrein presentment shall not be held elsewhere than in their own county courts, and that in manner following; We, or, if we should be out of the realm, our chief justiciar, will send two justiciaries through every county four times a year, who shall alone with four knights of the county chosen by the county, hold the said assizes in the county court, on the day and in the place of meeting of that court.

19. And if any of the said assizes cannot be taken on the day of the county court, let there remain of the knights and freeholders, who were present at the county court on that day, as many as may be required for the efficient making of judgments, according as the business be more or less.

20. A freeman shall not be amerced for a slight offense, except in accordance with the degree of the offense; and for a grave offense he shall be amerced in accordance with the gravity of the offense, yet saving always his "contentment"; and a merchant in the same way, saving his "merchandise"; and a villein shall be amerced in the same way, saving his "wainage" if they have fallen into our mercy: and none of the aforesaid amercements shall be imposed except by the oath of honest men of the neighborhood.

21. Earls and barons shall not be amerced except through their peers, and only in accordance with the degree of the offense.

22. A clerk shall not be amerced in respect of his lay holding except after the manner of the others aforesaid; further, he shall not be amerced in accordance with the extent of his ecclesiastical benefice.

23. No village or individual shall be compelled to make bridges at river banks, except those who from of old were legally bound to do so.

24. No sheriff, constable, coroners, or others of our bailiffs, shall hold pleas of our Crown.

25. All counties, hundred, wapentakes, and trithings (except our demesne manors) shall remain at the old rents, and without any additional payment.

26. If anyone holding of us a lay fief shall die, and our sheriff or bailiff shall exhibit our letters patent of summons for a debt which the deceased owed us, it shall be lawful for our sheriff or bailiff to attach and enroll the chattels of the deceased, found upon the lay fief, to the value of that debt, at the sight of law worthy men, provided always that nothing whatever be thence removed until the debt which is evident shall be fully paid to us; and the residue shall be left to the executors to fulfill the will of the deceased; and if there be nothing due from him to us, all the chattels shall go to the deceased, saving to his wife and children their reasonable shares.

27. If any freeman shall die intestate, his chattels shall be distributed by the hands of his nearest kinsfolk and friends, under supervision of the Church, saving to every one the debts which the deceased owed to him.

28. No constable or other bailiff of ours shall take corn or other provisions from anyone without immediately tendering money therefor, unless he can have postponement thereof by permission of the seller.

29. No constable shall compel any knight to give money in lieu of castle-guard, when he is willing to perform it in his own person, or (if he himself cannot do it from any

reasonable cause) then by another responsible man. Further, if we have led or sent him upon military service, he shall be relieved from guard in proportion to the time during which he has been on service because of us.

30. No sheriff or bailiff of ours, or other person, shall take the horses or carts of any freeman for transport duty, against the will of the said freeman.

31. Neither we nor our bailiffs shall take, for our castles or for any other work of ours, wood which is not ours, against the will of the owner of that wood.

32. We will not retain beyond one year and one day, the lands those who have been convicted of felony, and the lands shall thereafter be handed over to the lords of the fiefs.

33. All kydells for the future shall be removed altogether from Thames and Medway, and throughout all England, except upon the seashore.

34. The writ which is called praecipe shall not for the future be issued to anyone, regarding any tenement whereby a freeman may lose his court.

35. Let there be one measure of wine throughout our whole realm; and one measure of ale; and one measure of corn, to wit, "the London quarter"; and one width of cloth (whether dyed, or russet, or "halberget"), to wit, two ells within the selvedges; of weights also let it be as of measures.

36. Nothing in future shall be given or taken for a writ of inquisition of life or limbs, but freely it shall be granted, and never denied.

37. If anyone holds of us by fee-farm, either by socage or by burage, or of any other land by knight's service, we will not (by reason of that fee-farm, socage, or burgage), have the wardship of the heir, or of such land of his as if of the fief of that other; nor shall we have wardship of that fee-farm, socage, or burgage, unless such fee-farm owes knight's service. We will not by reason of any small serjeancy which anyone may hold of us by the service of rendering to us knives, arrows, or the like, have wardship of his heir or of the land which he holds of another lord by knight's service.

38. No bailiff for the future shall, upon his own unsupported complaint, put anyone to his "law", without credible witnesses brought for this purposes.

39. No freemen shall be taken or imprisoned or disseised or exiled or in any way destroyed, nor will we go upon him nor send upon him, except by the lawful judgment of his peers or by the law of the land.

40. To no one will we sell, to no one will we refuse or delay, right or justice.

41. All merchants shall have safe and secure exit from England, and entry to England, with the right to tarry there and to move about as well by land as by water, for buying and selling by the ancient and right customs, quit from all evil tolls, except (in time of war) such merchants as are of the land at war with us. And if such are found in our land at the beginning of the war, they shall be detained, without injury to their bodies or goods, until information be received by us, or by our chief justiciar, how the merchants of our land found in the land at war with us are treated; and if our men are safe there, the others shall be safe in our land.

42. It shall be lawful in future for anyone (excepting always those imprisoned or outlawed in accordance with the law of the kingdom, and natives of any country at war with us, and merchants, who shall be treated as if above provided) to leave our kingdom and to return, safe and secure by land and water, except for a short period in time of war, on grounds of public policy- reserving always the allegiance due to us.

43. If anyone holding of some escheat (such as the honor of Wallingford, Nottingham, Boulogne, Lancaster, or of other escheats which are in our hands and are baronies) shall die, his heir shall give no other relief, and perform no other service to us than he would have done to the baron if that barony had been in the baron's hand; and we shall hold it in the same manner in which the baron held it.

44. Men who dwell without the forest need not henceforth come before our justiciaries of the forest upon a general summons, unless they are in plea, or sureties of one or more, who are attached for the forest.

45. We will appoint as justices, constables, sheriffs, or bailiffs only such as know the law of the realm and mean to observe it well.

46. All barons who have founded abbeys, concerning which they hold charters from the kings of England, or of which they have long continued possession, shall have the wardship of them, when vacant, as they ought to have.

47. All forests that have been made such in our time shall forthwith be disafforsted; and a similar course shall be followed with regard to river banks that have been placed "in defense" by us in our time.

48. All evil customs connected with forests and warrens, foresters and warreners, sheriffs and their officers, river banks and their wardens, shall immediately by inquired into in each county by twelve sworn knights of the same county chosen by the honest men of the same county, and shall, within forty days of the said inquest, be utterly abolished, so as never to be restored, provided always that we previously have intimation thereof, or our justiciar, if we should not be in England.

49. We will immediately restore all hostages and charters delivered to us by Englishmen, as sureties of the peace of faithful service.

50. We will entirely remove from their bailiwicks, the relations of Gerard of Athee (so that in future they shall have no bailiwick in England); namely, Engelard of Cigogne, Peter, Guy, and Andrew of Chanceaux, Guy of Cigogne, Geoffrey of Martigny with his brothers, Philip Mark with his brothers and his nephew Geoffrey, and the whole brood of the same.

51. As soon as peace is restored, we will banish from the kingdom all foreign born knights, crossbowmen, serjeants, and mercenary soldiers who have come with horses and arms to the kingdom's hurt.

52. If anyone has been dispossessed or removed by us, without the legal judgment of his peers, from his lands, castles, franchises, or from his right, we will immediately restore them to him; and if a dispute arise over this, then let it be decided by the five and twenty barons of whom mention is made below in the clause for securing the peace. Moreover, for all those possessions, from which anyone has, without the lawful judgment of his peers, been disseised or removed, by our father, King Henry, or by our brother, King Richard, and which we retain in our hand (or which as possessed by others, to whom we are bound to warrant them) we shall have respite until the usual term of crusaders; excepting those things about which a plea has been raised, or an inquest made by our order, before our taking of the cross; but as soon as we return from the expedition, we will immediately grant full justice therein.

53. We shall have, moreover, the same respite and in the same manner in rendering justice concerning the disafforestation or retention of those forests which Henry our father and Richard our broter afforested, and concerning the wardship of lands which are of the fief of another (namely, such wardships as we have hitherto had by reason of a fief which anyone held of us by knight's service), and concerning abbeys founded on other fiefs than our own, in which the lord of the fee claims to have right; and when we have returned, or if we desist from our expedition, we will immediately grant full justice to all who complain of such things.

54. No one shall be arrested or imprisoned upon the appeal of a woman, for the death of any other than her husband.

55. All fines made with us unjustly and against the law of the land, and all amercements, imposed unjustly and against the law of the land, shall be entirely remitted,

or else it shall be done concerning them according to the decision of the five and twenty barons whom mention is made below in the clause for securing the pease, or according to the judgment of the majority of the same, along with the aforesaid Stephen, archbishop of Canterbury, if he can be present, and such others as he may wish to bring with him for this purpose, and if he cannot be present the business shall nevertheless proceed without him, provided always that if any one or more of the aforesaid five and twenty barons are in a similar suit, they shall be removed as far as concerns this particular judgment, others being substituted in their places after having been selected by the rest of the same five and twenty for this purpose only, and after having been sworn.

56. If we have disseised or removed Welshmen from lands or liberties, or other things, without the legal judgment of their peers in England or in Wales, they shall be immediately restored to them; and if a dispute arise over this, then let it be decided in the marches by the judgment of their peers; for the tenements in England according to the law of England, for tenements in Wales according to the law of Wales, and for tenements in the marches according to the law of the marches. Welshmen shall do the same to us and ours.

57. Further, for all those possessions from which any Welshman has, without the lawful judgment of his peers, been disseised or removed by King Henry our father, or King Richard our brother, and which we retain in our hand (or which are possessed by others, and which we ought to warrant), we will have respite until the usual term of crusaders; excepting those things about which a plea has been raised or an inquest made by our order before we took the cross; but as soon as we return (or if perchance we desist from our expedition), we will immediately grant full justice in accordance with the laws of the Welsh and in relation to the foresaid regions.

58. We will immediately give up the son of Llywelyn and all the hostages of Wales, and the charters delivered to us as security for the peace.

59. We will do towards Alexander, king of Scots, concerning the return of his sisters and his hostages, and concerning his franchises, and his right, in the same manner as we shall do towards our owher barons of England, unless it ought to be otherwise according to the charters which we hold from William his father, formerly king of Scots; and this shall be according to the judgment of his peers in our court.

60. Moreover, all these aforesaid customs and liberties, the observances of which we have granted in our kingdom as far as pertains to us towards our men, shall be observed b all of our kingdom, as well clergy as laymen, as far as pertains to them towards their men.

61. Since, moveover, for God and the amendment of our kingdom and for the better allaying of the quarrel that has arisen between us and our barons, we have granted all these concessions, desirous that they should enjoy them in complete and firm endurance forever, we give and grant to them the underwritten security, namely, that the barons choose five and twenty barons of the kingdom, whomsoever they will, who shall be bound with all their might, to observe and hold, and cause to be observed, the peace and liberties we have granted and confirmed to them by this our present Charter, so that if we, or our justiciar, or our bailiffs or any one of our officers, shall in anything be at fault towards anyone, or shall have broken any one of the articles of this peace or of this security, and the offense be notified to four barons of the foresaid five and twenty, the said four barons shall repair to us (or our justiciar, if we are out of the realm) and, laying the transgression before us, petition to have that transgression redressed without delay. And if we shall not have corrected the transgression (or, in the event of our being out of the realm, if our justiciar shall not have corrected it) within forty days, reckoning from the time it has been intimated to us (or to our justiciar, if we should be out of the realm), the four barons aforesaid shall refer that matter to the rest of the five and twenty barons,

and those five and twenty barons shall, together with the community of the whole realm, distrain and distress us in all possible ways, namely, by seizing our castles, lands, possessions, and in any other way they can, until redress has been obtained as they deem fit, saving harmless our own person, and the persons of our queen and children; and when redress has been obtained, they shall resume their old relations towards us. And let whoever in the country desires it, swear to obey the orders of the said five and twenty barons for the execution of all the aforesaid matters, and along with them, to molest us to the utmost of his power; and we publicly and freely grant leave to everyone who wishes to swear, and we shall never forbid anyone to swear. All those, moveover, in the land who of themselves and of their own accord are unwilling to swear to the twenty five to help them in constraining and molesting us, we shall by our command compel the same to swear to the effect foresaid. And if any one of the five and twenty barons shall have died or departed from the land, or be incapacitated in any other manner which would prevent the foresaid provisions being carried out, those of the said twenty five barons who are left shall choose another in his place according to their own judgment, and he shall be sworn in the same way as the others. Further, in all matters, the execution of which is entrusted,to these twenty five barons, if perchance these twenty five are present and disagree about anything, or if some of them, after being summoned, are unwilling or unable to be present, that which the majority of those present ordain or command shall be held as fixed and established, exactly as if the whole twenty five had concurred in this; and the said twenty five shall swear that they will faithfully observe all that is aforesaid, and cause it to be observed with all their might. And we shall procure nothing from anyone, directly or indirectly, whereby any part of these concessions and liberties might be revoked or diminished; and if any such things has been procured, let it be void and null, and we shall never use it personally or by another.

62. And all the will, hatreds, and bitterness that have arisen between us and our men, clergy and lay, from the date of the quarrel, we have completely remitted and pardoned to everyone. Moreover, all trespasses occasioned by the said quarrel, from Easter in the sixteenth year of our reign till the restoration of peace, we have fully remitted to all, both clergy and laymen, and completely forgiven, as far as pertains to us. And on this head, we have caused to be made for them letters testimonial patent of the lord Stephen, archbishop of Canterbury, of the lord Henry, archbishop of Dublin, of the bishops aforesaid, and of Master Pandulf as touching this security and the concessions aforesaid.

63. Wherefore we will and firmly order that the English Church be free, and that the men in our kingdom have and hold all the aforesaid liberties, rights, and concessions, well and peaceably, freely and quietly, fully and wholly, for themselves and their heirs, of us and our heirs, in all respects and in all places forever, as is aforesaid. An oath, moreover, has been taken, as well on our part as on the art of the barons, that all these conditions aforesaid shall be kept in good faith and without evil intent.

Given under our hand - the above named and many others being witnesses - in the meadow which is called Runnymede, between Windsor and Staines, on the fifteenth day of June, in the seventeenth year of our reign.

APPENDIX 2

THE DECLARATION OF INDEPENDENCE, 1776

(4-7-1976)

When in the course of human events, it becomes necessary for one people to dissolve the political bands which have connected them with another, and to assume among the powers of the earth, the separate and equal station to which the Laws of nature and of Nature's God entitled them, a decent respect to the opinions of mankind requires that they should declared the cause which impel them to the separation.

We hold these truths to be self-evident, that all men are created equal, that they are endowed by their Creator with certain unalienable Rights, that among these are Life, Liberty and the pursuit of Happiness—that to secure these rights, Governments are instituted among men, deriving their just powers from the consent of the governed, - That whenever any form of Government becomes destructive of these ends, it is the Right of the people to alter or to abolish it, and to institute new Government, laying its foundation on such principles and organising its powers in such form , as to them shall seem most likely to effect their safety and Happiness. Prudence, indeed, will dictate that Governments long established should not be changed for light and transient causes; and accordingly all experience hath shown, that mankind are more disposed to suffer, while evils are sufferable, than to right themselves by abolishing the forms to which they are accustomed. But when a long train of abuses and usurpation, pursuing invariably the same object evinces a design to reduce them under absolute Despotism, it is their right, it is their duty, to throw off such Government, and to provide new Guards for their future security. Such has been the patient sufferance of these Colonies; and such is now the necessity, which constrains them to alter their former Systems of Government. The history of the present King of Great Britain is a history of repeated injuries and usurpation, all having in direct object the establishment of an absolute Tyranny over these States. To prove this, let facts be submitted to a candid world. He has refused his Assent to Laws, the most wholesome and necessary for the public good.

He has forbidden his Governors to pass Laws of immediate and pressing importance, unless suspended in their operation till his Assent should be obtained; and when so suspended, he has utterly neglected to attend to them.

He has refused to pass other Laws for the accommodation of large districts of people, unless those people would relinquish the right of Representation in the Legislature, a right inestimable to them and formidable to tyrants only.

He has called together legislative bodies at places unusual, uncomfortable, and distant from the depository of their public records, for the sole purpose of fatiguing them into compliance with his measures.

He has dissolved Representative Houses repeatedly, for opposing with manly firmness his invasions on the rights of the people.

He has refused for a long time, after such dissolution, to cause others to be elected; whereby the Legislative powers, incapable of Annihilation, have returned to the People at large for their exercise; the State remaining in the meantime exposed to all the dangers of invasion from without, and convulsions within.

He has endeavoured to prevent the population of these States; for that purpose obstructing the Laws for Naturalisation of Foreigners; refusing to pass orders to encourage their migrations hither, and raising the conditions of new Appropriations of Lands.

He has obstructed the Administration of Justice, by refusing his assent to Laws for establishing Judiciary powers.

He has made Judges dependent on his will alone, for the tenure of their offices, and the amount and payment of their salaries.

He has erected a multitude of New Offices, and sent hither swarms of Officers to harass our people, and eat out their substance.

He has kept among us, in times of peace, Standing armies without the consent of our Legislatures.

He has affected to render the military independent of and superior to the civil power.

He has combined with others to subject us to a jurisdiction foreign to our Constitution, and unacknowledged by our laws; giving his assent to their Acts of pretended Legislation;

For quartering large bodies of armed troops among us.

For protecting them, by a mock trial, from punishment for any Murders which they should commit on the Inhabitants of these States;

For cutting off our Trade with all parts of the world:

For imposing Taxes on us without our consent:

For depriving us in many cases, of the benefits of Trial by Jury;

For transporting us beyond seas to be tried for pretended offences;

For abolishing the free system of English laws in a neighbouring Province, establishing therein an Arbitrary Government, and enlarging its boundaries so as to render it at once an example and fit instrument for introducing the same absolute rule into these colonies;

For taking away our Charters, abolishing our most valuable Laws, and altering fundamentally the Forms of our Governments.

For suspending our own Legislatures, and declaring themselves invested with power to legislate for us in all cases whatsoever.

He has abdicated Government here, by declaring us out of his protection and waging war against us.

He has plundered our seas, ravaged our consents, burst our towns, and destroyed the lives of our people.

He is at this time transporting large Armies of foreign Mercenaries to complete the works of death, desolation and tyranny, already begun with circumstances of Cruelty and perfidy scarcely paralled in the most barbarous ages. and totally unworthy the Head of a civilised nation.

He has on constrained our fellow citizens taken captive on the high seas to bear Arms against their country, to become the executioners of their friends and Brethren, or to fall themselves by their hands.

He has excited domestic insurrections amongst us, and has endeavoured to bring on the inhabitants of our frontiers, the merciless Indian Savages, whose known rule of warfare, is an undistinguished destruction of all ages, sexes and conditions.

In every stage of these oppressions we have petitioned for redress in the most humble terms: Our repeated petitions have been answered only by repeated injury. A prince whose character is thus marked by every act which may define a Tyrant, is unfit to be the ruler of a free people.

Nor have we been wanting in attention to our British brethren. We have warned them from time-to-time of attempts by their Legislature to extend an unwarrantable jurisdiction over us. We have reminded them of the circumstances of our emigration and settlement here. We have appealed to their native justice and magnanimity, and we have conjured them by the ties of our common kindred to disallow these usurpation, which, would inevitably interrupt our connections and correspondence. They too have been deaf to the voice of justice and of consanguinity. We must, therefore, acquiesce in the necessity, which denounces our separation, and hold them, as we hold the rest of mankind, Enemies in War, in Peace Friends.

We, therefore, the Representative of the United States of America, in General Congress, Assembled, appealing to the Supreme Judge of the world for the rectitude of our intentions, do in the name, and by authority of the good people of these colonies, solemnly publish and declare, that these untied colonies are, and of right ought to be free and Independent States; that they are Absolved from all Allegiance to the British Crown, and that all political connection between them and the State of Great Britain, is and ought to be totally dissolved; and that as Free and Independent States, they have full power to levy war, conclude peace, contract Alliances, establish commerce, and to do all other acts and things which Independent States may of right do. And for the support of this Declaration, with a firm reliance on the protection of divine Providence, we mutually pledge to each other our Lives, our Fortunes and our sacred Honour.

APPENDIX 3

THE BILL OF RIGHTS OF CONSTITUTION OF THE UNITED STATES OF AMERICA

The Preamble to The Bill of Rights

Congress of the United States

begun and held at the City of New-York, on

Wednesday the fourth of March, one thousand seven hundred and eighty nine.

THE Conventions of a number of the States, having at the time of their adopting the Constitution, expressed a desire, in order to prevent misconstruction or abuse of its powers, that further declaratory and restrictive clauses should be added: And as extending the ground of public confidence in the Government, will best ensure the beneficent ends of its institution.

RESOLVED by the Senate and House of Representatives of the United States of America, in Congress assembled, two thirds of both Houses concurring, that the following Articles be proposed to the Legislatures of the several States, as amendments to the Constitution of the United States, all, or any of which Articles, when ratified by three fourths of the said Legislatures, to be valid to all intents and purposes, as part of the said Constitution; viz.

ARTICLES in addition to, and Amendment of the Constitution of the United States of America, proposed by Congress, and ratified by the Legislatures of the several States, pursuant to the fifth Article of the original Constitution.

Note: The following text is a transcription of the first ten amendments to the Constitution in their original form. These amendments were ratified December 15, 1791, and form what is known as the "Bill of Rights."

Amendment I

Congress shall make no law respecting an establishment of religion, or prohibiting the free exercise thereof; or abridging the freedom of speech, or of the press; or the right of the people peaceably to assemble, and to petition the Government for a redress of grievances.

Amendment II

A well regulated Militia, being necessary to the security of a free State, the right of the people to keep and bear Arms, shall not be infringed.

Amendment III

No Soldier shall, in time of peace be quartered in any house, without the consent of the Owner, nor in time of war, but in a manner to be prescribed by law.

Amendment IV

The right of the people to be secure in their persons, houses, papers, and effects, against unreasonable searches and seizures, shall not be violated, and no Warrants shall issue, but upon probable cause, supported by Oath or affirmation, and particularly describing the place to be searched, and the persons or things to be seized.

Amendment V

No person shall be held to answer for a capital, or otherwise infamous crime, unless on a presentment or indictment of a Grand Jury, except in cases arising in the land or naval forces, or in the Militia, when in actual service in time of War or public danger; nor shall any person be subject for the same offence to be twice put in jeopardy of life or limb; nor shall be compelled in any criminal case to be a witness against himself, nor be deprived of life, liberty, or property, without due process of law; nor shall private property be taken for public use, without just compensation.

Amendment VI

In all criminal prosecutions, the accused shall enjoy the right to a speedy and public trial, by an impartial jury of the State and district wherein the crime shall have been committed, which district shall have been previously ascertained by law, and to be informed of the nature and cause of the accusation; to be confronted with the witnesses against him; to have compulsory process for obtaining witnesses in his favor, and to have the Assistance of Counsel for his defence.

Amendment VII

In Suits at common law, where the value in controversy shall exceed twenty dollars, the right of trial by jury shall be preserved, and no fact tried by a jury, shall be otherwise re-examined in any Court of the United States, than according to the rules of the common law.

Amendment VIII

Excessive bail shall not be required, nor excessive fines imposed, nor cruel and unusual punishments inflicted.

Amendment IX

The enumeration in the Constitution, of certain rights, shall not be construed to deny or disparage others retained by the people.

Amendment X

The powers not delegated to the United States by the Constitution, nor prohibited by it to the States, are reserved to the States respectively, or to the people.

Amendment XI

Passed by Congress March 4, 1794. Ratified February 7, 1795.

Note: Article III, section 2, of the Constitution was modified by amendment 11.

The Judicial power of the United States shall not be construed to extend to any suit in law or equity, commenced or prosecuted against one of the United States by Citizens of another State, or by Citizens or Subjects of any Foreign State.

Amendment XII

Passed by Congress December 9, 1803. Ratified June 15, 1804.

Note: A portion of Article II, section 1 of the Constitution was superseded by the 12th amendment.

The Electors shall meet in their respective states and vote by ballot for President and Vice-President, one of whom, at least, shall not be an inhabitant of the same state with themselves; they shall name in their ballots the person voted for as President, and in distinct ballots the person voted for as Vice-President, and they shall make distinct lists of all persons voted for as President, and of all persons voted for as Vice-President, and of the number of votes for each, which lists they shall sign and certify, and transmit sealed to the seat of the government of the United States, directed to the President of the Senate; — the President of the Senate shall, in the presence of the Senate and House of Representatives, open all the certificates and the votes shall then be counted; — The person having the greatest number of votes for President, shall be the President, if such number be a majority of the whole number of Electors appointed; and if no person have such majority, then from the persons having the highest numbers not exceeding three on the list of those voted for as President, the House of Representatives shall choose immediately, by ballot, the President. But in choosing the President, the votes shall be taken by states, the representation from each state having one vote; a quorum for this purpose shall consist of a member or members from two-thirds of the states, and a majority of all the states shall be necessary to a choice. [And if the House of Representatives shall not choose a President whenever the right of choice shall devolve upon them, before the fourth day of March next following, then the Vice-President shall act as President, as in case of the death or other constitutional disability of the President. —]* The person having the greatest number of votes as Vice-President, shall be the Vice-President, if such number be a majority of the whole number of Electors appointed, and if no person have a majority, then from the two highest numbers on the list, the Senate shall choose the Vice-President; a quorum for the purpose shall consist of two-thirds of the whole number of Senators, and a majority of the whole number shall be necessary to a choice. But no person constitutionally ineligible to the office of President shall be eligible to that of Vice-President of the United States.

**Superseded by section 3 of the 20th amendment.*

Amendment XIII

Passed by Congress January 31, 1865. Ratified December 6, 1865.

Note: A portion of Article IV, section 2, of the Constitution was superseded by the 13th amendment.

Section 1. Neither slavery nor involuntary servitude, except as a punishment for crime whereof the party shall have been duly convicted, shall exist within the United States, or any place subject to their jurisdiction.

Section 2. Congress shall have power to enforce this article by appropriate legislation.

Amendment XIV

Passed by Congress June 13, 1866. Ratified July 9, 1868.

Note: Article I, section 2, of the Constitution was modified by section 2 of the 14th amendment.

Section 1. All persons born or naturalized in the United States, and subject to the jurisdiction thereof, are citizens of the United States and of the State wherein they reside. No State shall make or enforce any law which shall abridge the privileges or immunities of citizens of the United States; nor shall any State deprive any person of life, liberty, or property, without due process of law; nor deny to any person within its jurisdiction the equal protection of the laws.

Section 2. Representatives shall be apportioned among the several States according to their respective numbers, counting the whole number of persons in each State, excluding Indians not taxed. But when the right to vote at any election for the choice of electors for President and Vice-President of the United States, Representatives in Congress, the Executive and Judicial officers of a State, or the members of the Legislature thereof, is denied to any of the male inhabitants of such State, being twenty-one years of age,* and citizens of the United States, or in any way abridged, except for participation in rebellion, or other crime, the basis of representation therein shall be reduced in the proportion which the number of such male citizens shall bear to the whole number of male citizens twenty-one years of age in such State.

Section 3. No person shall be a Senator or Representative in Congress, or elector of President and Vice-President, or hold any office, civil or military, under the United States, or under any State, who, having previously taken an oath, as a member of Congress, or as an officer of the United States, or as a member of any State legislature, or as an executive or judicial officer of any State, to support the Constitution of the United States, shall have engaged in insurrection or rebellion against the same, or given aid or comfort to the enemies thereof. But Congress may by a vote of two-thirds of each House, remove such disability.

Section 4. The validity of the public debt of the United States, authorized by law, including debts incurred for payment of pensions and bounties for services in suppressing insurrection or rebellion, shall not be questioned. But neither the United States nor any State shall assume or pay any debt or obligation incurred in aid of insurrection or rebellion against the United States, or any claim for the loss or emancipation of any slave; but all such debts, obligations and claims shall be held illegal and void.

Section 5. The Congress shall have the power to enforce, by appropriate legislation, the provisions of this article.

**Changed by section 1 of the 26th amendment.*

Amendment XV

Passed by Congress February 26, 1869. Ratified February 3, 1870.

Section 1. The right of citizens of the United States to vote shall not be denied or abridged by the United States or by any State on account of race, color, or previous condition of servitude—

Section 2. The Congress shall have the power to enforce this article by appropriate legislation.

Amendment XVI

Passed by Congress July 2, 1909. Ratified February 3, 1913.

Note: Article I, section 9, of the Constitution was modified by amendment 16.

The Congress shall have power to lay and collect taxes on incomes, from whatever source derived, without apportionment among the several States, and without regard to any census or enumeration.

Amendment XVII

Passed by Congress May 13, 1912. Ratified April 8, 1913.

Note: Article I, section 3, of the Constitution was modified by the 17th amendment.

The Senate of the United States shall be composed of two Senators from each State, elected by the people thereof, for six years; and each Senator shall have one vote. The electors in each State shall have the qualifications requisite for electors of the most numerous branch of the State legislatures.

When vacancies happen in the representation of any State in the Senate, the executive authority of such State shall issue writs of election to fill such vacancies: *Provided*, That the legislature of any State may empower the executive thereof to make temporary appointments until the people fill the vacancies by election as the legislature may direct.

This amendment shall not be so construed as to affect the election or term of any Senator chosen before it becomes valid as part of the Constitution.

Amendment XVIII

Passed by Congress December 18, 1917. Ratified January 16, 1919. Repealed by amendment 21.

Section 1. After one year from the ratification of this article the manufacture, sale, or transportation of intoxicating liquors within, the importation thereof into, or the exportation thereof from the United States and all territory subject to the jurisdiction thereof for beverage purposes is hereby prohibited.

Section 2. The Congress and the several States shall have concurrent power to enforce this article by appropriate legislation.

Section 3. This article shall be inoperative unless it shall have been ratified as an amendment to the Constitution by the legislatures of the several States, as provided in the Constitution, within seven years from the date of the submission hereof to the States by the Congress.

Amendment XIX

Passed by Congress June 4, 1919. Ratified August 18, 1920.

The right of citizens of the United States to vote shall not be denied or abridged by the United States or by any State on account of sex.

Congress shall have power to enforce this article by appropriate legislation.

Amendment XX

Passed by Congress March 2, 1932. Ratified January 23, 1933.

Note: Article I, section 4, of the Constitution was modified by section 2 of this amendment. In addition, a portion of the 12th amendment was superseded by section 3.

Section 1. The terms of the President and the Vice President shall end at noon on the 20th day of January, and the terms of Senators and Representatives at noon on the 3rd day of January, of the years in which such terms would have ended if this article had not been ratified; and the terms of their successors shall then begin.

Section 2. The Congress shall assemble at least once in every year, and such meeting shall begin at noon on the 3d day of January, unless they shall by law appoint a different day.

Section 3. If, at the time fixed for the beginning of the term of the President, the President elect shall have died, the Vice President elect shall become President. If a President shall not have been chosen before the time fixed for the beginning of his term, or if the President elect shall have failed to qualify, then the Vice President elect shall act as President until a President shall have qualified; and the Congress may by law provide for the case wherein neither a President elect nor a Vice President shall have qualified, declaring who shall then act as President, or the manner in which one who is to act shall be selected, and such person shall act accordingly until a President or Vice President shall have qualified.

Section 4. The Congress may by law provide for the case of the death of any of the persons from whom the House of Representatives may choose a President whenever the right of choice shall have devolved upon them, and for the case of the death of any of the persons from whom the Senate may choose a Vice President whenever the right of choice shall have devolved upon them.

Section 5. Sections 1 and 2 shall take effect on the 15th day of October following the ratification of this article.

Section 6. This article shall be inoperative unless it shall have been ratified as an amendment to the Constitution by the legislatures of three-fourths of the several States within seven years from the date of its submission.

Amendment XXI

Passed by Congress February 20, 1933. Ratified December 5, 1933.

Section 1. The eighteenth article of amendment to the Constitution of the United States is hereby repealed.

Section 2. The transportation or importation into any State, Territory, or Possession of the United States for delivery or use therein of intoxicating liquors, in violation of the laws thereof, is hereby prohibited.

Section 3. This article shall be inoperative unless it shall have been ratified as an amendment to the Constitution by conventions in the several States, as provided in the Constitution, within seven years from the date of the submission hereof to the States by the Congress.

Amendment XXII

Passed by Congress March 21, 1947. Ratified February 27, 1951.

Section 1. No person shall be elected to the office of the President more than twice, and no person who has held the office of President, or acted as President, for more than two years of a term to which some other person was elected President shall be elected to the office of President more than once. But this Article shall not apply to any person holding the office of President when this Article was proposed by Congress, and shall not prevent any person who may be holding the office of President, or acting as President, during the term within which this Article becomes operative from holding the office of President or acting as President during the remainder of such term.

Section 2. This article shall be inoperative unless it shall have been ratified as an amendment to the Constitution by the legislatures of three-fourths of the several States within seven years from the date of its submission to the States by the Congress.

Amendment XXIII

Passed by Congress June 16, 1960. Ratified March 29, 1961.

Section 1. The District constituting the seat of Government of the United States shall appoint in such manner as Congress may direct:

A number of electors of President and Vice President equal to the whole number of Senators and Representatives in Congress to which the District would be entitled if it were a State, but in no event more than the least populous State; they shall be in addition to those appointed by the States, but they shall be considered, for the purposes of the election of President and Vice President, to be electors appointed by a State; and they shall meet in the District and perform such duties as provided by the twelfth article of amendment.

Section 2. The Congress shall have power to enforce this article by appropriate legislation.

Amendment XXIV

Passed by Congress August 27, 1962. Ratified January 23, 1964.

Section 1. The right of citizens of the United States to vote in any primary or other election for President or Vice President, for electors for President or Vice President, or for Senator or Representative in Congress, shall not be denied or abridged by the United States or any State by reason of failure to pay poll tax or other tax.

Section 2. The Congress shall have power to enforce this article by appropriate legislation.

Amendment XXV

Passed by Congress July 6, 1965. Ratified February 10, 1967.

Note: Article II, section 1, of the Constitution was affected by the 25th amendment.

Section 1. In case of the removal of the President from office or of his death or resignation, the Vice President shall become President.

Section 2. Whenever there is a vacancy in the office of the Vice President, the President shall nominate a Vice President who shall take office upon confirmation by a majority vote of both Houses of Congress.

Section 3. Whenever the President transmits to the President pro tempore of the Senate and the Speaker of the House of Representatives his written declaration that he is unable to discharge the powers and duties of his office, and until he transmits to them a written declaration to the contrary, such powers and duties shall be discharged by the Vice President as Acting President.

Section 4. Whenever the Vice President and a majority of either the principal officers of the executive departments or of such other body as Congress may by law provide, transmit to the President pro tempore of the Senate and the Speaker of the House of Representatives their written declaration that the President is unable to discharge the powers and duties of his office, the Vice President shall immediately assume the powers and duties of the office as Acting President.

Thereafter, when the President transmits to the President pro tempore of the Senate and the Speaker of the House of Representatives his written declaration that no inability exists, he shall resume the powers and duties of his office unless the Vice President and a majority of either the principal officers of the executive department or of such other body as Congress may by law provide, transmit within four days to the President pro tempore of the Senate and the Speaker of the House of Representatives their written declaration that the President is unable to discharge the powers and duties of his office. Thereupon Congress shall decide the issue, assembling within forty-eight hours for that purpose if not in session. If the Congress, within twenty-one days after receipt of the latter written declaration, or, if Congress is not in session, within twenty-one days after Congress is required to assemble, determines by two-thirds vote of both Houses that the President is unable to discharge the powers and duties of his office, the Vice President shall continue to discharge the same as Acting President; otherwise, the President shall resume the powers and duties of his office.

Amendment XXVI

Passed by Congress March 23, 1971. Ratified July 1, 1971.

Note: Amendment 14, section 2, of the Constitution was modified by section 1 of the 26th amendment.

Section 1. The right of citizens of the United States, who are eighteen years of age or older, to vote shall not be denied or abridged by the United States or by any State on account of age.

Section 2. The Congress shall have power to enforce this article by appropriate legislation.

Amendment XXVII

Originally proposed Sept. 25, 1789. Ratified May 7, 1992.

No law, varying the compensation for the services of the Senators and Representatives, shall take effect, until an election of representatives shall have intervened.

APPENDIX 4

THE FRENCH DECLARATION OF THE RIGHTS OF MAN AND CITIZEN

Decreed by the National Assembly, on 20, 21, 23, 24 and 26 August, 1789, approved by the King.

The representatives of the French People, constituted in a national Assembly considering that ignorance, forgetfulness and disrespect for the rights of man are the sole cause of public misfortune and the corruption of governments, have decided to set out, in a solemn declaration, the natural, sacred and inalienable rights of man; such that this declaration, constantly present the minds of the members of the body politic, will remind them continually of their rights and power; such that the acts of the legislative and executive powers, being subject at any instant to comparison with the aim of any political institution, will be better respected; such that the demands of citizens, henceforth based on simple and indisputable principles, shall always contribute to the maintenance of the Constitution and to the happiness of all consequently, the National Assembly recognises and declares, in the presence and under the auspices of the Supreme Being, the following rights of man and citizen.

Articles:

1. Men are born free and remain free and equal in rights. Social distinctions can be based only on public utility.

2. The aim of every political association is the preservation of the natural and imprescriptible rights of man. These rights are liberty, property, security, and resistance to oppression.

3. The sources of all sovereignty resides essentially in the nation; no body, no individual can exercise authority that does not proceed from it in plain terms.

4. Liberty consists in the power to do anything that does not injure others; accordingly, the exercise of the rights of each man has no limits except those that secure the enjoyment of these same rights to the other members of society. These limits can be determined only by law.

5. The law has only the rights to forbid such actions as are injurious to society. Nothing can be forbidden that is not interdicted by the law, and no one can be constrained to do that which it does not order.

6. Law is the expression of the general will. All citizens have the right to take part personally, or by their representatives, and its formation. It must be the same for all, whether it protects or punishes. All citizens, being equal in its eyes, art equally eligible to all public dignities, places, and employments, according to their capacities, and without other distinction than that of their virtues and talents.

7. No man can be accused, arrested, or detained, except in the cases determined by the law and according to the forms it has prescribed. Those who procure, expedite, execute, or cause arbitrary orders to be executed, ought to be punished: but every citizen summoned were seized in virtue of the law ought to render instant obedience; he makes himself guilty by resistance.

8. The law ought only to establish penalties that are strict and obviously necessary, and no one can be punished except in virtue of a law established and promulgated prior to the offense and legally applied.

9. Every man being presumed innocent until he has been pronounced guilty, if it is thought indispensable to arrest him, all severity that may not be necessary to secure his person ought to be strictly suppressed by law.

10. No one should be disturbed on account of his opinions, even religious, provided their manifestation does not upset the public order established by law.

11. The free communication of ideas and opinions is one of the most precious of the rights of man; every citizen can then freely speak, write, and print, subject to responsibility for the abuse of this freedom in the cases is determined by law.

12. The guarantee of the rights of man and citizen requires a public force; this force then is instituted for the advantage of all and not for the personal benefit of those to whom it is entrusted.

13. A general tax is indispensable for the maintenance of the public force and for the expenses of administration; it ought to be equally apportioned among all citizens according to their means.

14. All the citizens have a right to ascertain, by themselves or by their representatives, the necessity of the public tax, to consent to it freely, to follow the employment of it, and to determine the quota, the assessment, the collection, and the duration of it.

15. Society has the right to call for an account of his administration by every public agent.

16. Any society in which the guarantee of the rights is not secured, or the separation of powers not determined, has no constitution at all.

17. Property being a sacred to and inviolable right, no one can be deprived of it, unless illegally established public necessity evidently demands it, under the condition of a just and prior indemnity.

APPENDIX 5

UNIVERSAL DECLARATION OF HUMAN RIGHTS, 1948[1]

PREAMBLE

Whereas recognition of the inherent dignity and of the equal and inalienable rights of all members of the human family is the foundation of freedom, justice and peace in the world,

Whereas disregard and contempt for human rights have resulted in barbarous acts which have outraged the conscience of mankind, and the advent of a world in which human beings shall enjoy freedom of speech and belief and freedom from fear and want has been proclaimed as the highest aspiration of the common people.

Whereas it is essential, if man is not to be compelled to have recourse, as a last resort, to rebellion against tyranny and oppression, that human rights should be protected by the rule of law,

Whereas it is essential to promote the development of friendly relations between nations,

Whereas the peoples of the United Nations have in the Charter reaffirmed their faith in fundamental human rights, in the dignity and worth of the human person and in the equal rights of men and women and have determined to promote social progress and better standards of life in larger freedom,

Whereas Member States have pledged themselves to achieve, in co-operation with the United Nations, the promotion of universal respect for and observance of human rights and fundamental freedoms,

Whereas a common understanding of these rights and freedoms is of the greatest importance for the full realization of this pledge,

Now, Therefore THE GENERAL ASSEMBLY proclaims THIS UNIVERSAL DECLARATION OF HUMAN RIGHTS as a common standard of achievement for all peoples and all nations, to the end that every individual and every organ of society, keeping this Declaration constantly in mind, shall strive by teaching and education to promote respect for these rights and freedoms and by progressive measures, national and international, to secure their universal and effective recognition and observance, both among the peoples of Member States themselves and among the peoples of territories under their jurisdiction.

Article 1

All human beings are born free and equal in dignity and rights. They are endowed with reason and conscience and should act towards one another in a spirit of brotherhood.

Article 2

Everyone is entitled to all the rights and freedoms set forth in this Declaration, without distinction of any kind, such as race, colour, sex, language, religion, political or other opinion, national or social origin, property, birth or other status. Furthermore, no distinction shall be made on the basis of the political, jurisdictional or international status of the country or territory to which a person belongs, whether it be independent, trust, non-self-governing or under any other limitation of sovereignty.

Article 3

Everyone has the right to life, liberty and security of person.

---

1. Adopted and proclaimed by General Assembly resolution 217A(III) of 1C December, 1948.

Article 4

No one shall be held in slavery or servitude; slavery and the slave trade shall be prohibited in all their forms.

Article 5

No one shall be subjected to torture or to cruel, inhuman or degrading treatment or punishment.

Article 6

Everyone has the right to recognition everywhere as a person before the law.

Article 7

All are equal before the law and are entitled without any discrimination to equal protection of the law. All are entitled to equal protection against any discrimination in violation of this Declaration and against any incitement to such discrimination.

Article 8

Everyone has the right to an effective remedy by the competent national tribunals for acts violating the fundamental rights granted him by the constitution or by law.

Article 9

No one shall be subjected to arbitrary arrest, detention or exile.

Article 10

Everyone is entitled in full equality to a fair and public hearing by an independent and impartial tribunal, in the determination of his rights and obligations and of any criminal charge against him.

Article 11

1. Everyone charged with a penal offence has the right to be presumed innocent until proved guilty according to law in a public trial at which he has had all the guarantees necessary for his defence.

2. No one shall be held guilty of any penal offence on account of any act or omission which did not constitute a penal offence, under national or international law, at the time when it was committed. Nor shall a heavier penalty be imposed than the one that was applicable at the time the penal offence was committed.

Article 12

No one shall be subjected to arbitrary interference with his privacy, family, home or correspondence, nor to attacks upon his honour and reputation. Everyone has the right to the protection of the law against such interference or attacks.

Article 13

1. Everyone has the right to freedom of movement and residence within the borders of each state.

2. Everyone has the right to leave any country, including his own, and to return to his country.

Article 14

1. Everyone has the right to seek and to enjoy in other countries asylum from persecution.

2. This right may not be invoked in the case of prosecutions genuinely arising from non-political crimes or from acts contrary to the purposes and principles of the United Nations.

Article 15

1. Everyone has the right to a nationality.

2. No one shall be arbitrarily deprived of his nationality nor denied the right to change his nationality.

Article 16

1. Men and women of full age, without any limitation due to race, nationality or religion, have the right to marry and to found a family. They are entitled to equal rights as to marriage, during marriage and at its dissolution.

2. Marriage shall be entered into only with the free and full consent of the intending spouses.

3. The family is the natural and fundamental group unit of society and is entitled to protection by society and the State.

Article 17

1. Everyone has the right to own property alone as well as in association with others.

2. No one shall be arbitrarily deprived of his property.

Article 18

Everyone has the right to freedom of thought, conscience and religion; this right includes freedom to change his religion or belief, and freedom, either alone or in community with others and in public or private, to manifest his religion or belief in teaching, practice, worship and observance.

Article 19

Everyone has the right to freedom of opinion and expression; this right includes freedom to hold opinions without interference and to seek, receive and impart information and ideas through any media and regardless of frontiers.

Article 20

1. Everyone has the right to freedom of peaceful assembly and association. 58

2. No one may be compelled to belong to an association. 59

Article 21

1. Everyone has the right to take part in the government of his country, directly or through freely chosen representatives.

2. Everyone has the right of equal access to public service in his country. 62

3. The will of the people shall be the basis of the authority of government; this will shall be expressed in periodic and genuine elections which shall be by universal and equal suffrage and shall be held by secret vote or by equivalent free voting procedures.

Article 22

Everyone, as a member of society, has the right to social security and is entitled to realization, through national effort and international co-operation and in accordance with the organization and resources of each State, of the economic, social and cultural rights indispensable for his dignity and the free development of his personality.

Article 23

1. Everyone has the right to work, to free choice of employment, to just and favourable conditions of work and to protection against unemployment.

2. Everyone, without any discrimination, has the right to equal pay for equal work.

3. Everyone who works has the right to just and favourable remuneration ensuring for himself and his family an existence worthy of human dignity, and upplemented, if necessary, by other means of social protection.

4. Everyone has the right to form and to join trade unions for the protection of his interests.

Article 24

Everyone has the right to rest and leisure, including reasonable limitation of working hours and periodic holidays with pay.

Article 25

1. Everyone has the right to a standard of living adequate for the health and well-being of himself and of his family, including food, clothing, housing and medical care and necessary social services, and the right to security in the event of unemployment, sickness, disability, widowhood, old age or other lack of livelihood in circumstances beyond his control.

2. Motherhood and childhood are entitled to special care and assistance. All children, whether born in or out of wedlock, shall enjoy the same social protection.

Article 26

1. Everyone has the right to education. Education shall be free, at least in the elementary and fundamental stages. Elementary education shall be compulsory. Technical and professional education shall be made generally available and higher education shall be equally accessible to all on the basis of merit.

2. Education shall be directed to the full development of the human personality and to the strengthening of respect for human rights and fundamental freedoms. It shall promote understanding, tolerance and friendship among all nations, racial or religious groups, and shall further the activities of the United Nations for the maintenance of peace.

3. Parents have a prior right to choose the kind of education that shall be given to their children.

Article 27

1. Everyone has the right freely to participate in the cultural life of the community, to enjoy the arts and to share in scientific advancement and its benefits.

2. Everyone has the right to the protection of the moral and material interests resulting from any scientific, literary or artistic production of which he is the author.

Article 28

Everyone is entitled to a social and international order in which the rights and freedoms set forth in this Declaration can be fully realized.

Article 29

1. Everyone has duties to the community in which alone the free and full development of his personality is possible.

2. In the exercise of his rights and freedoms, everyone shall be subject only to such limitations as are determined by law solely for the purpose of securing due recognition and respect for the rights and freedoms of others and of meeting the just requirements of morality, public order and the general welfare in a democratic society.

3. These rights and freedoms may in no case be exercised contrary to the purposes and principles of the United Nations.

Article 30

Nothing in this Declaration may be interpreted as implying for any State, group or person any right to engage in any activity or to perform any act aimed at the destruction of any of the rights and freedoms set forth herein.

APPENDIX 6

INTERNATIONAL COVENANT ON CIVIL AND POLITICAL RIGHTS, 1966[1]

PREAMBLE

THE STATES PARTIES TO THE PRESENT COVENANT

Considering that, in accordance with the principles proclaimed in the Charter of the United Nations, recognition of the inherent dignity and of the equal and inalienable rights of all members of the human family is the foundation of freedom, justice and peace in the world,

Recognizing that these rights derive from the inherent dignity of the human person,

Recognizing that, in accordance with the Universal Declaration of Human Rights, the ideal of free human beings enjoying civil and political freedom and freedom from fear and want can only be achieved if conditions are created whereby everyone may enjoy his civil and political rights, as well as his economic, social and cultural rights,

Considering the obligation of States under the Charter of the United Nations to promote universal respect for and observance of, human rights and freedoms,

Realizing that the individual, having duties to other individuals and to the community to which he belongs, is under a responsibility to strive for the promotion and observance of the rights recognized in the present Covenant,

Agree upon the following Articles:

PART I

Article 1

1. All peoples have the right of self-determination. By virtue of that right they freely determine their political status and freely pursue their economic, social and cultural development.

2. All peoples may, for their own ends, freely dispose of their natural wealth and resources without prejudice to any obligations arising out of international economic co-operation, based upon the principle of mutual benefit, and international law. In no case may a people be deprived of it its own means of subsistence.

3. The States Parties to the present Covenant, including those having responsibility for the administration of Non-Self-Governing and Trust Territories, shall promote the realization of the right of self-determination, and shall respect that right, in conformity with the provisions of the Charter of the United Nations.

PART II

Article 2

1. Each State Party to the present Covenant undertakes to respect and to ensure to all individuals within its territory and subject to its jurisdiction the rights recognized in the present Covenant, without distinction of any kind, such as race, colour, sex, language, religion, political or other opinion, national or social origin, property, birth or other status.

2. Where not already provided for by existing legislative or other measures, each State Party to the present Covenant undertakes to take the necessary steps, in accordance with its constitutional processes and with the provisions of the present Covenant, to

---

1. Opened for signature at New York dated 19th December, 1966.

adopt such legislative or other measures as may be necessary to give effect to the rights recognized in the present Covenant.

3. Each State Party to the present Covenant undertakes:

(a) to ensure that any person whose rights or freedoms as herein recognized are violated shall have an effective remedy, notwithstanding that the violation has been committed by persons acting in an official capacity;

(b) to ensure that any person claiming such a remedy shall have his right thereto determined by competent judicial, administrative or legislative authorities, or by any other competent authority provided for by the legal system of the State, and to develop the possibilities of judicial remedy;

(c) to ensure that the competent authorities shall enforce such remedies when granted.

Article 3

The States Parties to the present Covenant undertake to ensure the equal right of men and women to the enjoyment of all civil and political rights set forth in the present Covenant.

Article 4

1. In time of public emergency which threatens the life of the nation and the existence of which is officially proclaimed, the States Parties to the present Covenant may take measures derogating from their obligations under the present Covenant to the extent strictly required by the exigencies of the situation, provided that such measures are not inconsistent with their other obligations under international law and do not involve discrimination solely on the ground of race, colour, sex, language, religion or social origin.

2. No derogation from Articles 6, 7, 8 (paragraphs 1 and 2), 11 ,15, 16 and 18 may be made under this provision.

3. Any State Party to the present Covenant availing itself of the right of derogation shall immediately inform the other States Parties to the present Covenant, through the intermediary of the Secretary-General of the United Nations, of the provisions from which it has derogated and of the reasons by which it was actuated. A further communication shall be made, through the same intermediary, on the date on which it terminates such derogation.

Article 5

1. Nothing in the present Covenant may be interpreted as implying for any State, group or person any right to engage in any activity or perform any act aimed at the destruction of any of the rights and freedoms recognized herein or at their limitation to a greater extent than is provided for in the present Covenant.

2. There shall be no restriction upon or derogation from any of the fundamental human rights recognized or existing in any State Party to the present Covenant pursuant to law, conventions, regulations or custom on the pretext that the present Covenant does not recognize such rights or that it recognizes them to a lesser extent.

PART III

Article 6

1. Every human being has the inherent right to life. This right shall be protected by law. No one shall be arbitrarily deprived of his life.

2. In countries which have not abolished the death penalty, sentence of death may be imposed only for the most serious crimes in accordance with the law in force at the time of the commission of the crime and not contrary to the provisions of the present Covenant and to the Convention on the Prevention and Punishment of the Crime of

Genocide. This penalty can only be carried out pursuant to a final judgement rendered by a competent court.

3. When deprivation of life constitutes the crime of genocide, it is understood that nothing in this Article shall authorize any State Party to the present Covenant to derogate in any way from any obligation assumed under the provisions of the Convention on the Prevention and Punishment of the Crime of Genocide.

4. Anyone sentenced to death shall have the right to seek pardon or commutation of the sentence. Amnesty, pardon or commutation of the sentence of death may be granted in all cases.

5. Sentence of death shall not be imposed for crimes committed by persons below eighteen years of age and shall not be carried out on pregnant women.

6. Nothing in this Article shall be invoked to delay or to prevent the abolition of capital punishment by any State Party to the present Covenant.

Article 7

No one shall be subjected to torture or to cruel, inhuman or degrading treatment or punishment. In particular, no one shall be subjected without his free consent to medical or scientific experimentation.

Article 8

1. No one shall be held in slavery; slavery and the slave-trade in all their forms shall be prohibited.

2. No one shall be held in servitude.

3. (a) No one shall be required to perform forced or compulsory labour

(b) Paragraph 3 (a) shall not be held to preclude, in countries where imprisonment with hard labour may be imposed as a punishment for a crime, the performance of hard labour in pursuance of a sentence to such punishment by a competent court.

(c) For the purpose of this paragraph the term "forced or compulsory labour" shall not include:

- (i) any work or service, not referred to in sub-paragraph (b), normally required of a person who is under detention in consequence of a lawful order of a court, or of a person during conditional release from such detention;
- (ii) any service of a military character and, in countries where conscientious objection is recognized, any national service required by law of conscientious objectors;
- (iii) any service exacted in cases of emergency or calamity threatening the life or well-being of the community;
- (iv) any work or service which forms part of normal civil obligations.

Article 9

1. Everyone has the right to liberty and security of person. No one shall be subjected to arbitrary arrest or detention. No one shall be deprived of his liberty except on such grounds and in accordance with such procedure as are established by law.

2. Anyone who is arrested shall be informed, at the time of arrest, of the reasons for his arrest and shall be promptly informed of any charges against him.

3. Anyone arrested or detained on a criminal charge shall be brought promptly before a judge or other officer authorized by law to exercise judicial power and shall be entitled to trial within a reasonable time or to release. It shall not be the general rule that persons awaiting trial shall be detained in custody, but release may be subject to guarantees to appear for trial, at any other stage of the judicial proceedings, and, should occasion arise, for execution of the judgement.

4. Anyone who is deprived of his liberty by arrest or detention shall be entitled to take proceedings before a court, in order that that court may decide without delay on the lawfulness of his detention and order his release if the detention is not lawful.

5. Anyone who has been the victim of unlawful arrest or detention shall have an enforceable right to compensation.

Article 10

1. All persons deprived of their liberty shall be treated with humanity and with respect for the inherent dignity of the human person.

2. (a) Accused persons shall, save in exceptional circumstances, be segregated from convicted persons and shall be subject to separate treatment appropriate to their status as unconvicted persons;

(b) Accused juvenile persons shall be separated from adults and brought as speedily as possible for adjudication.

3. The penitentiary system shall comprise treatment of prisoners the essential aim of which shall be their reformation and social rehabilitation. Juvenile offenders shall be segregated from adults and be accorded treatment appropriate to their age and legal status.

Article 11

No one shall be imprisoned merely on the ground of inability to fulfil a contractual obligation.

Article 12

1. Everyone lawfully within the territory of a State shall, within that territory, have the right to liberty of movement and freedom to choose his residence.

2. Everyone shall be free to leave any country, including his own.

3. The above-mentioned rights shall not be subject to any restrictions except those which are provided by law, are necessary to protect national security, public order (ordre public), public health or morals or the rights and freedoms of others, and are consistent with the other rights recognized in the present Covenant.

4. No one shall be arbitrarily deprived of the right to enter his own country.

Article 13

An alien lawfully in the territory of a State Party to the present Covenant may be expelled therefrom only in pursuance of a decision reached in accordance with law and shall, except where compelling reasons of national security otherwise require, be allowed to submit the reasons against his expulsion and to have his case reviewed by, and be represented for the purpose before, the competent authority or a person or persons especially designated by the competent authority.

Article 14

1. All persons shall be equal before the courts and tribunals. In the determination of any criminal charge against him, or of his rights and obligations in a suit at law, everyone shall be entitled to a fair and public hearing by a competent, independent and impartial tribunal established by law. The Press and the public may be excluded from all or part of a trial for reasons of morals, public order *(ordre public)* or national security in a democratic society, or when the interest of the private lives of the parties so requires, or to the extent strictly necessary in the opinion of the court in special circumstances where publicity would prejudice the interests of justice; but any judgement rendered in a criminal case or in a suit at law shall be made public except where the interest of juvenile persons otherwise requires or the proceedings concern matrimonial disputes or the guardianship of children.

2. Everyone charged with a criminal offence shall have the right to be presumed innocent until proved guilty according to law.

3. In the determination of any criminal charge against him, everyone shall be entitled to the following minimum guarantees, in full equality:

(a) to be informed promptly and in detail in a language which he understands of the nature and cause of the charge against him;

(b) to have adequate time and facilities for the preparation of his defence and to communicate with counsel of his own choosing;

(c) to be tried without undue delay;

(d) to be tried in his presence, and to defend himself in person or through legal assistance of his own choosing; to be informed, if he does not have legal assistance, of this right; and to have legal assistance assigned to him, in any case where the interests of justice so require, and without payment by him in any such case if he does not have sufficient means to pay for it;

(e) to examine, or have examined the witnesses against him and to obtain the attendance and examination of witnesses on his behalf under the same conditions as witnesses against him;

(f) to have the free assistance of an interpreter if he cannot understand or speak the language used in court;

(g) not to be compelled to testify against himself or to confess guilt.

4. In the case of juvenile persons, the procedure shall be such as will take account of their age and the desirability of promoting their rehabilitation.

5. Everyone convicted of a crime shall have the right to his conviction and sentence being reviewed by a higher tribunal according to law.

6. When a person has by a final decision been convicted of a criminal offence and when subsequently his conviction has been reversed or he has been pardoned on the ground that a new or newly discovered fact shows conclusively that there has been a miscarriage of justice, the person who has suffered punishment as a result of such conviction shall be compensated according to law, unless it is proved that the non-disclosure of the unknown fact in time is wholly or partly attributable to him.

7. No one shall be liable to be tried or punished again for an offence for which he has already been finally convicted or acquitted in accordance with the law and penal procedure of each country.

Article 15

1. No one shall be held guilty of any criminal offence on account of any act or omission which did not constitute a criminal offence, under national or international law, at the time when it was committed. Nor shall a heavier penalty be imposed than the one that was applicable at the time when the criminal offence was committed. If, subsequent to the commission of the offence, provision is made by law for the imposition of a lighter penalty, the offender shall benefit thereby.

2. Nothing in this Article shall prejudice the trial and punishment of any person for any act or omission which, at the time when it was committed was criminal according to the general principles of law recognized by the community of nations.

Article 16

Everyone shall have the right to recognition everywhere as a person before the law.

Article 17

1. No one shall be subjected to arbitrary or unlawful interference with his privacy, family, home or correspondence, nor to unlawful attacks on his honour and reputation.

2. Everyone has the right to the protection of the law against such interference or attacks.

Article 18

1. Everyone shall have the right to freedom of thought, conscience and religion. This right shall include freedom to have or to adopt a religion or belief of his choice, and freedom, either individually or in community with others and in public or private, to manifest his religion or belief in worship, observance, practice and teaching.

2. No one shall be subject to coercion which would impair his freedom to have or to adopt a religion or belief of his choice.

3. Freedom to manifest one's religion or beliefs may be subject only to such limitations as are prescribed by law and are necessary to protect public safety, order, health, or morals or the fundamental rights and freedoms of others.

4. The States Parties to the present Covenant undertake to have respect for the liberty of parents and, when applicable, legal guardians to ensure the religious and moral education of their children in conformity with their own convictions.

Article 19

1. Everyone shall have the right to hold opinions without interference.

2. Everyone shall have the right to freedom of expression; this right shall include freedom to seek, receive and impart information and ideas of all kinds, regardless of frontiers, either orally, in writing or in print, in the form of art, or through any other media of his choice.

3. The exercise of the rights provided for in paragraph 2 of this Article carries with it special duties and responsibilities. It may therefore be subject to certain restrictions, but these shall only be such as are provided by law and are necessary:

(a) for respect of the rights or reputations of others;

(b) for the protection of national security or of public order *(ordre public)*, or of public health or morals.

Article 20

1. Any propaganda for war shall be prohibited by law.

2. Any advocacy of national, racial or religious hatred that constitutes incitement to discrimination, hostility or violence shall be prohibited by law.

Article 21

The right of peaceful assembly shall be recognized. No restrictions may be placed on the exercise of this right other than those imposed in conformity with the law and which are necessary in a democratic society in the interests of national security or public safety, public order (ordre public), the protection of public health or morals or the protection of the rights and freedoms of others.

Article 22

1. Everyone shall have the right to freedom of association with others, including the right to form and join trade unions for the protection of his interests.

2. No restrictions may be placed on the exercise of this right other than those which are prescribed by law and which are necessary in a democratic society in the interests of national security or public safety, public order (ordre public), the protection of public health or morals or the protection of the rights and freedoms of others. This Article shall not prevent the imposition of lawful restrictions on members of the armed forces and of the police in their exercise of this right.

3. Nothing in this Article shall authorize States Parties to the International Labour Organisation Convention of 1948 concerning Freedom of Association and Protection of

the Right to Organize to take legislative measures which would prejudice, or to apply the law in such a manner as to prejudice, the guarantees provided for in that Convention.

Article 23

1. The family is the natural and fundamental group unit of society and is entitled to protection by society and the State.

2. The right of men and women of marriageable age to marry and to found a family shall be recognized.

3. No marriage shall be entered into without the free and full consent of the intending spouses.

4. States Parties to the present Covenant shall take appropriate steps to ensure equality of rights and responsibilities of spouses as to marriage, during marriage and at its dissolution. In the case of dissolution, provision shall be made for the necessary protection of any children.

Article 24

1. Every child shall have, without any discrimination as to race, colour sex, language, religion, national or social origin, property or birth, the right to such measures of protection as are required by his status as a minor, on the part of his family, society and the State.

2. Every child shall be registered immediately after birth and shall have a name.

3. Every child has the right to acquire a nationality.

Article 25

Every citizen shall have the right and the opportunity, without any of the distinctions mentioned in Article 2 and without unreasonable restrictions:

(a) to take part in the conduct of public affairs, directly or through freely chosen representatives;

(b) to vote and to be elected at genuine periodic elections which shall be by universal and equal suffrage and shall be held by secret ballot, guaranteeing the free expression of the will of the electors;

(c) to have access, on general terms of equality, to public service in his country.

Article 26

All persons are equal before the law and are entitled without any discrimination to the equal protection of the law. In this respect, the law shall prohibit any discrimination and guarantee to all persons equal and effective protection against discrimination on any ground such as race, colour, sex, language, religion, political or other opinion, national or social origin, property, birth or other status.

Article 27

In those States in which ethnic, religious or linguistic minorities exist persons belonging to such minorities shall not be denied the right, in community with the other members of their group, to enjoy their own culture, to profess and practise their own religion, or to use their own language.

PART IV

Article 28

1. There shall be established a Human Rights Committee (hereafter referred to in the present Covenant as the Committee). It shall consist of eighteen members and shall carry out the functions hereinafter provided.

2. The Committee shall be composed of nationals of the States Parties to the present Covenant who shall be persons of high moral character and recognized competence in

the field of human rights, consideration being given to the usefulness of the participation of some persons having legal experience.

3. The members of the Committee shall be elected and shall serve in their personal capacity.

Article 29

1. The members of the Committee shall be elected by secret ballot from a list of persons possessing the qualifications prescribed in Article 28 and nominated for the purpose by the States Parties to the present Covenant.

2. Each State Party to the present Covenant may nominate not more than two persons. These persons shall be nationals of the nominating State.

3. A person shall be eligible for renomination.

Article 30

1. The initial election shall be held not later than six months after the date of the entry into force of the present Covenant.

2. At least four months before the date of each election to the Committee other than an election to fill a vacancy declared in accordance with Article 34, the Secretary-General of the United Nations shall address a written invitation to the States Parties to the present Covenant to submit their nominations for membership of the Committee within three months.

3. The Secretary-General of the United Nations shall prepare a list in alphabetical order of all the persons thus nominated, with an indication of the States Parties which have nominated them, and shall submit it to the States Parties to the present Covenant no later than one month before the date of each election.

4. Elections of the members of the Committee shall be held at a meeting of the States Parties to the present Covenant convened by the Secretary-General of the United Nations at the Headquarters of the United Nations. At that meeting, for which two thirds of the States Parties to the present Covenant shall constitute a quorum, the persons elected to the Committee shall be those nominees who obtain the largest number of votes and an absolute majority of the votes of the representatives of States Parties present and voting.

Article 31

1. The Committee may not include more than one national of the same State.

2. In the election of the Committee, consideration shall be given to equitable geographical distribution of membership and to the representation of the different forms of civilization and of the principal legal systems.

Article 32

1. The members of the Committee shall be elected for a term of four years. They shall be eligible for re-election if renominated. However, the terms of nine of the members elected at the first election shall expire at the end of two years; immediately after the first election, the names of these nine members elected at the first election shall expire at the end of two years; immediately after the first election, the names of these nine members shall be chosen by lot by the Chairman of the meeting referred to in Article 30, paragraph 4.

2. Elections at the expiry of office shall be held in accordance with the preceding Articles of this part of the present Covenant.

Article 33

1. If, in the unanimous opinion of the other members, a member of the Committee has ceased to carry out his functions for any cause other than absence of a temporary character, the Chairman of the Committee shall notify the Secretary-General of the United Nations, who shall then declare the seat of that member to be vacant.

2. In the event of the death or the resignation of a member of the Committee, the Chairman shall immediately notify the Secretary-General of the United Nations, who shall declare the seat vacant from the date of death or the date on which the resignation takes effect.

Article 34

1. When a vacancy is declared in accordance with Article 33 and if the term of office of the member to be replaced does not expire within six months of the declaration of the vacancy, the Secretary-General of the United Nations shall notify each of the States Parties to the present Covenant, which may within two months submit nominations in accordance with Article 29 for the purpose of filling the vacancy.

2. The Secretary-General of the United Nations shall prepare a list in alphabetical order of the persons thus nominated and shall submit it to the States Parties to the present Covenant. The election to fill the vacancy shall then take place in accordance with the relevant provisions of this part of the present Covenant.

3. A member of the Committee elected to fill a vacancy declared in accordance with Article 33 shall hold office for the remainder of the term of the member who vacated the seat on the Committee under the provisions of that Article.

Article 35

The members of the Committee shall, with the approval of the General Assembly of the United Nations, receive emoluments from United Nations resources on such terms and conditions as the General Assembly may decide, having regard to the importance of the Committee's responsibilities.

Article 36

The Secretary-General of the United Nations shall provide the necessary staff and facilities for the effective performance of the functions of the Committee under the present Covenant.

Article 37

1. The Secretary-General of the United Nations shall convene the initial meeting of the Committee at the Headquarters of the United Nations.

2. After its initial meeting, the Committee shall meet at such times as shall be provided in its rules of procedure.

3. The Committee shall normally meet at the Headquarters of the United Nations or at the United Nations Office at Geneva.

Article 38

Every member of the Committee shall, before taking up his duties, make a solemn declaration in open committee that he will perform his functions impartially and conscientiously.

Article 39

1. The Committee shall elect its officers for a term of two years. They may be re-elected.

2. The Committee shall establish its own rules of procedure, but these rules shall provide, *inter alia*, that—

(a) twelve members shall constitute a quorum;

(b) decisions of the Committee shall be made by a majority vote of the members present.

Article 40

1. The States Parties to the present Covenant undertake to submit reports on the measures they have adopted which give effect to the rights recognized herein and on the progress made in the enjoyment of those rights:

(a) within one year of the entry into force of the present Covenant for the States Parties concerned;

(b) thereafter whenever the Committee so requests.

2. All reports shall be submitted to the Secretary-General of the United Nations, who shall transmit them to the Committee for consideration. Reports shall indicate the factors and difficulties, if any, affecting the implementation of the present Covenant.

3. The Secretary-General of the United Nations may, after consultation with the Committee, transmit to the specialized agencies concerned copies of such parts of the reports as may fall within their field of competence.

4. The Committee shall study the reports submitted by the States Parties to the present Covenant. It shall transmit its reports, and such general comments as it may consider appropriate, to the States Parties. The Committee may also transmit to the Economic and Social Council these comments along with the copies of the reports it has received from States Parties to the present Covenant.

5. The States Parties to the present Covenant may submit to the Committee observations on any comments that may be made in accordance with paragraph 4 of this Article.

Article 41

1. A State Party to the present Covenant may at any time declare under this Article that it recognizes the competence of the Committee to receive and consider communications to the effect that a State Party claims that another State Party is not fulfilling its obligations under the present Covenant. Communications under this Article may be received and considered only if submitted by a State Party which has made a declaration recognizing in regard to itself the competence of the Committee. No communication shall be received by the Committee if it concerns a State Party which has not made such a declaration. Communications received under this Article shall be dealt with in accordance with the following procedure:

(a) if a State Party to the present Covenant considers that another State Party is not giving effect to the provisions of the present Covenant, it may, by written communication, bring the matter to the attention of that State Party. Within three months after the receipt of the communication, the receiving State shall afford the State which sent the communication an explanation or any other statement in writing clarifying the matter, which should include, to the extent possible and pertinent, reference to domestic procedures and remedies taken, pending, or available in the matter.

(b) if the matter is not adjusted to the satisfaction of both States Parties concerned within six months after the receipt by the receiving State of the initial communication, either State shall have the right to refer the matter to the Committee, by notice given to the Committee and to the other State.

(c) the Committee shall deal with a matter referred to it only after it has ascertained that all available domestic remedies have been invoked and exhausted in the matter, in conformity with the generally recognized principles of international law. This shall not be the rule where the application of the remedies is unreasonably prolonged.

(d) the Committee shall hold closed meetings when examining communications under this Article.

(e) subject to the provisions of sub-paragraph (c), the Committee shall make available its good offices to the States Parties concerned with a view to a friendly solution of the matter on the basis of respect for human rights and fundamental freedoms as recognized in the present Covenant.

(f) In any matter referred to it, the Committee may call upon the States Parties concerned, referred to in sub-paragraph (b), to supply any relevant information.

(g) the States Parties concerned, referred to in sub-paragraph (b), shall have the right to be represented when the matter is being considered in the Committee and to make submissions orally and/or in writing.

(h) the Committee shall, within twelve months after the date of receipt of notice under sub-paragraph (b), submit a report:

(i) if a solution within the terms of sub-paragraph (e) is reached, the Committee shall confine its report to a brief statement of the facts and of the solution reached;

(ii) if a solution within the terms of sub-paragraph (e) is not reached, the Committee shall confine its report to a brief statement of the facts; the written submissions and record of the oral submissions made by the States Parties concerned shall be attached to the report. In every matter, the report shall be communicated to the States Parties concerned.

2. The provisions of this Article shall come into force when ten States Parties to the present Covenant have made declarations under paragraph 1 of this Article. Such declarations shall be deposited by the States Parties with the Secretary-General of the United Nations, who shall transmit copies thereof to the other States Parties. A declaration may be withdrawn at any time by notification to the Secretary-General. Such a withdrawal shall not prejudice the consideration of any matter which is the subject of a communication already transmitted under this Article; no further communication by any State Party shall be received after the notification of withdrawal of the declaration has been received by the Secretary-General, unless the State Party concerned had made a new declaration.

Article 42

1. (a) If a matter referred to the Committee in accordance with Article 41 is not resolved to the satisfaction of the States Parties concerned, the Committee may, with the prior consent of the States Parties concerned, appoint an *ad hoc* Conciliation Commission (hereinafter referred to as the Commission). The good offices of the Commission shall be made available to the States Parties concerned with a view to an amicable solution of the matter on the basis of respect for the present Covenant;

(b) The Commission shall consist of five persons acceptable to the States Parties concerned. If the States Parties concerned fail to reach agreement within three months on all or part of the composition of the Commission the members of the Commission concerning whom no agreement has been reached shall be elected by secret ballot by a two-thirds majority vote of the Committee from among its members.

2. The members of the Commission shall serve in their personal capacity. They shall not be nationals of the States Parties concerned, or of a State not party to the present Covenant, or of a State Party which has not made a declaration under Article 41.

3. The Commission shall elect its own Chairman and adopt its own rules of procedure.

4. The meetings of the Commission shall normally be held at the Headquarters of the United Nations or at the United Nations Office at Geneva. However, they may be held at such other convenient places as the Commission may determine in consultation with the Secretary-General of the United Nations and the States Parties concerned.

5. The secretariat provided in accordance with Article 36 shall also service the commissions appointed under this Article.

6. The information received and collated by the Committee shall be made available to the Commission and the Commission may call upon the States Parties concerned to supply any other relevant information.

7. When the Commission has fully considered the matter, but in any event not later than twelve months after having been seized of the matter, it shall submit to the Chairman of the Committee a report for communication to the States Parties concerned:

(a) if the Commission is unable to complete its consideration of the matter within twelve months, it shall confine its report to a brief statement of the status of its consideration of the matter;

(b) if an amicable solution to the matter on the basis of respect for human rights as recognized in the present Covenant is reached, the Commission shall confine its report to a brief statement of the facts and of the solution reached;

(c) if a solution within the terms of sub-paragraph (b) is not reached, the Commission's report shall embody its findings on all questions of fact relevant to the issues between the States Parties concerned, and its views on the possibilities of an amicable solution of the matter. This report shall also contain the written submissions and a record of the oral submissions made by the States Parties concerned;

(d) if the Commission's report is submitted under sub-paragraph (c), the States Parties concerned shall, within three months of the receipt of the report, notify the Chairman of the Committee whether or not they accept the contents of the report of the Commission.

8. The provisions of this Article are without prejudice to the responsibilities of the Committee under Article 41.

9. The States Parties concerned shall share equally all the expenses of the members of the Commission in accordance with estimates to be provided by the Secretary-General of the United Nations.

10. The Secretary-General of the United Nations shall be empowered to pay the expenses of the members of the Commission, if necessary, before reimbursement by the States Parties concerned, in accordance with paragraph 9 of this Article.

Article 43

The members of the Committee, and of the *ad hoc* conciliation commissions which may be appointed under Article 42, shall be entitled to the facilities, privileges and immunities of experts on mission for the United Nations as laid down in the relevant sections of the Convention on the Privileges and Immunities of the United Nations.

Article 44

The provisions for the implementation of the present Covenant shall apply without prejudice to the procedures prescribed in the field of human rights by or under the constituent instruments and the conventions of the United Nations and of the specialized agencies and shall not prevent the States Parties to the present Covenant from having recourse to other procedures for settling a dispute in accordance with general or special international agreements in force between them.

Article 45

The Committee shall submit to the General Assembly of the United Nations, through the Economic and Social Council, an annual report on its activities.

PART V

Article 46

Nothing in the present Covenant shall be interpreted as impairing the provisions of the Charter of the United Nations and of the constitutions of the specialized agencies which define the respective responsibilities of the various organs of the United Nations and of the specialized agencies in regard to the matters dealt with in the present Covenant.

Article 47

Nothing in the present Covenant shall be interpreted as impairing the inherent right of all peoples to enjoy and utilize fully and freely their natural wealth and resources.

PART VI

Article 48

1. The present Covenant is open for signature by any State Member of the United Nations or member of any of its specialized agencies, by any State Party to the Statute of the International Court of Justice, and by any other State which has been invited by the General Assembly of the United Nations to become a party to the present Covenant.

2. The present Covenant is subject to ratification. Instruments of ratification shall be deposited with the Secretary-General of the United Nations.

3. The present Covenant shall be open to accession by any State referred to in paragraph 1 of this Article.

4. Accession shall be effected by the deposit of an instrument of accession with the Secretary-General of the United Nations.

5. The Secretary-General of the United Nations shall inform all States which have signed this Covenant or acceded to it of the deposit of each instrument of ratification or accession.

Article 49

1. The present Covenant shall enter into force three months after the date of the deposit with the Secretary-General of the United Nations of the thirty-fifth instrument of ratification or instrument of accession.

2. For each State ratifying the present Covenant or acceding to it after the deposit of the thirty-fifth instrument of ratification or instrument of accession, the present Covenant shall enter into force three months after the date of the deposit of its own instrument of ratification or instrument of accession.

Article 50

The provisions of the present Covenant shall extend to all parts of federal States without any limitations or exceptions.

Article 51

1. Any State Party to the present Covenant may propose an amendment and file it with the Secretary-General of the United Nations. The Secretary-General of the United Nations shall thereupon communicate any proposed amendments to the States Parties to the present Covenant with a request that they notify him whether they favour a conference of States Parties for the purpose of considering and voting upon the proposals. In the event that at least one third of the States Parties favours such a conference, the Secretary-General shall convene the conference under the auspices of the United Nations. Any amendment adopted by a majority of the States Parties present and voting at the conference shall be submitted to the General Assembly of the United Nations for approval.

2. Amendments shall come into force when they have been approved by the General Assembly of the United Nations and accepted by a two-thirds majority of the States Parties to the present Covenant in accordance with their respective constitutional processes.

3. When amendments come into force, they shall be binding on those States Parties which have accepted them, other States Parties still being bound by the provisions of the present Covenant and any earlier amendment which they have accepted.

Article 52

Irrespective of the notifications made under Article 48, paragraph 5, the Secretary-General of the United Nations shall inform all States referred to in paragraph 1 of the same Article of the following particulars:

(a) signatures, ratifications and accessions under Article 48;

(b) the date of the entry into force of the present Covenant under Article 49 and the date of the entry into force of any amendments under Article 51.

Article 53

1. The present Covenant, of which the Chinese, English, French, Russian and Spanish texts are equally authentic, shall be deposited in the archives of the United Nations.

2. The Secretary-General of the United Nations shall transmit certified copies of the present Covenant to all States referred to in Article 48.

APPENDIX 7

INTERNATIONAL COVENANT ON ECONOMIC, SOCIAL AND CULTURAL RIGHTS, 1966[1]

The States Parties to the present Covenant,

Considering that, in accordance with the principles proclaimed in the Charter of the United Nations, recognition of the inherent dignity and of the equal and inalienable rights of all members of the human family is the foundation of freedom, justice and peace in the world,

Recognizing that these rights derive from the inherent dignity of the human person,

Recognizing that, in accordance with the Universal Declaration of Human Rights, the ideal of free human beings enjoying freedom from fear and want can only be achieved if conditions are created whereby everyone may enjoy his economic, social and cultural rights, as well as his civil and political rights,

Considering the obligation of States under the Charter of the United Nations to promote universal respect for, and observance of, human rights and freedoms,

Realizing that the individual, having duties to other individuals and to the community to which he belongs, is under a responsibility to strive for the promotion and observance of the rights recognized in the present Covenant,

Agree upon the following Articles:

PART I

Article 1

1. All peoples have the right of self-determination. By virtue of that right they freely determine their political status and freely pursue their economic, social and cultural development.

2. All peoples may, for their own ends, freely dispose of their natural wealth and resources without prejudice to any obligations arising out of international economic co-operation, based upon the principle of mutual benefit, and international law. In no case may a people be deprived of its own means of subsistence.

3. The States Parties to the present Covenant, including those having responsibility for the administration of Non-Self-Governing and Trust Territories, shall promote the realization of the right of self-determination, and shall respect that right, in conformity with the provisions of the Charter of the United Nations.

PART II

Article 2

1. Each State Party to the present Covenant undertakes to take steps, individually and through international assistance and co-operation, especially economic and technical, to the maximum of its available resources, with a view to achieving progressively the full realization of the rights recognized in the present Covenant by all appropriate means, including particularly the adoption of legislative measures.

2. The States Parties to the present Covenant undertake to guarantee that the rights enunciated in the present Covenant will be exercised without discrimination of any kind as to race, colour, sex, language, religion, political or other opinion, national or social origin, property, birth or other status.

---

1. Done on 16th December, 1966 and came into force on 23rd March, 1976.

3. Developing countries, with due regard to human rights and their national economy, may determine to what extent they would guarantee the economic rights recognized in the present Covenant to non-nationals.

Article 3

The States Parties to the present Covenant undertake to ensure the equal right of men and women to the enjoyment of all economic, social and cultural rights set forth in the present Covenant.

Article 4

The States Parties to the present Covenant recognize that, in the enjoyment of those rights provided by the State in conformity with the present Covenant, the State may subject such rights only to such limitations as are determined by law only in so far as this may be compatible with the nature of these rights and solely for the purpose of promoting the general welfare in a democratic society.

Article 5

1. Nothing in the present Covenant may be interpreted as implying for any State, group or person any right to engage in any activity or to perform any act aimed at the destruction of any of the rights or freedoms recognized herein, or at their limitation to a greater extent than is provided for in the present Covenant.

2. No restriction upon or derogation from any of the fundamental human rights recognized or existing in any country in virtue of law, conventions, regulations or custom shall be admitted on the pretext that the present Covenant does not recognize such rights or that it recognizes them to a lesser extent.

PART III

Article 6

1. The States Parties to the present Covenant recognize the right to work, which includes the right of everyone to the opportunity to gain his living by work which he freely chooses or accepts, and will take appropriate steps to safeguard this right.

2. The steps to be taken by a State Party to the present Covenant to achieve the full realization of this right shall include technical and vocational guidance and training programmes, policies and techniques to achieve steady economic, social and cultural development and full and productive employment under conditions safeguarding fundamental political and economic freedoms to the individual.

Article 7

The States Parties to the present Covenant recognize the right of everyone to the enjoyment of just and favourable conditions of work, which ensure, in particular:

(a) remuneration which provides all workers, as a minimum, with:

   (i) fair wages and equal remuneration for work of equal value without distinction of any kind, in particular women being guaranteed conditions of work not inferior to those enjoyed by men, with equal pay for equal work;

   (ii) a decent living for themselves and their families in accordance with the provisions of the present Covenant;

(b) safe and healthy working conditions;

(c) equal opportunity for everyone to be promoted in his employment to an appropriate higher level, subject to no considerations other than those of seniority and competence;

(d) rest, leisure and reasonable limitation of working hours and periodic holidays with pay, as well as remuneration for public holidays.

Article 8

1. The States Parties to the present Covenant undertake to ensure:

(a) the right of everyone to form trade unions and join the trade union of his choice, subject only to the rules of the organization concerned, for the promotion and protection of his economic and social interests. No restrictions may be placed on the exercise of this right other than those prescribed by law and which are necessary in a democratic society in the interests of national security or public order or for the protection of the rights and freedoms of others;

(b) the right of trade unions to establish national federations or confederations and the right of the latter to form or join international trade-union organizations;

(c) the right of trade unions to function freely subject to no limitations other than those prescribed by law and which are necessary in a democratic society in the interests of national security or public order or for the protection of the rights and freedoms of others;

(d) the right to strike, provided that it is exercised in conformity with the laws of the particular country.

2. This Article shall not prevent the imposition of lawful restrictions on the exercise of these rights by members of the armed forces or of the police or of the administration of the State.

3. Nothing in this Article shall authorize States Parties to the International Labour Organisation Convention of 1948 concerning Freedom of Association and Protection of the Right to Organize to take legislative measures which would prejudice, or apply the law in such a manner as would prejudice, the guarantees provided for in that Convention.

Article 9

The States Parties to the present Covenant recognize the right of everyone to social security, including social insurance.

Article 10

The States Parties to the present Covenant recognize that:

1. The widest possible protection and assistance should be accorded to the family, which is the natural and fundamental group unit of society, particularly for its establishment and while it is responsible for the care and education of dependent children. Marriage must be entered into with the free consent of the intending spouses.

2. Special protection should be accorded to mothers during a reasonable period before and after childbirth. During such period working mothers should be accorded paid leave or leave with adequate social security benefits.

3. Special measures of protection and assistance should be taken on behalf of all children and young persons without any discrimination for reasons of parentage or other conditions. Children and young persons should be protected from economic and social exploitation. Their employment in work harmful to their morals or health or dangerous to life or likely to hamper their normal development should be punishable by law. States should also set age limits below which the paid employment of child labour should be prohibited and punishable by law.

Article 11

1. The States Parties to the present Covenant recognize the right of everyone to an adequate standard of living for himself and his family, including adequate food, clothing and housing, and to the continuous improvement of living conditions. The States Parties will take appropriate steps to ensure the realization of this right, recognizing to this effect the essential importance of international co-operation based on free consent.

2. The States Parties to the present Covenant, recognizing the fundamental right of everyone to be free from hunger, shall take, individually and through international co-operation, the measures, including specific programmes, which are needed:

(a) to improve methods of production, conservation and distribution of food by making full use of technical and scientific knowledge, by disseminating knowledge of the principles of nutrition and by developing or reforming agrarian systems in such a way as to achieve the most efficient development and utilization of natural resources;

(b) taking into account the problems of both food-importing and food-exporting countries, to ensure an equitable distribution of world food supplies in relation to need.

Article 12

1. The States Parties to the present Covenant recognize the right of everyone to the enjoyment of the highest attainable standard of physical and mental health.

2. The steps to be taken by the States Parties to the present Covenant to achieve the full realization of this right shall include those necessary for:

(a) the provision for the reduction of the still birth-rate and of infant mortality and for the healthy development of the child;

(b) the improvement of all aspects of environmental and industrial hygiene;

(c) the prevention, treatment and control of epidemic, endemic, occupational and other diseases;

(d) the creation of conditions which would assure to all medical service and medical attention in the event of sickness.

Article 13

1. The States Parties to the present Covenant recognize the right of everyone to education. They agree that education shall be directed to the full development of the human personality and the sense of its dignity, and shall strengthen the respect for human rights and fundamental freedoms. They further agree that education shall enable all persons to participate effectively in a free society, promote understanding, tolerance and friendship among all nations and all racial, ethnic or religious groups, and further the activities of the United Nations for the maintenance of peace.

2. The States Parties to the present Covenant recognize that, with a view to achieving the full realization of this right:

(a) primary education shall be compulsory and available free to all;

(b) secondary education in its different forms, including technical and vocational secondary education, shall be made generally available and accessible to all by every appropriate means, and in particular by the progressive introduction of free education;

(c) higher education shall be made equally accessible to all, on the basis of capacity by every appropriate means, and in particular by the progressive introduction of free education;

(d) fundamental education shall be encouraged or intensified as far as possible for those persons who have not received or completed the whole period of their primary education;

(e) the development of a system of schools at all levels shall be actively pursued, an adequate fellowship system shall be established, and the material conditions of teaching staff shall be continuously improved.

3. The States Parties to the present Covenant undertake to have respect for the liberty of parents and, when applicable, legal guardians, to choose for their children

schools, other than those established by the public authorities, which conform to such minimum educational standards as may be laid down or approved by the State and to ensure the religious and moral education of their children in conformity with their own convictions.

4. No part of this Article shall be construed so as to interfere with the liberty of individuals and bodies to establish and direct educational institutions, subject always to the observance of the principles set forth in paragraph I of this Article and to the requirement that the education given in such institutions shall conform to such minimum standards as may be laid down by the State.

Article 14

Each State Party to the present Covenant which, at the time of becoming a Party, has not been able to secure in its metropolitan territory or other territories under its jurisdiction compulsory primary education, free of charge, undertakes, within two years, to work out and adopt a detailed plan of action for the progressive implementation, within a reasonable number of years, to be fixed in the plan, of the principle of compulsory education free of charge for all.

Article 15

1. The States Parties to the present Covenant recognize the right of everyone:

(a) to take part in cultural life;

(b) to enjoy the benefits of scientific progress and its applications;

(c) to benefit from the protection of the moral and material interests resulting from any scientific, literary or artistic production of which he is the author.

2. The steps to be taken by the States Parties to the present Covenant to achieve the full realization of this right shall include those necessary for the conservation, the development and the diffusion of science and culture.

3. The States Parties to the present Covenant undertake to respect the freedom indispensable for scientific research and creative activity.

4. The States Parties to the present Covenant recognize the benefits to be derived from the encouragement and development of international contacts and cooperation in the scientific and cultural fields.

PART IV

Article 16

1. The States Parties to the present Covenant undertake to submit in conformity with this part of the Covenant reports on the measures which they have adopted and the progress made in achieving the observance of the rights recognized herein.

2. (a) All reports shall be submitted to the Secretary-General of the United Nations, who shall transmit copies to the Economic and Social Council for consideration in accordance with the provisions of the present Covenant.

(b) The Secretary-General of the United Nations shall also transmit to the specialized agencies copies of the reports, or any relevant parts therefrom, from States Parties to the present Covenant which are also members of these specialized agencies in so far as these reports, or parts therefrom, relate to any matters which fall within the responsibilities of the said agencies in accordance with their constitutional instruments.

Article 17

1. The States Parties to the present Covenant shall furnish their reports in stages, in accordance with a programme to be established by the Economic and Social Council within one year of the entry into force of the present Covenant after consultation with the States Parties and the specialized agencies concerned.

2. Reports may indicate factors and difficulties affecting the degree of fulfilment of obligations under the present Covenant.

3. Where relevant information has previously been furnished to the United Nations or to any specialized agency by any State Party to the present Covenant, it will not be necessary to reproduce that information, but a precise reference to the information so furnished will suffice.

Article 18

Pursuant to its responsibilities under the Charter of the United Nations in the field of human rights and fundamental freedoms, the Economic and Social Council may make arrangements with the specialized agencies in respect of their reporting to it on the progress made in achieving the observance of the provisions of the present Covenant falling within the scope of their activities. These reports may include particulars of decisions and recommendations on such implementation adopted by their competent organs.

Article 19

The Economic and Social Council may transmit to the Commission on Human Rights for study and general recommendation or as appropriate for information the reports concerning human rights submitted by States in accordance with Articles 16 and 17, and those concerning human rights submitted by the specialized agencies in accordance with Article 18.

Article 20

The States Parties to the present Covenant and the specialized agencies concerned may submit comments to the Economic and Social Council on any general recommendation under Article 19 or reference to such general recommendation in any report of the Commission on Human Rights or any documentation referred to therein.

Article 21

The Economic and Social Council may submit from time to time to the General Assembly reports with recommendations of a general nature and a summary of the information received from the States Parties to the present Covenant and the specialized agencies on the measures taken and the progress made in achieving general observance of the rights recognized in the present Covenant.

Article 22

The Economic and Social Council may bring to the attention of other organs of the United Nations, their subsidiary organs and specialized agencies concerned with furnishing technical assistance any matters arising out of the reports referred to in this part of the present Covenant which may assist such bodies in deciding, each within its field of competence, on the advisability of international measures likely to contribute to the effective progressive implementation of the present Covenant.

Article 23

The States Parties to the present Covenant agree that international action for the achievement of the rights recognized in the present Covenant includes such methods as the conclusion of conventions, the adoption of recommendations, the furnishing of technical assistance and the holding of regional meetings and technical meetings for the purpose of consultation and study organized in conjunction with the Governments concerned.

Article 24

Nothing in the present Covenant shall be interpreted as impairing the provisions of the Charter of the United Nations and of the constitutions of the specialized agencies which define the respective responsibilities of the various organs of the United Nations and of the specialized agencies in regard to the matters dealt with in the present Covenant.

Article 25

Nothing in the present Covenant shall be interpreted as impairing the inherent right of all peoples to enjoy and utilize fully and freely their natural wealth and resources.

PART V

Article 26

1. The present Covenant is open for signature by any State Member of the United Nations or member of any of its specialized agencies, by any State Party to the Statute of the International Court of Justice, and by any other State which has been invited by the General Assembly of the United Nations to become a party to the present Covenant.

2. The present Covenant is subject to ratification. Instruments of ratification shall be deposited with the Secretary-General of the United Nations.

3. The present Covenant shall be open to accession by any State referred to in paragraph I of this Article.

4. Accession shall be effected by the deposit of an instrument of accession with the Secretary-General of the United Nations.

5. The Secretary-General of the United Nations shall inform all States which have signed the present Covenant or acceded to it of the deposit of each instrument of ratification or accession.

Article 27

1. The present Covenant shall enter into force three months after the date of the deposit with the Secretary-General of the United Nations of the thirty-fifth instrument of ratification or instrument of accession.

2. For each State ratifying the present Covenant or acceding to it after the deposit of the thirty-fifth instrument of ratification or instrument of accession, the present Covenant shall enter into force three months after the date of the deposit of its own instrument of ratification or instrument of accession.

Article 28

The provisions of the present Covenant shall extend to all parts of federal States without any limitations or exceptions.

Article 29

1. Any State Party to the present Covenant may propose an amendment and file it with the Secretary-General of the United Nations. The Secretary-General shall thereupon communicate any proposed amendments to the States Parties to the present Covenant with a request that they notify him whether they favour a conference of States Parties for the purpose of considering and voting upon the proposals. In the event that at least one third of the States Parties favours such a conference, the Secretary-General shall convene the conference under the auspices of the United Nations. Any amendment adopted by a majority of the States Parties present and voting at the conference shall be submitted to the General Assembly of the United Nations for approval.

2. Amendments shall come into force when they have been approved by the General Assembly of the United Nations and accepted by a two-thirds majority of the States Parties to the present Covenant in accordance with their respective constitutional processes.

3. When amendments come into force they shall be binding on those States Parties which have accepted them, other States Parties still being bound by the provisions of the present Covenant and any earlier amendment which they have accepted.

Article 30

Irrespective of the notifications made under Article 26, paragraph 5, the Secretary-General of the United Nations shall inform all States referred to in paragraph I of the same Article of the following particulars:

(a) signatures, ratifications and accessions under Article 26;

(b) the date of the entry into force of the present Covenant under Article 27 and the date of the entry into force of any amendments under Article 29.

Article 31

1. The present Covenant, of which the Chinese, English, French, Russian and Spanish texts are equally authentic, shall be deposited in the archives of the United Nations.

2. The Secretary-General of the United Nations shall transmit certified copies of the present Covenant to all States referred to in Article 26.

APPENDIX 8

ENGLISH BILL OF RIGHTS, 1689

An Act Declaring the Rights and Liberties of the Subject and Settling the Succession of the Crown.

Whereas the Lords Spiritual and Temporal and Commons assembled at Westminster, lawfully, fully and freely representing all the estates of the people of this realm, did upon the thirteenth day of February in the year of our Lord one thousand six hundred eighty-eight (old style date) present unto their Majesties, then called and known by the names and style of William and Marry, prince and princess of Orange, being present in their proper persons, a certain declaration in writing made by the said Lords and Commons in the words following, *viz*:

Whereas the late King James the Second, by the assistance of divers evil counsellors, judges and ministers employed by him, did endeavour to subvert and extirpate the Protestant religion and the laws and liberties of this kingdom;

"By assuming and exercising a power of dispensing with and suspending of laws and the execution of laws without consent of Parliament;

By committing and prosecuting divers worthy prelates for humbly petitioning to be excused from concurring to the said assumed power;

By issuing and causing to be executed a commission under the great seal for erecting Court called the Court of Commissioners for Ecclesiastical Causes;

By levying money for and to the use of the Crown by pretence of prerogative for other time and in other manner than the same was granted by Parliament;

By raising and keeping a standing army within this kingdom in time of peace without consent of Parliament, and quartering soldiers contrary to law;

By causing several good subjects being Protestants to be disarmed at the same time when papists were both armed and employed contrary to law;

By violating the freedom of election of members to serve in Parliament;

By prosecutions in the Court of King's Bench for matters and causes cognisable only in Parliament, and by divers other arbitrary and illegal courses;

And whereas of late years partial corrupt and unqualified persons have been returned and served on juries in trials, and particularly divers jurors in trials for high treason which were not freeholders;

And excessive bail hath been required of persons committed in criminal cases to elude the benefit of the laws made for the liberty of the subjects;

And excessive fines have been imposed;

And illegal and cruel punishments inflicted;

And several grants and promises made of fines and forfeitures before any conviction or judgment against the persons upon whom the same were to be levied;

All which are utterly and directly contrary to the known laws and statutes and freedom of this realm;

And whereas the said Late King James the Second having abdicated the government and the throne being thereby vacant, his Highness the prince of Orange (whom it hath pleased Almighty God to make the glorious instrument of delivering this kingdom from property and arbitrary power) did (by the advice of the Lords Spiritual and Temporal and divers principal persons of the Commons) cause letters to be written to the Lords Spiritual and Temporal being Protestants, and other letters to the several counties, cities, universities, boroughs and cinque ports, for the choosing of such persons to represent them as were of right to be sent to Parliament, to meet and sit at West Minister upon the two and twentieth day of January in this year one thousand six hundred eighty and eight (old style date), in order to such an establishment as that their religion, laws and liberties might not again be in danger of being subverted, upon which letters elections having been accordingly made.

And thereupon the said Lords Spiritual and Temporal and Commons, pursuant to their respective letters and elections, being now assembled in a full and free representative of this nation, taking into their most serious consideration the best means for attaining the ends aforesaid, do in the first place (as their ancestors in like case have usually done) for the vindicating the asserting their ancient rights and liberties declare.

That the pretended power of suspending the laws or the execution of laws by regal authority without consent of Parliament is illegal;

That the pretended power of dispensing with laws or the execution of laws by regal authority, as it hath been assumed and exercised of late, is illegal;

That the commission for erecting the late Court of Commissioners for Ecclesiastical Causes, and all other commissions and courts of like nature, are illegal and pernicious;

The levying money for or to the use of the Crown by pretence of prerogative, without grant of Parliament, for longer time, or in other manner than the same is or shall be granted, is illegal;

That it is the right of the subjects to petition the king, and all commitments and prosecutions for such petitioning are illegal;

That the raising or keeping a standing army within the kingdom in time of peace, unless it be with consent of Parliament, is against law;

That the subjects which are Protestants may have arms for their defence suitable to' their conditions and as allowed by law;

That election of members of Parliament ought to be free;

That the freedom of speech and debates or proceedings in Parliament ought not to be impeached or questioned in any Court or place out of Parliament;

That excessive bail ought not to be required, nor excessive fines imposed, nor cruel and unusual punishments inflicted;

That jurors ought to be duly empanelled and returned, and jurors which pass upon men in trials for high treason ought to be free-holders;

That all grants and promises of fines and forfeitures of particular persons before conviction are illegal and void;

And that for redress of all grievances, and for the amending, strengthening and preserving of the laws, Parliaments ought to be held frequently.

And they do claim, demand and insist upon all and singular the premises as their undoubted rights and liberties, and that no declarations, judgments, doings or proceedings to the prejudice of the people in any of the said premises ought in any wise to be drawn hereafter into consequence or example; to which demand of their rights they are particularly encouraged by the declaration of His Highness the Prince of Orange as being the only means for obtaining a full redress and remedy their in. Having therefore an entire confidence that his said Highness the Prince of Orange will perfect the deliverance so far advanced by him, and will still preserve them from the violation of their rights which they have here asserted, and from all other attempts upon their religion, rights and liberties, the said Lords Spiritual and Temporal and Commons assembled at West minister do resolve that William and Mary, Prince and Princess of Orange, be and be declared king and queen of England, France and Ireland and the dominions thereunto belonging , to hold the crown and royal dignity of the said kingdoms and dominions to them, the said prince and princess, during their lives and the life of the survivor to them, and that the sole and full exercise of the regal power be only in and executed by the said Prince of Orange in the names of the said prince and princess during their joint lives, and after their deceases the said crown and royal dignity of the same kingdoms and dominions to be to the heirs of the body of the said princess, and for default of such issue to the Princess Anne of Denmark and the heirs of her body, and for default of such issue to the heirs of the body of the said prince of Orange, And the Lords Spiritual and Temporal and Commons do pray the said prince and princess to accept the same accordingly.

And that the oaths hereafter mentioned be taken by all persons of whom the oaths have allegiance and supremacy might be required by law, instead of them; and that the said oaths of allegiance and supremacy be abrogated.

I, A.B., do sincerely promise and swear that I will be faithful and bear true allegiance to their Majesties King William and Queen Mary. So help me God.

I, A.B., do swear that I do from my heart abhor, detest and abjure as impious and heretical this damnable doctrine and position, that princes ex-communicated or deprived by the Pope or any authority of the see of Rome may be deposed or murdered by their subjects or any other whatsoever. And I do declare that no foreign prince, person, prelate, state or potentate hath or ought to have any jurisdiction, power, superiority, pre-eminence or authority, ecclesiastical or spiritual, within this realm. So held me God.

Upon which their said majesties did accept the crown and royal dignity of the kingdoms of England, France and Ireland, and the dominions thereunto belonging, according to the resolution and desire of the said Lords and Commons contained in the said declaration. And thereupon their majesties were pleased that the said Lords Spiritual and Temporal and Commons, being the two Houses of Parliament, should continue to sit, and with their Majesties' royal concurrence make effectual provision for the settlement of the religion, laws and liberties of this kingdom, so that the same for the future might not be in danger again of being subverted, to which the said Lords Spiritual and Temporal and Commons did agree, and proceed to act accordingly. Now in pursuance of the premises the said Lords Spiritual and Temporal and Commons in Parliament assembled, for the rectifying, confirming and establishing the said declaration and the articles, clauses, matters and things therein contained by the force of law made in due form by authority of Parliament, do pray that it may be declared and enacted that all and singular the rights and liberties asserted and claimed in the said declaration are the true, ancient, and indubitable rights and liberties of the people of this kingdom, and so shall be esteemed, allowed, adjudged, deemed and taken to be; and that all and every the particulars aforesaid shall be firmly and strictly holden and observed as they are expressed in the said declaration, and all officers and ministers whatsoever shall serve their majesties and their successors according to the same in all time to come. And the said Lords Spiritual and Temporal and Commons, seriously considering how it hath pleased Almighty God in his marvellous providence and merciful goodness to this nation to provide and preserve their said Majesties' royal persons most happily to reign over us upon the throne of their ancestors, for which they render unto him from the bottom of their hearts their humblest thanks and praises, do truly, firmly, assuredly and in the sincerity of their hearts thinks, and do hereby recognise, acknowledge and declare, that King James the Second having abdicated the government, and their Majesties having accepted the crown and royal dignity as aforesaid, their said Majesties did become, were , are and of right ought to be by the laws of this realm our sovereign liege lord and lady, king and queen of England, France and Ireland and the dominions thereunto belonging , in and to whose princely persons the royal state, crown and dignity of the said realms with all honours, styles, titles, realities, prerogatives, powers, jurisdictions and authorities to the same belonging and appertaining are most fully, rightfully and entirely invested and incorporated, united and annexed. And for preventing all questions and divisions in this realm by reason of any pretended titles to the sworn, and for preserving a certainty in the succession thereof, in the upon which the unity, peace, tranquillity and safety of this nation doth under God wholly consist and depend, the said Lords Spiritual and Temporal and Commons do beseech their Majesties that it may be enacted, established and declared, that the crown and regal government of the said kingdoms and dominions, with all and singular the premises thereunto belonging and appertaining, shall be and continue to their said Majesties and the survivor of them during their lives and the life of the survivor of them, and that the entire, perfect and full exercise of the regal power and government be only in and executed by his Majesty in the names of both their Majesties during their joint lives; and after their deceases the said crown and premises shall be and remain to the heirs of the body of her Majesty, and for default of such issue to her Royal Highness the Princess Annex of Denmark and the heirs of the body of her said Majesty; and thereunto the said Lords Spiritual and Temporal and Commons do in the name of all the people aforesaid most humbly and faithfully submit themselves, their heirs and posterities for ever, and do faithfully promise that they will stand to, maintain and defend their said Majesties, and also the utmost of their powers with their lives and estates against all persons whatsoever that shall attempt anything to the contrary. And whereas it hath been found by experience that it is inconsistent with the safety and welfare of this Protestant kingdom to be governed by a popish prince, or by any king or queen marrying a papist, the said Lords Spiritual and Temporal and Commons do further pray that it may be enacted, that all and every person and persons this, are or shall be reconciled to or shall hold communion with the see or church of Rome, or shall profess the popish religion, or shall marry a papist, shall be excluded and be for ever incapable to inherit, possess or enjoy the crown and government of this realm and Ireland and the dominions thereunto belonging or any part of the same, or to have, use or exercise any real power, authority or jurisdiction within the same; and in all and every such case or cases the people of these realms shall be and are hereby absolved of their allegiance; and the said crown and government shall from time to time descend to and be enjoyed by such person or persons being Protestants as should have inherited and enjoyed the same in case the said person or persons so reconciled, holding communion or professing or marrying as aforesaid were naturally dead; and that every king and queen of this realm who at any time hereafter shall come to and succeed in the imperial crown of this kingdom shall on the first day of the meeting of the first Parliament next after his or her coming to the crown, sitting in his or her throne in the House of Peers in the presence of the Lords and Commons therein assembled, or at his or her coronation before such person or persons who shall administer the coronation oath to him or her at the time of his or her taking the said oath (which shall first happen), make, subscribe and audibly repeat the declaration mentioned in the statute made in the thirtieth year of the reign of King Charles the Second entitled, an Act for the more effectual preserving the king's person and government by disabling papists from sitting in either House of Parliament- But it shall happen that such king or queen upon his or her succession to the crown of this realm shall be under the age of twelve years, then every such king or queen shall make, subscribe and audibly repeat the same declaration at his or her coronation or the first day of the meeting of the first Parliament as aforesaid which shall first happen after such king or queen shall have attained the said age of twelve years. All which their Majesties are contented and pleased shall be declared, enacted and established by authority of this present Parliament, and shall stand, remain and be the law of this realm for ever; and the same are by their said Majesties, by and with the advice and consent of the Lords Spiritual and Temporal and Commons in Parliament assembled and by the authority of the same, declared, enacted and established accordingly.

II. And be it further declared and enacted by the authority aforesaid, that from and after this present session of Parliament no dispensation by *non-obstante* of or to any statute or any part thereof shall be allowed, but that the same shall be held void and of no effect, except a dispensation be allowed of in such statute, and except in such cases as shall be specially provided for by one or more bill or bills to be passed during this present session of Parliament.

III. Provided that no charter or grant or pardon granted before the three and twentieth day of October in the year of our Lord one thousand six hundred eighty–nine shall be in any ways impeached or invalidated by this Act, but that the same shall be and remain of the same force and effect in law and no other than as if this Act had never been made.

BIBLIOGRAPHY

(A list of Articles mentioned or consulted by the Author of this Book)

Each Scholar mentioned below has contributed with special competence on the Essay in his field. In addition many other Authorities in variety of fields have given me the benefit of their specialized knowledge. I acknowledge my gratefulness to them.

1. Law Relating to Protection of Human Rights under the Indian Constitution by Justice Palok Basu.
2. Protection of Human Rights, National and International Perspectives by Khwaja A Muntaqim.
3. Human Rights in the Changing World edited by Justice E.S. Venkataramaiah.
4. Times of India, English Daily, New Delhi.
5. Human Rights Year Book, 2009 and 2011 edited by P.H. Parekh.
6. Constitution of India by V.N. Shukla.
7. Law Relating to Protection of Human Rights, Dr. S.K. Awasthi and R.P. Kataria.

SUBJECT INDEX

C

Compensation for Violation of Human Rights
- brutality, 30
- damages for breach of civil law, 29
- death in Police custody, 30
- human life and damage, 29
- scientific and upgraded mode of investigation, 30
- investigation or interrogation, 30
- monetary benefits, 29
- prohibit torture, 30
- sovereign immunity, 28
- suits and proceedings, 28
- torture for extracting information, 30

Corporate Governance
- animal farm, 37
- banking, insurance, 35
- child labours, 35
- corporate level integrity, 35
- covering the tanks, 35
- customs, 34
- cutting of green young trees, 35
- defense less employees, 35
- deforestation, 35
- diversity and ethnicity, 39
- environmental hazards, 35
- excessive use, 35
- global multinational companies, 34
- global warming, 35
- globalization of the businesses, 34
- Indian Forests Act, 36
- industrial pollution, 35
- international market, 34
- laws and norms, 34
- market/management pressure, 35
- misuse of electricity, 35
- non-governmental organisation, 35
- outsourcing of jobs, 39
- private security forces, 38
- rival corporations, 35
- social responsibility of business and industry, 34
- traditional relationship between government and business, 34
- transportation facilities, 34
- Union Carbide India Limited, 36
- vehicular pollution, 35
- water undrinkable and poisonous, 36
- wells and ponds for construction, 35

Custodial Crimes
- Air Force, 51
- Army, 51
- atmospheric pressure, 51
- beating, 52
- confessional statement, 49
- custodial death, 49
- custodial rapes, 49
- dacoity, 50
- defence forces, 51
- direction for grant of bail to person apprehending arrest, 56
- DNA test, 52
- electric shocks, 52
- environmental coercion, 51
- extract information, 54
- extreme physical pain, 54
- final hearing, 57
- forensic test, 52
- grant of anticipatory bail, 49
- investigating agencies, 49
- job security, 60
- lie detector, 52
- medical evidence, 53
- mental agony, 54
- mental anguish, 54
- misuse of custodial interrogation, 49
- murder, 50
- narco test, 52
- navy, 51
- period of custody, 53
- physical threats, 51
- police lock-up, 51
- prevention of torture, 54
- protection against arrest and detention, 58
- protection from illegal action, 58
- protection in respect of conviction for offence, 48
- reasons for arrest, 50
- robbery, 50
- stripping, 52
- tape records, 52
- third degree methods, 49
- tiring interrogative prolixity, 51
- torture in police custody, 47
- VIP duties, 60
- voluntarily causing grievous hurt, 59
- well-trained police force, 60
- woman police officers, 55

D

Directive Principles of State Policy of Indian Constitution
- education to children, 99
- encourage settlement of international disputes, 100
- equal justice and free legal aid, 97
- fundamental duties, 100
- honourable relations between nations, 100

improve public health, 99
living wage, 98
maternity relief, 98
organise agriculture and animal husbandry, 100
participation of workers in management of industries, 99
promote harmony, 101
promotion of educational and economic interests of SCs and STs, 99
promotion of international peace and security, 100
protect forests, 101
protect natural environment, 101
protect rivers, 101
protect wild life, 101
protection of forest and wild life, 100
protection of monuments, 100
right to work, 98
separation of judiciary from executive, 100
standard of living, 99
Uniform Civil Code, 99
village panchayats, 98

E

Education to Children
abilities to communicate, 41
additional knowledge and skills, 45
children's mother tongue, 45
develop learning environment, 42
domestic ethnic cultures, 41
economic capacity and development, 43
free and government-funded, 41
India Sarva Siksha Abhiyan (SSA), 44
international cooperation and peace, 41
international solidarity and cooperation, 41
migrant children, 45
primary education, 41
private schools, 45
protection from physical violence, 42
secondary education, 41
stop all forms of physical and humiliating punishment, 42
technical and professional education, 40
transportation and mid-day meals, 43

F

Fundamental Rights of Indian Constitution
equal pay for equal work, 83
equality of opportunity, 83
freedom as to payment of taxes, 92
freedom of conscience and free profession, 90
freedom of speech, 85
freedom to manage religious affairs, 91
grounds of religion, 83
power of high courts to issue certain writs, 94
prohibition of employment of children in factories, 90
prohibition of traffic in human beings and forced labour, 89
protection against arrest and detention, 87
protection against un-employment, 83
protection of interests of minorities, 92
protection of life and personal liberty, 87
remedies for enforcement of rights, 94
right of minorities to establish and administer educational institutions, 93
right to equal access to public services, 83

H

Historical Background
augmentation of human resources, 2
clean water, 3
environmental pollution, 3
establishing the institution, 2
fostering social reforms, 2
human dignity, 2
international brotherhood, 3
linkage of human development, 2
mechanism to attain human dignity, 1
philosophy of value, 1
poverty and illiteracy, 3
protecting national unity and integrity, 2
right of self-preservation, 1
right to education, 3
right to health, 3
right to procreate, 1
rights relating to dignity, 1
rights relating to liberty, 1
rights relating to life, 1
root for human development, 2
shape political society, 1
single world family, 3
spirit of democracy, 2
terrorism and communal clashes, 3
unpolluted air, 3
Vasudhaiva Kutumbakam, 1
wars and nuclear weapons, 3

Horizon of Human Rights
equal treatment, 33
fair and impartial trial, 32
legal rights of man and woman, 31
observation home, 33
protect the rights of children, 33
rights relating to liberty, 31
standards of civilization, 31

Human Rights and Children
age of innocence, 6
child labour, 5

child trafficking, 5
death due to disease, 6
drug abuse, 5
education, 6
exploitation, 6
forced to survive in brothels, 5
forced to survive in dance bars, 5
forced to survive in factories, 5
forced to survive in guesthouses, 5
free education to child, 7
hazardous employment, 5
health services, 6
lack of drinking water, 6
lack of food, 6
mid-day-meals and transportation, 7
no school fee, 6
not engaged/employed at Dhabas, 4
not engaged/employed at tea stalls, 4
priority for adult responsibility, 7
protection against discrimination, 4
pulling rickshaw, 4
quality elementary education, 6
servant at stationery shops, 4
servants at home, 4
sexual exploitation, 5
shelter, 6
shortage of medicine, 6
supremacy of children, 4
textbooks, 7
traffic in human beings, 5
uniforms, 7

Human Rights and Detainee
children and juveniles, 63
degrading treatment or punishment, 63
diplomatic mission, 65
domestic law, 67
ethnic or social origin, 63
food, 62
health, 62
medical care and treatment, 66
medical examination, 66
nursing mothers, 63
parents or guardians, 65
pregnant women, 63
religion or religious belief, 63
sick or handicapped persons, 63
treated in a humane manner, 63

Human Rights and Women
awareness, 11
bigamy of marriage, 14
Common Civil Code, 14
complaint mechanism, 11
complaints committee, 11
criminal proceedings, 11
disciplinary action, 11
forced pregnancy, 8
forced prostitution, 8
rape, 8
sexual harassment
demand or request for sexual favours, 10
physical contact and advances, 10
sexually coloured remarks, 10
showing pornography, 10
unwelcome physical, 10
verbal or non-verbal conduct of sexual nature, 10
sexual slavery, 8
special counsellor, 11
support service, 11
suppression of immoral traffic in women and girls, 9
third party harassment, 11
Uniform Civil Code, 14
welfare and providing relief to women, 13
workers' initiative, 11

I

Indian Constitution
clean and decent surroundings, 76
Dalits Tribals, 75
economic and political democracy, 75
electricity, 76
environment education, 76
equality, 75
fraternity, 75
justice, 75
liberty, 75
medial care, 76
protects the rights of children and women, 74
provide facilities and opportunities, 75
pure air and water, 76
right to food, 76
right to water, 76
roads, 76
safe and decent structure, 76
sanitation, 76
shelter, 76
social democracy, 75
sufficient light, 76

J

Judiciary in protection of Human Rights
bonded labour, 110
economically disadvantaged position, 111
education and medical aid, 109
interrogation centre or other lock-up, 113
Legal Aid Organisation, 113
living conditions in prisons, 110
medical examination, 114
police control room, 114
Public Interest Litigation, 108
right to breathe fresh air, 107
right to clothing, 107
right to food, 107

right to shelter, 107
secular or secularism, 113
social discrimination against
Harijans, 109
Social Interest Litigation, 108
usurpation of natural resources, 110

L

Law Enforcing Officials, 24
arbitrariness handcuffing, 25
confession, 27
examination of witnesses, 27
extortion, 26
feeling of superiority, 24
human rights and custodial crimes, 25
inhuman or degrading treatment, 24
instigate or tolerate, 24
International Code of Conduct, 24
murder, 26
persons against illegal acts, 24
Police Code of Conduct, 27
public emergency, 25
ravages of power, 24
search of arrested persons, 27
smuggling of arms and ammunition, 26
State of war, 24
terrorist and disruptive activities, 26
threat of war, 24
threat to national security, 24

N

National Human Rights Commission
adequate power of State, 102
associations of doctors, 102
associations of journalists, 102
associations of lawyers, 102
autonomy from government, 102
discovery and production of
document, 104
illegal detention by police, 105
inquiry report, 106
lathi charge, 105
pluralism in membership, 102
police and para-military force, 104
regional political party, 106
social and professional organisations, 102
sufficient resources, 102
trade unions, 102

P

Physically disabled and AIDS/HIV-affected persons
awareness campaigns, 77
blindness, 77
blindness or low vision, 77
candidates to appear in Civil Service
Examinatiom, 80
counselling, 79
employment and health care, 81
hearing impairment, 77
legal protection, 81
leprosy cured, 77
locomotor disability, 77
low vision, 77
medical and paramedical staff, 80
medical and social rehabilitation, 79
mental illness, 77
mental retardation, 77
National AIDS Control Organization, 80
physical therapy, 78
placement services, 79
post-natal care of mother and child, 77
right to economic and social security, 79
right to live with their families, 79
right to proper medical care, 78
social boycott or social exclusion, 81
vocational training and rehabilitation, 79

Public Interest Litigation
bandhua mazdoor, 70
child labour exploitation, 70
considerable amount of favourtism, 70
corruption, 70
disadvantaged and unprivileged
persons, 73
ecological destruction, 72
enforcement of fundamental rights, 70
farmers, 73
Legal Service Corporation, 70
mazdoors, 73
nepotism, 70
opportunities for self-development, 72
people of weaker sections, 70
poor and weaker persons, 70
sexual harassment of women, 70
social activists and journalists, 70
tenure of punishment, 70

R

Religious Harmony
community affair, 22
convention against torture, 20
cultural heritage, 22
democratic, 20
educated/intellectual persons, 22
elimination of racial discrimination, 20
emotionally stabilizing factor, 21
freedom to change religion, 20
ideological pluralism, 19
intermediate colleges, 22
liberty of expression, 19
liberty of faith, 19
liberty of thought, 19
literal inerrancy of Scripture, 19
money suffocates democracy, 19
muscle power, 19
national education policy, 22
national integration, 22

national interest transcending religious, 21
national or social origin, 20
national unity and integrity, 21
principle of religious tolerance and brotherhood, 22
religion misused by political leaders, 22
republic, 20
role of education, 21
Sarv Dharam Sam Bhav, 22
secondary schools, 22
secular, 20
socialist, 20
traditional orthodox religious beliefs, 19
universities, 22

Rule of Law
action of Government, 16
administrative efficiency, 17
ceaseless enforcement, 17
democratically elected Legislature, 15
discriminate people, 18
duties and functions, 18
financial autonomy, 18
independent Judiciary, 15
Indian legal system, 18
liberty and security, 16
maintenance of law, 17
monopoly of wisdom, 17
protect the basic human rights, 17
right to judicial remedy, 16
un-fettered legislative power, 15

S

Statutes/Conventions/Declarations
American Declaration of Independence, *1776*, 3
Bill of Rights of Constitution of the United States of America, 3
Child Labour (Prohibition and Regulation) Act, *1986*, 7
Child Marriage Restraint Act, *1929*, 9
Children (Pledging of Labour) Act, *1933*, 7
Convention on the Political Rights of Women, 8
Crown Proceedings Act, *1947*, 28
Dowry Prohibition Act, *1961*, 9
Draft of Rights, *1689*, 3
English Bill of Rights, 1689, 3
Environmental (Protection) Act, *1986*, 36
Equal Remuneration Act, *1976*, 9
French Declaration of the Rights of the Man and of the Citizen, *1789*, 3
Hindu Adoption and Maintenance Act, *1956*, 9
Hindu Marriage Act, *1955*, 9
Hindu Minority and Guardianship Act, *1956*, 9
Hindu Succession Act, *1956*, 9
Industrial Employment (Standing Orders) Act, *1946*, 10
International Covenant and Economic, Social and Cultural Rights, *1966*, 3, 32
International Covenant of Civil and Political Rights, *1966* (ICPR), 3, 32
Maternity Benefit Act, *1961*, 9
Medical Termination of Pregnancy Act, *1971*, 9
Motor Transport Workers Act, *1961*, 7
Plantation Labour Act, *1951*, 7
Protection of Human Rights Act, *1993*, 1
Right of Children to Free and Compulsory Education (RTE) Act, *2009*, 6, 43
Special Marriage Act, *1954*, 9
Universal Declaration of Human Rights, *1948* (UDHR), 3, 32

•••

Raj Kumar Gupta born on 3rd June, 1954 at Jagatdal , District 24-Parganas (North), West Bengal. Graduated from Allahabad University and passed Law Degree from T.D. Post Graduate College, Jaunpur, U.P.

He joined legal profession in June 1977, and is presently Advocate of Supreme Court of India.

He is the Secretary of United Lawyers Association, New Delhi and President of Mahabir Agrahari Foundation (Regd.), Delhi.

He is a Life member of Indian Law Institute (Deemed University), Delhi, Life Member of Bar Association of India, Delhi and Member of International Law Association, (Regional Branch India), Delhi.

Numerous Articles are published in English, Hindi and Bengali Journals/Magazines on legal and constitutional issues authored by him.

He has authored a Hindi poetry book "Prayaschit" published in 2005 and "Babu Brish Bhan Ji, Great Freedom Fighter" in English published in 2010.